IT'S NOT OKAY
TO BE A CANNIBAL

IT'S
NOT
OKAY
TO BE A
CANNIBAL

*How to Keep Addiction
from Eating Your Family Alive*

Andrew T. Wainwright AND Robert Poznanovich
AND THE National Intervention Team AT
Addiction Intervention Resources

Hazelden
Center City, Minnesota 55012-0176

1-800-328-0094
1-651-213-4590 (Fax)
www.hazelden.org

ISBN: 978-1-59285-370-0

Editor's note: The stories in this book are based on actual experiences. The names and details have been changed to protect
the privacy of the people involved. In some cases, composites
have been created.

17 16 15 14 13 7 6 5 4 3
Cover design by Theresa Gedig
Interior design and typesetting by Prism Publishing Center

Dedication

To the parents and family members of the AIR staff with gratitude. Because you had the courage to pick up the phone and take action, we are here to answer the phone when the next person calls.

CONTENTS

ACKNOWLEDGMENTS

We want to thank the intervention teams at Addiction Intervention Resources—everyone from the people who answer the phones to the people who book the plane tickets and balance our books. It is such a meaningful way to make a living, and every person on this team has helped save lives.

We wish to thank all the treatment centers we work with, especially Hazelden and Fellowship Club, with whom we have enjoyed a strong friendship, and to whom we owe our own personal recovery. Ten years into this we still find ourselves addicted to miracles and stand amazed at the power of a program of recovery to turn broken lives around.

We wish to thank writer Mike Finley for his help in writing this book. Mike was creative, often funny, and always engaged. He pushed us to build the book around strong stories and made many contributions to the thinking and tone of the project.

Finally, we wish to thank the moms and dads, brothers and sisters, friends and colleagues of cannibals who came to us and told us truths that families don't like to share. It is because of their courage and honesty that thousands of sick people are well today.

NOTE TO READERS

This is a book for families of addicts who are wondering how to help the people they love—or, barring that, to keep the family from being destroyed by the addict. The solutions we offer are for all kinds of addictions—drugs, alcohol, and other destructive compulsions.

There are many titles about addiction intervention. What makes our approach different is that

- we emphasize the family first and the addict second,
- we advocate profound clarity—what some call "tough love,"
- we see intervention and treatment as the best solution to the addiction problems that torment our society,
- we have mounted a campaign of "house-to-house fighting" to help one family at a time find relief.

This book is for families whose addicted loved ones are no longer functioning as "normal" people and have crossed a line into unacceptable behavior. We use the word *cannibal* throughout this book to denote the behavior of someone who lives in a state of advanced addiction. The point is not that addicts literally eat other people, but cannibalism is an apt metaphor for what addiction does to individuals and families. Our aim is not to denigrate loved ones who have fallen victim to addiction but to reveal the damage that addiction does every day to millions of families.

When we use the word *we* in this book, it means the larger we of AIR and the intervention and consulting teams we lead. Sometimes, we mean the addiction field generally. Many people's stories and wisdom appear in these pages, not just those of the authors and staff at AIR.

These are true stories about real addicts and their families, but names, locations, and circumstances have been changed to protect privacy. If we say Steve was a pipe fitter in Pittsburgh, his name is not really Steve, and if he is in the pipe fitting trade at all, it is miles and miles from Pittsburgh.

The field of addiction has its own vernacular, which can sometimes be confusing. We have tried to minimize this confusion by treating all addicts—alcoholics, other drug users, and people with compulsive disorders—roughly the same. We use the terms *addict* and *cannibal* to describe people struggling with a deadly illness. The illness takes hundreds of different forms, with no two alike. There are important differences between the many kinds of addiction. We lump them together because, for our purposes, the similarities are more important than the differences.

We used mostly male pronouns in this book. We did this mainly to keep our sentences simple. Finally, a matter of tone. This is a collection of stories and lessons from deep in the trenches of our addicted society. Sometimes we employ humor in telling these stories. We do not do this because addiction is funny. It is not. But the experiences of families with addiction involve many paradoxes. If we could not laugh at these paradoxes some of the time, we would be crying all of the time.

1

THE CANNIBAL
ON THE BALCONY

Addiction involves losing all sense of shame, and addicts are able do things that ordinary people would never dare do. Addicts—let's face it—live more colorful lives than most of us do. For this reason, they can be kind of fascinating.

After a recent meeting of our national addiction consulting team, we took time to recall the more memorable interventions we'd been part of during the previous year. Many of the stories were sad, some were depraved yet humorous, and many more were filled with hope and grace.

We talked about heroin addicts shooting up whiskey and others forced to drink "spit-back" methadone. We remembered alcoholics fleeing the scene of a hit-and-run, and others with livers so distended that they hung over their belts. We spoke of meth addicts who "tricked out" their girlfriends to pay for their next fix. And we recounted many sad stories of families who were destroyed by the actions of their addicted loved ones.

Someone in our group mentioned his favorite addict

excuse from the past year: "I don't remember a thing; I was in the middle of a lupus blackout." The addict didn't really have the disease lupus erythematosus. In truth, lupus doesn't even involve blackouts. It was all nonsense—and a great example of the outrageous way addicts think and manipulate.

But of all our stories, one stood out: Susie M., nineteen, a blond, green-eyed girl from a moneyed family living in the heart of Texas. She was a perfect example of the progress and horror of this disease.

From the outside looking in, Susie had everything. She was smart. She was beautiful. She had been a student at Emory in Atlanta—until she dropped out in the middle of her sophomore year.

That had been a year earlier. Since then she had been in one gigantic, expensive, downward spiral. Her mother had cut her off—she stopped paying rent on Susie's apartment, stopped subsidizing her bank account, and almost stopped believing anything she said. Susie hadn't bothered to pay the utilities, so there was no water or gas in her apartment.

Our intervention team consisted of Susie's mother, Eleanor, the point person for the intervention; Eleanor's second husband, Phil; Susie's fourteen-year-old brother, Peter; her best friend from high school, Marcia; the pastor from her former church, the Reverend Tom; and the interventionist, Brian.

We arrived at her apartment building around nine in the morning. It was a sunny, cloudless, Texas day.

It's Not Okay to Be a Cannibal

WHY DO WE INTERVENE IN THE MORNING?

Early morning is the best time to hold interventions and to make help available. First thing in the morning anything seems possible. By the afternoon, "tomorrow" always looks like a better option. In the morning most addicts have gotten at least some sleep, so chances are you will find them at their most sober point of the day. By scheduling interventions in the morning, we also have the better part of the day to get them to treatment before withdrawal symptoms set in.

We knocked on the door, and Susie opened it with the chain on. Although she was clearly pretty, she was a mess. Her complexion was pale and drawn, and it looked as though her hair had not been washed in weeks. An infected red spot surrounded a recently installed nose ring. She weighed maybe 95 pounds.

A common sign of crack use is filthy hands. Addicts use cigarette ash or copper scrub pads to filter the crack, and handling all that is dirty work. Fingers turn black and dirt gets lodged under the nails. They also have blisters on their fingers from the constant flicking of disposable lighters, as well as blisters on their lips from putting a hot glass pipe against them. It's not cold sores they're suffering from.

Susie had it all—dilated eyes, dirty hands, and blistered lips. Her eyes flared as she figured out why we had come. "I'm not going to talk to you," she said firmly. "You get the hell out of my place now!"

We peered over her shoulder. Perched on the edge of a green couch were three of her running partners. All three sat forward on the couch, shoulders hunched—sulking, sneaking ghosts, their eyes by turns angry and afraid.

THINGS THAT GIVE ADDICTS AWAY

Eyes sometimes reveal a person's drug of choice. People on speed have dilated pupils, like saucers. People addicted to opiates, like heroin, have tiny, pinlike pupils.

Intravenous drug addicts often wear long sleeves, even in the summer, to hide the sores and scarred veins on their arms.

Crack addicts are often skinny and dirty. Alcoholics' hands shake. People on benzodiazepines can lose control over their facial muscles, especially around their mouths.

"Sus, we need to talk to you," her mother said. "Please, honey."

"Why don't we sit down and talk this out?" Phil, Susie's stepdad, suggested. Susie would have none of it. "Get out!" she hissed, closing the door in our faces.

We regrouped, descending the stairs until we stood right below her apartment, next to a swimming pool filled with beautiful clear water. Susie stood inside the open glass doors on the balcony above us.

It's Not Okay to Be a Cannibal

We strained our necks and called up to her. "Susie, we love you," her brother, Peter, cried. Tom, the pastor, said, "We came to give you the help you need."

This went on for a full fifteen minutes—a crackhead version of the balcony scene from *Romeo and Juliet*. Susie literally held the high ground, always a tactically advantageous position. Here was this spoiled, affluent, intelligent young woman who had morphed into something closer to a cannibal—untamed, hostile, living outside the law. She shook her fist at us and cursed us like a sailor.

Her mother and stepfather wondered: What could we have done differently? We provided her with a beautiful home, the best schools, everything to ensure a wonderful life. What did we do wrong that caused her to transform into the monster in front of us today?

The answer: nothing.

Addiction is a disease and should be treated as such, not a proper parenting issue. The three Cs for parents looking to understand their addicted child are

- you didn't Cause it,
- you can't Control it,
- you're not the Cure.

THE CANNIBAL'S CREED

Over time, addicts lose their personalities. Although the real people are still there, inside, they are consistently outvoted and outgunned by their addiction, turning them into cannibals who devour their own families:

- **Cannibals lose interest in doing normal things.** Over time, healthy activities and roles (like holding down a job; earning a living; or being a spouse or partner, a parent, a citizen, or a friend) take a backseat to the need to secure alcohol or drugs.
- **Cannibals destroy the family's finances.** Even if they are able to hold down a job and draw a paycheck, money is still going to the drug or the addictive behavior. Innocent families lose their houses every day in drug seizures.
- **Cannibals destroy the family's reputation.** Stories get around about "things not being right" in the home. Addicts commit crimes to get money for drugs or the addictive behavior. There are too many embarrassments, too many public scenes. Eventually the family withdraws from the community and pulls the curtains around its shame.
- **Cannibals destroy the family's mental health.** It's bad enough that the cannibals themselves lose control and "go crazy." But they take their families with them. Addicted families are depressed, angry, secretive, codependent, and confused. Not one or some of these things. All of these things.
- **Addicts/cannibals live like parasites.** They feast on the family's resources—their home, their finances, and their sanity—until the family is gutted and empty. They stop at nothing, because addic-

It's Not Okay to Be a Cannibal

tion survives by feeding itself at the expense of others.

___

We knew how much Susie's parents were hurting and how much they cared for their daughter. Despite all the abuse they suffer, families usually feel great loyalty to the addict. People remember the sweet things their loved ones did and how likable they could be, before the addiction took control. The family usually feels enormous sympathy for the addict's struggle, and they want to meet the addict halfway . . . or three-quarters of the way . . . even 99 percent of the way, if that will help. Unfortunately going the extra mile for the addicted loved one doesn't usually benefit anyone. Sympathy alone doesn't get people well.

This day, yelling up from the courtyard at Susie, the family had their say. Her brother reminded her of the good times they had had as kids and what a good sister Susie could be. The minister reminded her of a mission trip she had been part of during her sophomore year of high school.

Eventually Susie just smiled, closed the glass doors, and disappeared inside the dark apartment. Our meeting was over.

There was some distress among the family. In their minds Susie had won, and everyone else had lost. Phil, the stepfather, was blunt about it: "Well, that was ridiculous. I doubt we'll ever see her again."

Brian corrected Phil. "Actually, this intervention is

going just fine. Let's regroup and talk this through a bit," he said.

Later, at home, Brian said, "The truth is, all interventions, when done properly, are successful. Today, by intervening, you have successfully broken the conspiracy of silence that has paralyzed this family. This paralysis is part of the disease of addiction, which is very much a family illness. As long as everyone around Susie was helping her to keep her secrets, she was free to continue getting high.

"But as of this morning," Brian said, "those secrets have disappeared. You did your part for someone you love who's in trouble. Susie made herself very clear. It's more important for her at the moment to continue getting high than to be a part of this family the way you need her to be—healthy and drug-free.

"Here is how I think this plays out. Probably by this afternoon Susie will start to make some phone calls, looking for the weak link in this family's newly developed boundaries. Susie doesn't actually want to live like this, nor does she want a life without her family. However, we have to prepare to answer those calls and to hold the line on this family's request that she go to treatment.

"But remember, even if Susie doesn't call today, she now knows that this family will no longer support her addiction but that you all will absolutely support anything to do with her recovery. We all make choices and as a family and as individuals we will walk forward from where we stand—you all, as a family, back to your lives,

It's Not Okay to Be a Cannibal

and Susie back to hers. Remember, this is a process not an event. I need you all to be strong, support one another, and be patient." Before we broke up for the day, we agreed on a plan of what to say when Susie does call.

Sure enough, a week later the phone rang at the family home. "Mom, it's Susie. I can't do this anymore. I'm really sorry about the other day. . . . Will you guys still help me?"

Eleanor rose to the occasion. "Susie, that's the news we've been waiting to hear. If you truly want to go to treatment, and you really mean it this time, then you give Brian a call."

And Susie did. As this book went to press, Susie had been clean and sober for two full years. And she's enrolled in school again, studying history.

The Conspiracy of Silence

In an intervention, the conspiracy of silence is destroyed. Family members stop keeping secrets—from one another and from the outside world. Each one states the consequences he has seen arise from the cannibal's actions, how this behavior has affected him, and how the relationship will change unless the cannibal accepts the help that is offered.

An intervention is often more of a declaration and an offer than it is a discussion. Once these words are spoken, the intervention is by definition a success, even if the addict chooses not to accept help that day.

Because the conspiracy of silence has been broken, the family is now unfettered, the cannibal has been identified and named, help has been proffered, and the chains of codependency have been broken.

The difference between life before and life after an intervention is this: *It is now possible to tell the truth.* And the truth is that it's not okay to be a cannibal. It's not okay to be an addict at the family's expense. It's not okay to hold your loved ones hostage to your addiction.

While the family may love the brother or father or daughter or son who occupies the same body as the cannibal, after the intervention they have gone to war against the cannibal. With this idea planted firmly in each family member's mind, the whole family takes a giant step toward healing.

A Message of Tough Love

The term *addiction intervention* is only about forty years old. Before then the general public imagined that an alcoholic or other addict had to hit "rock bottom" before change was possible. Hitting bottom meant he had to experience something dreadful in order to realize he had to change his ways. The "something dreadful" could be arrest, losing a job, illness, or causing injury to another. It's an extremely painful way for an addict to learn. Many die reaching rock bottom. For many, rock bottom is death.

What changed this philosophy was the work of Vernon Johnson, a minister from Minneapolis. Using his intuition as a pastor, Johnson helped an alcoholic parishioner seek treatment. The process he developed is the backbone of what we now call addiction intervention. It is also called the Johnson Model, because it originated in the intervention center he set up called the Johnson Institute.

It was Johnson who did an intervention on Betty Ford, the wife of former U.S. president Gerald Ford. Betty Ford became a spokesperson for the process, and one of the best-known treatment centers in the world today bears her name.

The remarkable discovery Johnson made is that a person who is talked into seeking help has the same success rate in recovery as someone who actively seeks recovery on his own.*

Addiction is a strange phenomenon. It has been described as the only disease that tells you that you don't have it. In many cases, the person who is afflicted with this illness is the last one to know how sick he or she is. Such is the power of the addict's denial.

Vernon Johnson changed the current thought about addiction. We are followers of his method, with a twist. Like him, we try to create a "false bottom" so the addict can break through his own encasement of denial. The twist is that, while most other intervention approaches are about the addict, ours is directed primarily at family. Our primary emphasis is on the family's health, not the addict's.

* J. Fearing, "Statistically Speaking: A Comparative Analysis of the Inpatient Chemical Dependency Treatment Experience between Professionally Intervened Patients and Self-Referred Patients," *Treatment Today* 8, no. 2 (1996): 10–11.

Addiction is a family disease, because it harms everyone in the family or household. It tears at our souls because we love the person trapped by the addiction and do not want to do anything to hurt him.

This book delivers a radical message of tough love: The person you love is sick, crazy, and overruled time after time by the cannibal who has taken up residence in his body. If you wish to save the person you love from the cannibal, you must first save yourself. Otherwise, the cannibal will eat all of you alive—not just the addict but your whole family.

Intervention is a hard prescription. By its very nature it causes everyone involved to feel extremely uncomfortable for a short time. But if you bear with us, we will show you why an intervention may be the best chance your family has to survive. And we'll show you the right and wrong ways to conduct an intervention.

This book differs radically from the so-called War on Drugs that our society has been waging for the past thirty-five years. That war is being waged largely as an advertising campaign, broadcasting a general message into every school, office, and home about the dangers of drugs. This campaign has failed to work. Why? Because it is an air war, directed from high above the people who are affected by it. It is a war conducted by governments and foundations and academics who are looking for global solutions to what is actually a household problem.

Our alternative is closer to home, down to earth, and far more powerful. We tell families that the way to win

It's Not Okay to Be a Cannibal

the war on addiction is to confront addicts with the truth, get them off the couch and into treatment, and not give them access to our lives until and unless they change.

If the War on Drugs is an air war, this is house-to-house fighting. It is intense, and it can be ugly. But it works. We've seen it work, time after time, for family after family.

The most heartening thing about this kind of fighting is the success rate. About 90 percent of interventions succeed—maybe not the first day, but over the following few months. That success rate is better than you will get for most life-threatening diseases. It is a miracle to families who may have felt paralyzed by the problem for many years.

The Problem with Freedom

In industrialized democracies, a primary social value is freedom. The principle that lives in the minds of most people is that we are free to do what we like.

Freedom is our glory. It is what drives much of our accomplishments and our high standard of living. But it can be a problematic concept. It applies equally to good and bad behaviors. All an addict is doing by shooting up heroin or exposing himself in the park is expressing personal freedom. If family members try to rein that freedom in, and say it is freedom run amok, the cannibal complains that his rights are being violated.

Addicts of every stripe believe that they are not

hurting anyone and if people would just leave them alone, the world would be a better, freer place. This thought is an excellent window through which we can examine the delusions of the addicted. It is a place in which they, and not the family members whose lives they attach themselves to parasitically, are the victims. We have heard addicts express this conviction as if they were constitutional scholars.

The truth is that we have the legal right to some addictions, such as alcohol, overeating, and gambling, while other substances and behaviors, like heroin and some sexual activities, are against the law.

Regardless of the addiction's legality, one thing is clear: It is not the family's responsibility to pay for the addiction. No family is obligated to pay for the cannibal's rent, to feed him, to do his laundry, to pay his health insurance premiums, or to lend him the family car.

Having an addict in the family should not mean the family can't ever have company over, or that the floor of one room should be strewn with dirty dishes, or that the family be unable to sleep because the addict insists on blasting his stereo at seventy decibels at four in the morning.

The addict is right. This is the land of the free. And it is very, very, very difficult to deprive another citizen of his freedom. That is one reason that homelessness is such a large problem in the United States. Many of these people are mentally ill or addicted, and there is no ready legal means to deprive them of their freedom.

No, we can't flip a switch and have our addicted

It's Not Okay to Be a Cannibal

loved ones carted off to the asylum, as people did a few generations ago. Those institutions don't exist any more. But there are actions families can take to decrease the amount of stress in their households, to increase feelings of safety and security, and to feel confident that they've done everything possible to wrest their loved ones from the grip of addiction.

There are no guarantees that intervention will get your loved one to stop using. But we have the power to fight this affliction. Our belief systems strongly influence the outcome of a situation. If we *believe* change is possible, then it becomes possible.

The following chart lists some basic truisms. Many people are stuck in the thinking patterns listed in column 1. Column 2 describes behaviors that will effect change.

WHAT DOESN'T WORK	WHAT DOES WORK
Expecting things to get better by themselves	Being proactive and taking responsible steps to improve the situation
Remaining silent about the things you know	Speaking up and out to anyone who will listen
Refusing to call the authorities and have them take your addict away	Involving knowledgeable professionals and asking for help
Destroying your family system (relationships, finances, respect) in an attempt to save one person	Making decisions based upon the greater good of the family as a whole, making help available to the addict, and setting livable boundaries

2

IT STARTS WITH
A PHONE CALL

It's 2:26 in the afternoon when the phone rings. It's a mother in Toronto. "My son Jeffrey is in over his head with meth," she says, and has to clear her throat.

In a given day we get a dozen calls like hers. The callers are usually a little shaky at first—as if they are finally saying out loud what they have wanted to say for a long time—but they gain strength as we talk.

"Yes, I have a problem. My husband is in jail for the next thirty days but he told me that he wants to change. Can you do an intervention on a person behind bars?"

"My daughter Shelley is down to ninety-four pounds. She just won't eat, and I'm scared she's going to die."

"Our dad is drinking again, and he won't talk to any of us. We don't know what to do."

"My son Mike spends all his time in his room playing online poker. I don't know where the money is coming from."

"We think our daughter might be involved in some very dark sexual stuff. Is there an intervention for that?"

"My fiancée has been buying Dilaudids over the Internet for the past few months. Can you help me?"

"My sisters and I want to help our mom, but we're afraid that if we confront her the shame will cause her to harm herself."

So the calls come in, with the callers always sad, always struggling, never sure what the next right thing to do is. The first words are the hardest ones. Once they are spoken, it's like ice cracking on a frozen pond. People want to know what they can do, what works. Soon, the questions come fast and furious.

ELEMENTS OF A SUCCESSFUL INTERVENTION

- **The phone call.** For many, admitting to someone outside the family that there is a problem is the hardest part.
- **The creation of a plan for intervention.** The intervention team—the interventionist, family members, and other people who are important to the addict—must meet to plan the intervention.
- **The intervention.** The team holds a family meeting with the addict. Here is the agenda for the meeting: we love you, we see you struggling in all the different areas of your life, and help is available today.
- **The moment of decision.** The addict is given a choice: accept the help available or agree to live by the new set of boundaries set out by the intervention team.

- **The follow-up.** Intervention is a process, not an event. It means the interventionist works with the family for several months.

Successful interventions begin with phone calls, usually from a family member—a spouse or partner, a parent or child. Sometimes an employer or friend makes the call. This phone call is the pivotal first step. People are vulnerable and afraid and alone, but now they have reached what we call the "jumping-off point."

Think of the ledge scene from *Butch Cassidy and the Sundance Kid*. With the posse close behind, Butch and Sundance find themselves at the edge of a cliff with the river far below. "I can't swim!" says Robert Redford. "Why, you crazy," Paul Newman says to him, "the fall'll probably kill ya!" Families may not know what lies ahead, but they know, as Butch and Sundance did, that the current situation is no longer tolerable and doing nothing is no longer an option.

So the phone call is the jumping-off point: "I can't do it like this anymore. There has to be a different way." It is a brave and loving thing to do.

People's fears, before they dial, are almost incapacitating. Is this the right thing to do? What if we end up doing more harm than good? What happens if we lift the rock from the family secrets? It's not easy to trust outsiders with family secrets. Few families want to be examined closely by strangers. Most families just want things to be "the way they used to be."

It's Not Okay to Be a Cannibal

People are right to feel cautious. It's a big deal to give up and say, "We can't handle this anymore. You'll have to help us, because we can't do it by ourselves."

"What Is an Intervention, Exactly?"

The word *intervention* has several meanings. Intervention, generally, is the process of inserting oneself into a situation to alter an action or condition, such as to help someone overcome an addiction. This sense of intervention is long term. Indeed, it is often a lifelong business.

More specifically, *an intervention* is what people call the short-term event—the often dramatic confrontation that focuses honesty and caring on an individual and his addiction. This meeting of the minds asks that the addict make a life choice between addiction and health.

We'll talk about the long-term intervention process in chapter 8. In the meantime, we will focus on the short-term event.

A proper intervention is a planned realignment of family power, in which power is taken away from the addict and given to the rest of the family.

An intervention redraws the map about what behavior is and is not okay inside a family.

The goal of an intervention is to move the family out of crisis and to make help available to the addicted individual.

In the best interventions, the lion's share of attention

is focused on helping the family. Family members learn they must take themselves off the roller-coaster ride of addiction. They learn to set healthy, livable boundaries. They begin to practice *not* enabling. The natural by-product of these efforts—of the family helping themselves, of the natural realignment of power, of attention being moved off of the addict—is that the addicted individual takes the offer of help more seriously.

Accepting this offer may happen on the day of the intervention or in the following weeks. Whether the addict accepts help or refuses it, a new set of operating procedures has been put in place that clearly defines what is okay and what is not okay inside a given family system. (See page 21.)

These are rules families live by. It is not easy to change the rules. They took a lifetime to develop, and it will take awhile to establish new ones.

"Is Every Addict a Cannibal?"

The cannibal image is somewhat problematic, because no one likes to think that their mom or brother or friend is anything like a cannibal.

Cannibal is admittedly a harsh metaphor. But we chose it for that reason—because there is almost no calculating the harm addicts do to the people whose lives they touch.

Not all addicts qualify as cannibals. But beware of the temptation to take your family addict off the hook. Families offer two rationalizations:

1. "The addict isn't bothering anyone."

There are addicts who are relatively harmless, and most addicts have no wish to harm anyone else. If you took an addict and dropped him off in the desert with a lifetime supply of the drug of his choice, he would not be a cannibal in the same sense as a heroin addict living

IT IS OKAY TO	IT IS NOT OKAY TO
love someone unconditionally and to want desperately for him to recover.	help a person stay sick by keeping his secrets, by bailing him out of the trouble that he earned, or by helping him avoid the consequences of his actions because it makes you feel better.
confront the disease of addiction head-on, to hold people accountable for their actions, and to do everything in your power to assist those who are powerless.	let people take advantage of you and then, with your silence, to approve their behavior.
ask for and to expect to be treated with decency and respect by the people you agree to share your life and resources with.	know what is going on and to do nothing. With knowledge comes responsibility. If someone is struggling with an addiction, it is your duty to help him.

in your home. But most people live in families and belong to communities. We are social creatures and need human interaction. Because of this interconnectedness, most addicts wind up cannibalizing someone's relationship or goodwill.

Another example of a harmless addict is the alcoholic who drinks at home after work. He is not out breaking laws. He is not stealing from his kids' piggy banks. His habit seems passive and contained. He certainly defends his drinking on these grounds. But talk to his family and you might hear a different story.

Here is a man who has not had an intimate conversation with his wife in ten years. Here is a man who has never been to his kids' sporting events or concerts. Here's a guy who requires everyone in the family to tiptoe around him and to make excuses for his drinking. He may think he's a nice guy, but his addiction imposes a tyranny on the people he is supposed to love. He is a cannibal, whether he likes the word or not.

Most addicts don't want to be cannibals. Many just want to be left alone so they can take drugs. Many regret the pain they inflict on some level, sometimes even consciously. But they're stuck. Their addiction forces them to choose a path that other people know is uncivilized and unhealthy. In the course of pursuing their addictions, they inevitably cannibalize.

2. "But this addict is really nice."

We once were asked to conduct an intervention on a young man who had spent the previous thirty days in jail. His name was Alex, and he was all of nineteen. He had a big problem with drinking, which resulted in his arrest. The team was waiting for him at the jailhouse door and took him directly to a nearby hotel for a family meeting.

Alex was very receptive and soft-spoken. He shook the interventionist's hand warmly and thanked him for being there. When the interventionist explained what the team had in mind, he nodded thoughtfully.

"I think that's a really good idea," he said.

When they got to the airport, he helped the interventionist with *his* bags.

And after he boarded the plane, ashamed, he apologized for smelling bad. "I've been wearing the same pants for a month," he said.

Alex was a dream intervention, and his recovery was just as successful. We met with him a year later. He had taken courses in film production at the local community college and was making a living with a local ad firm. He gave us the biggest smile we had ever seen, and he thanked us.

Was Alex a cannibal? Yes, he was. The month he spent in jail was for clubbing another fellow with a bottle in a bar fight.

Cannibals have good qualities and aren't uniformly offensive, but they have crossed the line separating acceptable behavior from unacceptable behavior. We

rejoiced in Alex's recovery. We also understood that it was 100 percent necessary if he were to continue to live.

HOW HARD IS IT TO INTERVENE?

Here are some jarring statistics:

- Only 1 in 10 families who calls us for help decides to go forward with us and intervene.
- Once we do intervene, our record is much better: 9 of every 10 addicts agree to get treatment.

Conclusion? It's 10 times harder to get a family to intervene with our company than it is to get an addict to surrender!

"What If He's Not an Addict?"

Sometimes, you can't be certain if your loved one is drinking or drugging. Something isn't right, but you can't pinpoint what it is. And you don't have definitive proof that a problem exists—no liquor bottles or drug paraphernalia have been left lying around. And perhaps your current relationship isn't so strong that you can ask him and expect an honest answer. Many people are particularly fearful of labeling young persons, because even if they are problem drinkers, they may grow out of it, right? Jumping to a false conclusion will only confirm their view of you as a hysterical parent.

It's Not Okay to Be a Cannibal

Many parents are ready to supply nonaddiction excuses for their child's behavior:

- "She's been depressed lately."
- "He has a learning disability."
- "She's always marched to a different drummer."
- "Her friends drink, so it's understandable if she has a drink every now and then."

Translation: Most of us would like the explanation to be something besides addiction.

These are all examples of denial, a form of codependency. Codependency means letting the cannibal's actions control your life or taking responsibility for his actions. Denial protects a loved one from the truth. It seems harmless enough, until family members can no longer tell what is true and what isn't.

SOMETHING STRANGE IS GOING ON HERE

Mental illness is widely recognized as a treatable disease, whereas addiction is seen as a moral choice.

Many families would rather have their loved one be *mentally ill* (historically very difficult to treat) than *addicted* to a substance or behavior (more treatable than almost any other major physical disease).

Why? Because mental illness is more socially acceptable than alcoholism or drug addiction:

- Mental illness arouses sympathy. "It's not his fault."
- Addiction arouses scorn. "This is just a matter of willpower. If he really wanted to quit, he would."

A father from North Carolina described his suspicions about his son:

"I'm pretty sure my son Simon is doing pot or something. He's acting very strange, and he avoids talking to me face-to-face. His grades have gone to hell, and he hangs around with a crowd that looks like trouble. Something isn't right. But I haven't seen any paraphernalia, so I don't have any actual evidence of abuse. How can I go forward when I'm not sure he's doing drugs? How do I know I'm not just a hysterical father? I don't want to hold an intervention and find out he's clean."

The man did not want to be embarrassed by being wrong. How foolish he would feel and how destructive it would be to his credibility as a trusting and loving parent if he staged a full-dress intervention, only to discover that his son was straight but he had talked himself into believing he's an addict!

But the issue goes deeper than embarrassment. The man knows he is taking a huge tactical risk by calling for an intervention. He can imagine his cannibal child turning the tables and saying something like the following:

It's Not Okay to Be a Cannibal

"You know, if you had just treated me with some respect and come to me directly, we could have talked this through like adults. But, because you have chosen to sneak around and ambush me with this intervention nonsense, I see I can no longer treat *you* with respect. By refusing to respect me, you have lost all of my respect. You know, it's ironic. I would absolutely have gone to treatment had you come to me directly. But now, after what you've done here, I don't think that will ever happen."

That's Cannibalism 101: turning the best intentions of others against them. The problem is that this confusion ("Is he using or isn't he?") freezes families in their tracks at the very moment they need to take action. The result of too much analysis is often . . . paralysis.

For instance, there is a major gray area between addictive behavior and mental illness. At the minimum, all addicts suffer from some kind of emotional problem. Addiction is rooted in feelings of compulsion, isolation, and self-deception that all of us feel from time to time, but in addictive personalities these feelings strike deeper and more irresistibly. We believe addicts are genetically predisposed to emotional problems, while others name and get through the emotion or don't take situations too personally. Most healthy nonaddicts can regulate these emotions; addicts don't. At the first sign of distress, up goes the white flag, and they are using.

At the other end of the spectrum are people with serious mental illnesses: personality disorders, bipolar disorder, or schizophrenia. Many people with serious mental illnesses self-medicate by using chemicals, which in turn often leads to dangerous compulsive behaviors. Thus the two universes of addiction and mental illness are constantly feeding off one another.

Oftentimes we are looking for a root problem when in reality they are coexisting. Is he mentally ill first and a cannibal later? Or is he an addict whose behavior deepened his latent mental illness? This is an important question because, while addiction intervention is very successful with addicts who have emotional problems, it is less successful for people whose primary problem is serious mental illness and who happen to abuse drugs. Addiction intervention may not be the best tool for people with multiple disorders. Staging an addiction intervention for someone who is unable to make a rational decision to seek help—people suffering from unmedicated schizophrenia or another serious mental illness—may be insufficient or miss the point entirely.

We were once asked to do an alcoholism intervention on a young Boston woman named Elise. Elise was indeed an alcoholic, but the moment we met her we realized her problems went beyond that. She was extremely disordered, stuffing used tampons under the cushions of the family sofa. Her family was so concerned about the booze she was putting away that they underestimated the extent of her mental illness.

A good interventionist will know enough going into

such an intervention to line up a facility that specializes in the treatment of mental illness, either on its own or paired with chemical dependency treatment.

This is why we strongly recommend that a mental illness intervention be conducted by people who understand what it means to have a co-occurring disorder, or a mental illness coupled with substance abuse. Many addictive behaviors, such as gambling, anorexia, and sexual addictions, have strong psychological components. Families need to recognize that more is going on here than "just" addictive behavior. Families dealing with any degree of psychological problems should seek an interventionist who understands how complex the situation is and who is familiar with the capabilities of various treatment centers, recommending one that is staffed to handle co-occurring disorders.

Mental illness isn't the only factor that can complicate an intervention. Some situations are so abusive—the addict is so violent—that a sit-down session with an interventionist is out of the question. In such cases, a call to the police is the best place to start.

SHELTER FROM THE STORM

Our typical intervention results in the addict being taken to the appropriate level of care. This could be a chemical or mental health assessment, a local hospital detox or psychiatric ward, or a residential treatment facility. Possibilities include the following:

- chemical dependency centers that address alcoholism and drug addiction as a primary diagnosis
- co-occurring disorder facilities that address a mental illness and an addiction—for instance, alcoholism plus schizophrenia
- treatment centers and psychiatric hospitals that address mental illness as a primary diagnosis
- facilities whose main focus is on specific behavioral issues such as compulsive gambling, sexual addiction, trauma, or eating disorders

What's most important is not to bog down and do nothing. Whatever the problem is, it's not going to go away by itself. Acting to break the chain of inaction will produce relief for everyone, including the cannibal.

"Is Addiction One Thing or Many Things?"

Every addict is a human being, and every human being is unique. Addiction experts agree, however, that there is a commonality in all addictions. Whether the problem is chemical abuse, sexual acting out, eating disorders, or any other of our long list of addictions, the characteristics, behavior patterns, and consequences to self and family are generally the same. The importance of addressing and treating the addiction, and managing recovery, is the same regardless of the type of addiction.

Addiction is a disease, plain and simple. Addiction can be defined as a compulsive physiological and psychological need for a particular substance or behavior. When

It's Not Okay to Be a Cannibal

ADDICTION ISN'T JUST DRUGS AND ALCOHOL

Listed below are various categories of addictive behaviors. Some of these behaviors are plainly cannibalistic and cry out for intervention. Others are considered "normal," but nevertheless cause immense damage to the afflicted individuals and to those with whom they have relationships. Before you cast stones at other people's character failings, see if you aren't susceptible to one of these.

Workaholism. Needing to immerse oneself in activity at all times; always having to exercise

Eating disorders. Anorexia, bulimia, overeating

Money compulsions. Overspending, gambling, hoarding, collecting, stealing

Health compulsions. Obsession with one's appearance; hypochondria, handwashing, fear of germs

Sexual addictions. Predation, pornography, promiscuity, exhibitionism, any other inappropriate sexual behaviors

Appearance obsessions. Inability to be happy with yourself as you are

Achievement addiction. The need to be the best at everything you do; when one's resume becomes one's religion

Religious addictions. Overemphasis on the form of religion, rather than its spiritual truth

Intellectual addictions. Having to filter every experience through the mind; overintellectualizing

Destructive social patterns. Choosing the wrong kinds of partners, "slumming"

Relationship addictions. Having to be in control all the time; always having to please others to feel okay about oneself

Activity addiction. Unhealthy preoccupation with anything: surfing the Net, sports, politics, video games

talking specifically about chemical dependency (alcoholism or other drug addiction) as a disease, we say that it is primary, progressive, chronic, and fatal if not treated. Simply put—left unchecked and untreated, it is fatal.

Having said that, the various addictions each pose unique dangers.

Heroin addiction enjoys a special place in the pantheon of drugs for the havoc it wreaks on the human body. The drug lowers blood pressure and decreases breathing but is actually less harmful to the organs than alcohol. With heroin, drug quality and dirty needles cause abscesses, cellulitis, and infection, but overdosing is the leading cause of death. The death rate for one group of heroin addicts who were studied was one hundred times the rate for the general population. Heroin users experience bodily infections; contamination of the heart, liver, and kidneys; pneumonia; tuberculosis; hepatitis; and HIV. In addition, they overdose—their blood pressures drop, their breathing grows shallow, their hearts stop beating—and they die.

DAMAGE TO THE BODY

"The day I arrived at treatment I looked in the mirror, and I was amazed at what had happened to my body. In school, six years before, I had been on the soccer team and weighed a healthy 175 pounds. Now I weighed 135 and looked like I was dying. My eyes were hollow and sunken. My skin was gray and all the pick marks on my face made it look

It's Not Okay to Be a Cannibal

like I had chicken pox. I had abscesses on my hands and forearms, which I covered by pulling my sleeves down over my fingers. I was so ashamed, I was glad my father was far away and didn't have to see me like this. When I tried to dial the phone to talk to him and let him know I was in treatment, my hands wouldn't stop shaking and I kept punching in wrong numbers."

The image from the media is that people commonly die detoxing from "hard drugs" like heroin. Actually, alcohol addiction poses the greatest danger of death during detoxification. Unmedicated detoxification from alcohol can produce delirium tremens (DTs)—uncontrollable tremors throughout the body—nausea, the sweats, visual and auditory hallucinations, seizure, and death.

"WET BRAIN"

One of our interventionists traveled to Hong Kong to fetch an American businessman who had been drinking for thirty-two years. The morning of the intervention, the man was calm, lucid, and well spoken. Three days later, however, well into a carefully monitored detox at a treatment center, something unraveled inside his brain. Recognizing that his condition was growing unstable, the medical staff moved him to a nearby hospital. He stayed there for several months, never rallying, never getting clear in his head.

His wife moved to the states and took a house nearby. Each day he asked for the car to be brought around so he could go home. He never understood that he was a long way from his home in Hong Kong. He couldn't stand by himself or walk. His memory was severely impaired.

The man had suffered severe, permanent alcoholic brain damage—often referred to as "wet brain." The intervention may have saved his life, but major physical damage was already done.

Methamphetamine (meth) is one of the most destructive drugs for three reasons. First, meth can be produced cheaply and easily, which means that on the street it is low cost and available. Second, it creates initial effects of euphoria, increased energy, and weight loss without apparent consequences, which makes prolonged use attractive. Extended use, however, consistently produces paranoia, aggressiveness, and marked delusion. Third, and finally, meth acts as a neurotoxin within the body. It causes increased heart rate and blood pressure, and its use can result in cardiovascular collapse and death. It causes permanent damage to the brain and blood vessels, which can produce strokes.

BUT DON'T LET A NEGATIVE DIAGNOSIS SCARE YOU

Methamphetamine, heroin, a bottle of Jack Daniel's a day? Don't lose heart. The body is a resilient or-

It's Not Okay to Be a Cannibal

ganism capable of repairing itself at an astonishing rate.

Addiction of every kind is treated successfully every day.

The true enemy is not the drugs or the alcohol but the physical dependence and mental obsession of addiction that turns friends and family into cannibals. The obsession is perfectly treatable.

Many, many, many users have overcome the cannibal within and are living happy, high-functioning lives.

Don't despair. As the mother of one teenage alcoholic told us, "I'm sure I have made a hundred phone calls trying to help Jamie. If it can help him get better, I'll make one hundred and one."

Benzodiazepines such as Valium and Xanax may be the hardest drugs to withdraw from. Users may experience a raft of symptoms, ranging from skin rash to metallic taste to constipation to chest pain to hallucinations. And withdrawal can last weeks, unlike alcohol withdrawal, which ends after a few days. The best way to withdraw from drugs or alcohol is under a doctor's supervision. Going "cold turkey," doing it yourself, is always very dangerous—a doctor should always be consulted.

Even behavioral compulsivity, which is too often considered less serious than heavy-duty substance addiction, can be life-threatening. Eating disorders, untreated, result in the death of about 20 percent of those afflicted.

Eating disorders are especially pernicious because, unlike every other addictive substance or activity, one cannot walk away from food and survive. Complete and total abstinence is not an option—you have to eat *something*. So the drug of choice is always under one's nose.

Gambling can lead to financial and emotional destruction of the family, to the commission of crimes, to divorce, and to suicide.

All addictions tear at the soul, causing anguish, anger, depression, and despair.

All addictions rupture the fabric of the family, leading to the disintegration of important relationships.

"Do We Dare?"

This is the question that troubles families the most. Do we dare confront our loved one? Do we dare risk losing what goodwill is left between us? Is she really an addict? Do we have the right to step in and save an adult freely making decisions for himself? What if the addict stops loving us?

What if he hurts himself? Do we have the guts to have the conversation that we need to have, to send the powerful message to the addict that things have changed and that they're never changing back?

These are powerful questions that go to the heart of successful intervention. They are also linked with fears that form the biggest obstacle to getting help for the cannibal.

It's Not Okay to Be a Cannibal

"How Do We Know When It's Time to Intervene?"

Economists have always used armloads of statistics to explain the effects of inflation and unemployment. We would read these numbers, wrinkle our faces, and wonder what they meant exactly. Then someone combined them into a single statistic called the Misery Index: how it feels when we are struggling to find work to earn money that doesn't buy what it used to.

Suddenly, people understood.

The same index applies when considering what to do with an addict in the family. When is it time to intervene? It's time when you can't bear to live with it another minute.

OBSTACLES TO INTERVENTION

Over the years, we have received tens of thousands of phone calls inquiring about intervention for a loved one. Of these, only a fraction lead to action. What holds people back?

- **Family denial.** Is it really that bad? Is now the right time? Families ask us to cosign their denial every day for a hundred different reasons.
- **Family fear.** Even though the cannibal lives with them and things are truly desperate, somehow, in the family's mind, taking action would only make matters worse. Change for the addict means

change for the family, too. For many families, this fear is paralyzing.

- **Addiction myths.** Much of what people think they know about addiction is wrong: the addict has to hit bottom, treatment doesn't work, the addict needs to want to be helped, it's a willpower issue.

"Doesn't the Addict Have to Hit Bottom?"

The phrase *hitting bottom/hitting rock bottom* goes back many decades to the notion that addicts can't change their course of action until it is clear to them, beyond any doubt, that their situation has become too terrible to ignore. The moment a person realizes he's in mortal danger, he has "hit bottom."

The idea that addicts have to hit bottom before they can recover—and the corollary idea that there is nothing anyone can do until that happens—is one the greatest fallacies about addiction among the general public. (The theory was, likewise, once accepted by professionals in the field.) Its persistence has contributed to the pain, suffering, and death of millions of addicts struggling with this disease. But it's just not true. Intervention has the same success rate regardless of the addict's willingness to seek help.

Consider what happens in the medical field. If someone is sick with cancer in the United States, we don't wait until tumors sprout visibly from the skin. If we do that, we have waited too long. The medical community has sufficiently educated the American public about the importance of early detection and treatment regarding cancer as a treatable disease. Catching it early helps save lives and avoids many serious consequences.

The single most dangerous misconception about addiction is that it's untreatable and that addicted people don't get better.

Prior to the founding of Alcoholics Anonymous, alcoholism was widely believed to be untreatable. This sense of addiction as an irreversible curse is still prevalent in many people's minds. Never mind that time and time again, addiction of every kind has been proven to be as susceptible to treatment as any other major chronic illness. Treatment works—but people don't believe it works. They missed one of the most important stories of our time—that intervention works.

Do addicts have to hit bottom? No! Early detection and action is as helpful with addiction as it is with cancer. Many argue that to do otherwise—to have the power to intervene and to choose to do nothing with it—is irresponsible and inhumane.

Smashing a car into a freeway embankment could qualify as hitting bottom. So could causing death or injury to another person, getting fired, or being arrested. A spouse leaving, a suspicious spot on an X-ray of a liver, or any event powerful enough to override the everyday delusion that addicts live with is hitting bottom. Hitting bottom means just that: overcoming delusion.

Some addicts are ready to hoist the white flag of surrender and define their own bottom. They have definitely arrived at the bottom and know it, and they are desperate for help. Other people have an idea that they have a problem but aren't sure yet how serious it is. They have not hit bottom yet and wonder if they have to.

The answer is wonderful: An addict doesn't have to hit bottom to get help. The right kind of help can in effect "raise the bottom." Performed properly, an intervention creates a bottom on the spot for the addict. Bottom, after all, is a synonym for pain. The truth for all addicts is that pain is the great motivator and that consequences get people sober. When the pain is great enough, even an addict will be forced to admit that it hurts. So an intervention involves the administration of a certain kind of pain—the truth.

Intervention does *not* require that something catastrophic first happen in the family. That's exactly what intervention is trying to prevent. Intervention tries to create a "false bottom" right now, right here, today—a clear, scripted bottom that is under control. Waiting for the addict to hit bottom on his own is extremely dangerous since no one can be certain what that bottom will be. The cannibal may find it more difficult to turn his life around in jail, in the hospital, or six feet under— the deepest bottom of all.

"How Can We Possibly Take These Measures?"

Most people know a cannibal who is a danger to those around him. They try to talk to him, and he tells them to mind their #^%$* business. They may have thoughts of walking away, but with knowledge comes responsibility. Friends and family are in a position where they are responsible for what they know. What do they do? They don't want to be an accomplice to vehicular manslaughter or breaking and entering.

The person concerned about a loved one's drunk driving or criminal activity may hesitate to call an interventionist, but the person most likely on the fence (or not even near it) is the one who lives with an addict whose behavior is not as extreme.

Is it fun having an addict in one's life? No. Addicts compel family members to take actions no one wants to take. Yet sometimes people are compelled by circumstances to act.

If you value your addicted loved one enough to step in and provide help, the chances of helping are much greater than if you stand back and do nothing.

It is not okay to recognize a dangerous situation and then do nothing about it. It is okay

- to inform the police if someone you know is impaired, refuses to stop, and gets in a car to drive. Call 911 with the name, make of car, license plate number, and direction the person is headed. You and a great many other innocent people deserve safe streets to drive on.
- to call the police and let them know your cannibal is running a meth lab out of his home. Drug production, sales, or distribution in any

form is illegal. If you are scared about the consequences of an addict's behavior, that is an even more important reason to call the authorities.

- to ask a family member who refuses to stop his illegal drug activities to leave your home, even if it means he must live on the street.
- to let people be hungry, homeless, and poor if that is the independent decision they have made. If they want to be the best alcoholic or addict they can be, then tell them to rent their own apartment, buy their own booze or drugs, and drink or use themselves to death there—not in your spare bedroom.
- to say no to pleas for assistance from an individual who refuses treatment, *no matter how desperate the story,* if it puts you or others at risk.

You robbed a gas station to support your meth habit and you need a place to hide out until the situation cools?

Tough luck.

You need a meal and some sleep? A warm safe place to kick your dope habit for three or four days?

Tough luck.

It's cold outside, you have nowhere to go, and I have to let you in even though you refuse to go to treatment?

No. I don't. Choices have consequences. Yours have landed you a bed at the Salvation Army tonight.

It's Not Okay to Be a Cannibal

"Can the Intervention Be Done in a Way That Doesn't Cause Pain?"

Even when the addict is dying for someone to step into his life and offer him a way out, the challenge of intervening remains a gruesome moment of truth for addict and family.

It isn't easy to say, "You have become a cannibal."

It isn't easy to list the terrible things the addict has done, to his face.

It isn't easy to deliver the ultimatum: "You can go on being an addict if you wish, but you have to do it somewhere else, with no help from us."

But the pain is part of the intervention's power. For cannibals, emotional pain is the great motivator. Consequences are what get people sober. Remember that the point is to create an "artificial bottom" that the addict can hit and a safe place to crash, as opposed to a jail, a hospital, a grave.

"What Will the Cannibal Do When We Confront Him?"

Some run out the door. Some storm and yell. Some threaten that, even if treated, they will resume their addiction the day they are released. Some are mortified with embarrassment and deny there is any kind of problem. Some break down in tears. Most addicts, however, go quietly. When that happens, it's because there is still a part of them that is not deluded, that knows they need help and that addiction is leading them toward death. There is often just enough of the person you love still in there—and that person steps forward, overrules the cannibal, and says, "Okay, I'm willing to give this a shot."

Susie, the cannibal in the first chapter, slammed the door in our faces the first day. But a week later she called us and agreed to enter treatment. The intervention was a success; it just took awhile.

Not all addicts go quietly into treatment. Some cling desperately to the illusion that they are still in control. They will use every means at their disposal to provoke in you feelings of guilt, disgust, embarrassment, protectiveness, and love.

"What If He Hurts Himself?"

That's what a guilt-ridden father from Albuquerque named Dan asked. Dan's son, Jake, was a classic coke-snorting cannibal who holed up in his room, got high, and let everything else in his life slide. He didn't even bother to hide his stuff—the whole room was a shrine to preparing and taking coke. And lest the father try anything, the son defiantly gave him this warning:

"If you try to intervene on me, I swear I'll blow my brains out. And you can clean the mess up."

Now, Dan wasn't the greatest father. His marriage to Jake's mom had broken up three years earlier. He was sad. He brooded. He didn't spend much time with his son after he entered the rebellious teen period. What

THINGS THAT WORK	THINGS THAT DON'T WORK
Getting help. You need a fresh set of eyes to see things clearly. Ask for help from all quarters and talk to professionals about the best help available.	**The status quo.** When nothing changes . . . nothing changes.
Clarity. Be explicit regarding new livable boundaries for you and your family. Be clear about supporting recovery not addiction.	**Enabling.** Don't protect an addict from the consequences of his addiction. Those consequences will be invaluable in the long-term plan to get him sober.
Support. Speak up and out. Join a group like Al-Anon. Realize you are not alone— help others realize that they are not alone.	**Secrecy.** Cannibalism thrives in silence.
Serenity. Relax. You did not cause the cannibalism. Neither do you have the power to control it. Try to define your life independent of someone else's disease.	**Chaos.** Be aware of your own codependency and unhealthy enmeshment. If your life is a mess, it's harder to help someone else.

could they do together? Listen to loud music and talk trash about other people?

Although Dan's relationship with Jake was no great shakes, the prospect of his son committing suicide made him quake with fear. How could he carry on if his actions resulted in the death of his only son? What would happen to his life if he opened Jake's door and found him twisting on a rope?

The AIR clinician Dan spoke to listened to all of his fears and took a deep breath. "It's strange," he said. "The question of suicide is the number one concern of families contemplating intervention," he said. "The idea of their good intentions leading to a catastrophic result is paralyzing—it freezes them just when they are on the verge of taking action.

"Addicts do commit suicide, but not often at this point in the addiction cycle. Suicide overtakes people who are in enormous, conscious pain—often people wishing to recover but failing because they don't get the guidance and support they need. There are people who have been in treatment numerous times, and for whatever reason, they are not able to change. Their situation is authentically tragic. Their sense of shame is absolute. Helpless to right themselves, they do the unthinkable and take their lives.

"Addicts in the cannibal stage are generally not consciously in pain. They generally do not feel shame. This is why we call them cannibals—they live beyond the pale of shame and sensitivity. Cannibals don't want to die; they want to keep getting high or giving in to their com-

It's Not Okay to Be a Cannibal

pulsions. The clear and present danger facing them is death not by suicide but by overdose."

Dan nodded at the distinction between a cannibal and a true suicide. There wasn't much question regarding which described Jake.

The interventionist continued. "Instead of worrying about the cannibal's sensibilities, families need to worry about their own.

"I have some advice for you, Dan, and I give it with some reluctance. I don't want you to think I am indifferent to suicide. I'm not. People do commit suicide, and the consequences are obviously dreadful. But right now you need to look at an even bigger picture. If you'll give me a chance, I'm going to lay it out for you."

First, the clinician said, label the threat as what it is: emotional blackmail. "I'm going to kill myself if you take my coke away" is a nakedly, brutally manipulative statement. As a negotiating strategy, it is hard to take seriously, because it takes out the negotiator. Suicide is the nuclear option. It ends everything. It kills the individual, and in a psychological sense, it kills the survivors as well. It is so profound that self-respecting people can not bring themselves to use it as a bargaining chip. It's a kind of cheating: "I'll take my ball and go home—permanently!"

"If an addict uses this ploy," the clinician said, "you can be very certain it is the cannibal talking, not the person you love. And the addict has no intention of dying. The addict just wants more time to use and will go to any lengths to get it. The cannibal experiences no shame using this tactic. It is the person whom you love, the sick and suffering addict imprisoned inside, who must pay for the consequences of the cannibal's tactics down the road.

"Don't misunderstand me," the clinician told Dan. "People take their lives every day, but they do it out of despair, which is a terrible thing. Cannibals don't do it if there is even a ghost of a chance to go on using.

"So I'm telling you, beware of manipulation. Threatening suicide may just be another way for the addict to get what he wants."

The clinician paused. "Now I want you to think of the larger picture. The threat of suicide is a side issue, a distraction. The larger issue is that Jake, your loved one, is already dying. Addiction to drugs or alcohol is a primary, progressive, chronic, fatal illness. It leads in one direction—toward dysfunction and death. The threat of death already hangs over Jake, but suicide isn't the primary problem. Addiction is.

"Finally, remember that addiction is a family illness. Addicts are masters at making us feel guilty, at paralyzing us with our own emotional fears, so they can keep getting what they want. I know Jake looks like your son to you. But he's in the grips of a monster, and the little kid you loved is no longer in charge. Instead, you have this monster saying, 'If you try to help me I'll hurt myself.'"

Four days later, sitting in his living room, surrounded by the interventionist, his ex-wife, his son's best friend, and Jake's stepsister, Dan said these words to counter his son's threat:

"Son, if that's your decision, to hurt yourself, I can't stop you. If you take your life, you will succeed in causing your mom and me the deepest pain we will ever know. You have that power, because we love you. You're our son.

"But there are a couple of things you need to know. Your mother and I see you struggling with this addiction. And we want to help. We'll do anything we can to get you right again.

"Now, you are a free agent. You have the right to see our concern for you as an act of aggression. Yes, we're getting in your face. Yes, we're messing with your life. I can understand that you don't like that and wish we would go away.

"But I have to ask you, do you think that's a good reason to die? Is that what your life is for, to snuff it out in an act of spite?'"

What gave Dan the courage to utter these daring words? It was something the interventionist said to him and the entire group at the pre-intervention meeting:

"Here's what you need to say to Jake. Tell him that his suicide may indeed prompt feelings of guilt in you. But that deep down, you know better. You didn't wish his death. You didn't cause his death. You couldn't stop him from doing what he did. It was Jake who did these things. It's his responsibility, not yours. It's profoundly sad, and you will cry many tears because of it. But you will also know that you did the right thing. You did all the work that could be done. You tried to save him from his addiction.

"And you must ask yourself, What if I do nothing, say nothing? Jake will continue to spiral downward, and he will likely wind up dead or in prison.

"Addiction is eminently treatable, but first some type of intervention must occur and second, some type of outside help must be put in place. Whether this outside assistance happens voluntarily or involuntarily doesn't matter—but it must happen if recovery is to occur. Doing nothing is no longer okay. Parents who do nothing, who turn away and let the addiction progress unimpeded, are ultimately complicit in the consequences of their inaction. The worst thing is for your child to die and for you to know you could have done more to help him."

"What If He Doesn't Go?"

What happens if the family holds the intervention, and the addict calmly informs you he won't go into treatment? Was the intervention a catastrophic failure?

No. It becomes an important day in everyone's life. It's the day that things changed. It's the day the family gets off the hook for their loved one's problem. It's the day they let go of the guilt of responsibility. It's the day they all get to walk back to their own lives, secure that they have now accomplished 100 percent of the work that is available to them in terms of treating this disease in their family. There will be good days and bad days ahead, but the hopefulness of the good will outweigh the anxieties of the bad.

Think of it this way: being discouraged because the addict says no is a subtle form of codependence. Once again, you're allowing the addict to determine how you feel. Those days are gone. Your family is getting better, no matter what the addict says or does. That's the new reality.

Even if things are unsuccessful, and the cannibal does not agree to accept help, the family will always know in their hearts and be able to say to one another: "We tried. We did the work we were able to do. We love our daughter, and we made the best offer we were able to make. In the face of all this, she turned us down. Her choice is her responsibility. We feel regret that the family did not get the response it most wanted—an unequivocal 'yes'—but not guilt."

When you have a loved one who is an addict, there are really only three things you can hope for:

1. The addict will wake up one morning and say, "That's it. I'm done. It's time to get clean." And of his own accord, he will either get counseling, avail himself of outpatient help, check in to an inpatient clinic, or just attend Twelve Step meetings and, one way or another, stay sober. This is the miracle cure, and it is what every stressed-out family hopes and prays for. Occasionally, it even happens.

2. Some external event that is bad but not too bad—getting arrested, getting a scary medical warning, or having some serious financial consequences—will prompt the addict to seek treatment.
3. The family can act together to alter the power imbalance. They can effect a paradigm shift and change how the family decides to act moving forward, independent of whether the addict goes to treatment.

A family is like a mobile that hangs from a ceiling. It may have five or six or seven parts, one for each person in the family, dangling on wires and all dependent on the others for stability. When there is a cannibal in the family, his part of the mobile is granted disproportionate weight in the minds of the family and seemingly outweighs all the other family members put together.

The result of a well-run intervention is that by the time it is over, the family has more properly arranged itself. They have learned to distribute weight, responsibility, and power accordingly. Suddenly, the balance of power shifts away from what the addict wants and toward what the family wants.

It is a defining characteristic of the disease of addiction that addicts wield disproportionate power in their households. This perceived power imbalance and the reactions based upon it keep families locked in the conspiracy of silence. An addicted fifteen-year-old girl can emotionally overpower her father, even if he's an offensive lineman on an NFL team. Why? Because the addict isn't concerned about the lineman's feelings. One-on-one, the girl will knock her lineman father on his emotional behind every single time, because he cares, while she—in the grip of her own cannibalism—does not.

But line the addict up against her entire family, single-minded and determined, and her tyranny may have met its match. This is especially true when the family has agreed on the terms of noncompliance.

THE ANSWER TO "NO, I WON'T GO."

If you decide *not* to accept help today, you are saying, in effect, that it is more important for you to be an addict than to be an active, healthy member of this family. While this decision makes us sad, we will honor it. But you need to know that our relationships will change in the following ways:

- We will do everything within our power to support your recovery.
- We will do everything in our power to cut off support for your addiction.
- We will no longer pay your bills.
- We will no longer feed or clothe or shelter you.
- We will not provide you with transportation.
- We will not insure you.
- We will no longer make excuses for your actions.
- We will be open and honest about the state of this family's situation regarding you with anyone

who asks, including friends, relatives, employers and employees, creditors, members of law enforcement, or anyone who is interested.

- We will tell them that it is terribly sad but true that you are struggling with addiction and that we have done everything in our power to make help available to you but that for today you have chosen a different path. We will be clear that our hopes for your recovery remain strong but dedication to the welfare of our family as a whole comes first. We can no longer allow one person's disease to make life unmanageable for the rest of us.

Do you see how intervention changes the rules of the game? The addict can still say no, but he can't have things stay the same.

3

CANNIBAL CAMOUFLAGE

One advantage addicts have is that they are always one or two or four steps ahead of us. They know they are addicts before we do. Long before we become suspicious, they are already hiding their tracks, inventing excuses, refilling bottles, altering their calendars, turning the tables on us so that things that go wrong are *our* fault, not theirs. They know that if we ever catch up to them, and deal with them with the level of suspicion that their behavior deserves, the jig is up. So they are continually throwing camouflage over their activities to keep us in the dark.

They are brilliant at doing this. Even people who never had a deceitful bone in their bodies become masters of deception.

A Short List of Lies

How do cannibals deceive? Let us count a few ways:

Hiding evidence. Stashing liquor bottles in the clothes hamper. Bag of pills behind the light switch cover plate.

Dope in the blazer pocket in the closet. Cocaine in the bedside Bible. Snickers bars beneath the bed.

Planting evidence. Setting a bottle in plain view, at a constant or a modestly diminishing level. Drinking alcohol from bottles and then refilling them with water.

Keeping up appearances. Dressing to blend in and not stand out. The shrewd addict goes to church every Sunday and wears a shined pair of shoes.

Hiding in plain sight. "So what if I put away a twelve-pack in an evening? Who am I hurting? Or if I snort a line or two or take a toke during the ball game? It's only on the weekends. I work hard; I deserve to relax. It's really no big deal."

Misdirecting. Calling your attention to the one thing he's doing right—ignoring the ten things that have gone hopelessly wrong.

Financial camouflage. Juggling finances; kiting checks; running up balances on numerous credit cards, some of them kept without a partner's or spouse's awareness.

Building firewalls. Belonging to several groups of friends. Going out with different friends on different nights helps to hide frequency and amounts.

It's Not Okay to Be a Cannibal

False abstinence. Playing the teetotaler at parties or in public. Drinking club soda at the neighbors' cocktail party—but sneaking a double before leaving home—and leaving early to get back to the bottle.

Playwriting. Creating a play about his suffering, anxieties, superhuman pressure, or how no one understands him to explain his need to drink or why he skipped work. "I have a really screwed up family that makes my life unmanageable." "My wife just doesn't understand me." "Why does everything bad happen to me?"

Busy, busy. Avoiding detection by being unavailable.

That explains it. Having an answer for everything. Losing weight because of anorexia or a crack habit? Tell them you're on a great new diet that really works.

The barking dog. Putting up a ferocious front to keep others away. Also known as the best defense is a good offense.

Threats of suicide. Manipulating the family to the maximum: "Don't try to save my life or I'll end it."

Depression. Using emotional problems as an excuse: "You'd drink too if you felt like I do every day." People hide behind other emotional afflictions, too: bipolar syndrome, anxiety disorder, anger problems.

Lying. Making up friends, jobs, homes, lifestyles, events.

Stealing. Doing whatever is necessary to maintain the fiction of financial stability.

Blame shifting. Working to convince others that he's not the one at fault. It's everyone's fault but his.

Deny, deny, deny. "That wasn't me you saw." "I didn't take your money." "If anyone in our family has a drinking problem, it's you, not me."

Bluffing. "Why would you accuse me of missing work today? Call Jim my boss. He'll tell you I spent the whole day working hard."

Manipulating. "I was just feeling so low. I lost heart for a moment. I'm doing better now."

Turning the tables. "Where was I? Why, I was looking for you! I was on the verge of calling the police. Don't ever do that to me again!"

The Stairway of Deception

The many ways addicts deceive can be illustrated with a graph. Draw a ladder of horizontal lines. Each line represents a moment in the relationship between you and your addict.

It's Not Okay to Be a Cannibal

Line 1 is the day the addict gets caught in his first misbehavior. At this point the addict already knows a lot more than you do. He knows that he's been using for some time. But it's no big deal; he can handle it. So he denies his secret activities to you, or he steers conversation away from it.

What do you do? You buy the story, of course. What kind of person doesn't cut a family member slack from time to time? You're on the same team, right? Especially at the outset, when there is no prior history of misbehavior.

And so it goes, with each failure. Each time, the addict knows 100 percent what is happening and the family member knows very little. As a result, the cannibal continually outsmarts the family member.

In real life, the dishonest behavior goes far beyond five lines on a table. It's dozens and hundreds of lines, a horrifying sequence of failures, free passes, and turning a blind eye to the cannibal's bad behavior as he violates law after law and each time comes up with a plausible explanation.

At each point, going down the ladder, the addict is three or four lines ahead of the family member. There is no way the family member, acting on his or her own, is ever going to catch up to the deception and delusion of the addict. The addict will always occupy a lower rung on the ladder, and thus will always have the tactical advantage—even as he cheats, lies, and steals.

How can a family member win at this terrible game?

There is only one way: united intervention, not by just one person, whom the addict can isolate, manipulate, and con, but by the entire family, who have so much

INCIDENT	CANNIBAL'S RESPONSE	YOUR RESPONSE
1. Stole $20 bill from wallet	"No, I didn't take anything."	"Oh, okay. I must have spent it myself."
2. Rolled automobile	"This maniac came out of nowhere!"	"Oh, my poor baby!"
3. Secretly removed money from savings account	"Honey, someone's swindling us. We're the victims of white-collar crime."	"Gee, that seems a little far-fetched."
4. Lost job	"Those people had it in for me from the get-go."	"But I don't understand. Why didn't you tell me this was happening?" ("I did, but you wouldn't listen!")
5. Arrested buying coke on the street	"It's *your* fault. If you'd loved me without all your judgment, I wouldn't need to do these things."	"Jerry, I think we have a problem."

It's Not Okay to Be a Cannibal

corroborative evidence of wrong-doing that even the most delusionary, deceptive cannibal is forced to run up the white flag.

To the previous chart, intervention adds a final line. This time it's the family's turn to spring the surprise on the cannibal:

INCIDENT	CANNIBAL'S RESPONSE	YOUR RESPONSE
6. Intervention	"You're all ganging up on me. I thought you loved me!"	"Jerry, we're done with that conversation. Let's talk about going to treatment."

And the beauty is, this line can be played at any point on the ladder, before the most damaging misbehaviors occur. The family simply needs to begin seeing through the camouflage that the cannibal throws up to obscure his behaviors.

We have seen addicts in the extreme stages fending off hallucinated insects and feeling in their mouths for the alien transmitters that were controlling their behavior. There are such extremes. But mostly, addicts don't look like cannibals. They hide their feral nature with a series of subtle and often attractive disguises. For openers, they look exactly like the person you have always loved. Like Hannibal Lecter, the arch-cannibal of books and movies—and an authentic addict to sadistic behavior—they can be sophisticated and genteel. They may retain a good sense of humor. They may espouse honorable causes. In many outward ways they can be normal, and even admirable.

Or they may not be any of these positive things. The key to their cannibalism is not how they appear to you but what they do when no one's looking. Alcoholics fool you by drinking more than you think they're drinking and by doing it on the sly. Overeaters have candy bars hidden in the underwear drawer and Oreos stashed beneath the bed. Gamblers and sex addicts live lives of outward self-control and inner lives of turmoil. So they hide.

The first rule of cannibal detection is to be suspicious. Stop looking with your eyes and start thinking with your brain. Ask yourself what the other person is really doing. Focus not on appearances, which can be explained away, but on behaviors, which are undeniable facts.

Focus not on how things *seem* but how they *are*. What are the facts? Do these facts jibe with your expectations, with house rules, with what normal families and law-abiding folks do? When direct questions to addicts receive indirect answers or outright lies, you can be sure something fishy is going on.

The Crossroads

Most of us don't like spying on our loved ones or calling their veracity into question. When it comes to something as important as the life of the family, however, you're at a crossroads. This crossroads requires you to make a tough choice:

EITHER	OR
You like things the way they are and want to keep the status quo.	You don't like things the way they are and want them to change.

If you choose the first road, nothing changes. You accept that the cannibal, based upon your previous experience with him, has no intentions of doing anything different any time soon. You also recognize that you have no immediate interest in changing yourself. The status quo is acceptable to you. Thus, your final consideration is how do I make the best of the mess I find myself in?

If, however, you choose the second road—you can't live with the status quo—then you *must* take action to change it. There are really only two things that can change. Either the cannibal can elect to behave differently, or you and the family can. The question becomes, "Are you ready to initiate change?"

If your answer is yes, then it is time for a new set of tactics. Until now the cannibal has been on the offensive. From this point on, you'll be on the offensive. "Magical thinking" based on dated paradigms of how things used to be, of how you expect them to be, or of how you know they could be are of no use to you now. You must deal with facts. You must go into the truth business. You must rely on the knowledge that thousands of other families have acquired through dealing with their loved ones' addictions.

In the world of addiction there is an unfortunate truism: Where there's smoke, there's usually fire.

Family and friends easily get caught up in codependence, enmeshment, and an infallible need to blindly enable people to stay sick. By extricating yourself from these traps, you can examine the situation clearly.

WORDS THAT IMPRISON

These concepts are sometimes used interchangeably to describe the deformation of family relationships in the presence of addiction. But each has a specific meaning:

- **Codependency.** Taking responsibility for the addict's behavior. Codependency destroys the ability to see and speak the truth. It turns family members into "coconspirators" with the cannibal.
- **Enabling.** Rescuing the addict from the consequences of his actions. Enablers are people who, seeing trouble all around, allow it to get worse. Families do this out of "love." But it is a love that keeps people sick longer and makes situations worse.
- **Enmeshment.** A painful and complicated tangling of personalities that is common to families struggling with addiction. Enmeshment is the

It's Not Okay to Be a Cannibal

blurring of boundaries that leaves individuals un-
sure where one person leaves off and another
begins.

"What's Really Going On?"

- Is it okay that my fourteen-year-old son has a
  lock on his door and won't allow anyone in?
- What's happening out in the garage where my
  husband seems to spend night after night
  cleaning and organizing?
- Is it really okay that my wife drives the kids to
  school after she's been smoking pot?
- Honestly now, where is all the money going?
- Is it normal that my daughter goes to the
  bathroom directly after every meal?
- My son put on forty-five pounds of muscle
  this winter working out. He looks really
  strong and healthy, but should I worry that
  it's a little unnatural?
- My daughter has cuts on her arms and her
  legs. Is it possible that she just scratches herself in her sleep like she tells me?
- My husband told me that he has developed
  narcolepsy, which explains why he falls asleep
  at the dinner table every night. Is it possible
  he lied to me about his doctor's diagnosis?
- My son's eyes are always red. He says its sea-
  sonal allergies, but it's the dead of winter.
  Should I be suspicious?

Ask yourself: Does that really make sense? Or do I just buy it to avoid confrontation?

THE CANNIBAL TWIST

No one enjoys asking hectoring questions, and cannibals are skilled at turning that dislike to their advantage. They are good at keeping you off balance, blaming you for their offenses. It's a nasty game of distracting you from the real problem at hand—their addiction. Here are examples of the cannibal twist (also known as another version of the hustle):

- "Why are you nagging me about this?"
- "You've changed lately—all these questions!"
- "The only problem this family has is your paranoia."

This "twisted" aspect of relationships with addicts is yet another reason why outside interventionists are effective.

Of course they try to turn the accusations around to reflect poorly on you. Cannibals are the best in the business at aggressive misdirection. In their defense, they don't know they're doing it—they're delusional, and they think your questions are genuinely inappropriate and indicative that something is wrong with *you*.

The best way to get inside the cannibal mind is to listen to them talk. They do not horrify themselves. Until they get on the road to recovery, they may feel no shame

It's Not Okay to Be a Cannibal

whatsoever. If you know any active addicts, they are very baffling. Why are they this way? How do you get through to them? What does it take to get them to stop lying—to you or to themselves?

Here are the true stories, told in their own words, of two cannibals in whose interventions we played a part. At the time of their telling, they are no longer cannibals. Or rather, the cannibal inside each has shrunk, allowing the real person to resume control. But they remember their using days well.

A Gentleman and a Dope Fiend

At the height of my addiction, I did whatever it took to get drugs. Before I became an actual member of a methadone clinic, I used to go down there and hang out. Of course if you belong to a methadone program, you're not supposed to be using. You're supposed to be in the program to get off the dope. You're supposed to take the methadone and drink it right there.

But some people want it both ways; they want to stay in the program and still be able to use. They play games with the rules; they cheat on their urine tests. They're looking to make a few bucks, always running some kind of game—welcome to the wonderful world of drug addiction. Oftentimes rather than drink the stuff themselves, they'll spit it into a take-away bottle and sell it to sick sidewalk junkies—like me.

You may be wondering, what kind of person buys something other people have just spit out? I'll tell you.

I was an upscale kid from Georgetown, in the nation's capital. My dad was a kind of diplomat/lawyer, who negotiated hostage release deals for the government. My mom, after they divorced when I was five, became a money manager for a major investment house. My parents were great to me but not so great to each other.

Seen from the outside, my little brother and I had it pretty good. We were surrounded by the good things of life. Good books. Good schools. And we were lucky. But life is funny—things can be great on the outside, but inside a kid can feel pretty bad and pretty lonely.

I did everything I could to hide how I felt. I had my first drink standing in the woods with three pals in the fall of my sophomore year at prep school. One of them had boosted a bottle of champagne from a wedding, and we stood and took turns drinking it down straight from the bottle. The next time it was my turn. I stole a fifth of Jack Daniels from my grandmother's house in Miami and packed it in with my shirts on my way back to school. The fifth was the price of admission to the cool crowd.

You could say I figured out who I was or at least who I thought I wanted to be. I wanted to be a cool guy who hung out with other cool guys and got high. But who was I really? I was a kid with little identity of my own, only the deep impressions of my parents' expectations.

For the rest of my using career I sought out and found those same types of guys I had that first drink

It's Not Okay to Be a Cannibal

with. When I went on to college, I formed a new group that felt like the old one. We did everything we could get our hands on: beer, pot, crack, hallucinogens, and eventually heroin.

After graduating from college and four years of hard-core heroin addiction, the cool wore off. I was coming apart. My feet were so swollen my shoes no longer fit. I had abscesses and sores on my arms and legs, which were always infected. To fight off these infections, I began copping another class of drugs on the street, antibiotics.

And my legs—I traced the veins on my legs and feet with a ballpoint pen when I could, so I was sure to find a place to hit when I was high.

That was when I started buying spit-back methadone. Believe me, when you know you're getting dope sick, when it feels like a small animal is trying to eat its way out of your stomach alive, swallowing another addict's saliva is the least of your worries. Spit-back never got me high. It just bought me time. And it kept me from getting sick for one more day.

What was my life like? I smoked crack to get up. Then I shot dope to level out before work. Then I'd make it to the methadone clinic over lunch and do it all over again a couple hours later. Then I'd crash, late at night, and in the morning, start it all over again. I'd slip my already-buttoned shirt from the day before over my head and fasten my already-tied tie.

Finally the morning came when I found myself in tears on the back porch, having a full mental breakdown.

I realized that no amount of money or drugs could fix the problem I had. I walked the six blocks down to the local hospital to check myself into detox. But when they left me alone in an examination room, which I had entered with every intention of getting straight, I fell apart and began rifling through the cabinets for drugs. Any drugs. The nurse called security and five minutes later I was back on the street. I was beyond help.

This is where my mother stepped in. She knew I was messed up but not this bad. She had me admitted to a locked ward at another hospital and intervened on me there. I agreed to go to treatment and went with them to the airport. But I still thought I was in control. When I found out it was a one-way ticket to the treatment center, I went nuts and slugged my mom! With the help of the intervention team they got me onto the plane, loaded me up with Valium, and as I sank into my seat, the cannibal phase of my life began to fade away.

Oh, the story goes on. I relapsed three times, threatened my ex-girlfriend with a shotgun, and disgraced myself in any number of ways before finally putting together some legitimate long-term sobriety. Even in recovery the cannibal never goes away entirely. He's always somewhere close at hand, biding his time, waiting for a moment of weakness. My job today is to do the work to maintain my sobriety, to work my program. As long as I keep it up, I keep the cannibal days behind me.

They say only a small percentage of heroin addicts clean up their hand for good. Looking back, my story

It's Not Okay to Be a Cannibal

gives me shivers but honestly, if I had it to do over, I wouldn't change a thing. I have a tremendous amount of gratitude for the life I live today and without my intervention, even without the fistfight at the airport, there is every chance that I could be ten years dead.

Man of the Year

I was raised in the shadow of Chicago's industrial east side, not far from the Indiana line. In the 1970s, the steel plants represented a ticket to the middle class for immigrants from Serbia, like my family, and other eastern European countries. Many in my family went into the mills, and more than a few worked hard in the heat of the molten steel and succumbed to lifetimes of drinking and dysfunction.

But I wanted none of that. I was going to escape the fate of the steel mills. I saw how many kids, even in high school, were headed nowhere because of alcohol. I saw them fall by the wayside. I even shoveled dirt on a few of their graves.

But that was for other people. For me, great things awaited. I had the itch of ambition. I wanted achievement, influence, personal wealth. I wanted to become somebody extraordinary. And I set out from college—I was voted "Man of the Year" by my graduating class—to accomplish just that.

I embarked on a career in business. It was the early days of personal computers, and I rose quickly to become a big shot in the marketing department of one of the fastest-growing companies, based in Chicago.

I was smart—about what consumers wanted and about what competing companies were failing to do. I loved the game aspect of out-thinking the other guys, there in my company and the other companies, too. My campaigns were aggressive and clever, snatching customers away right under competitors' noses. I was cocky.

In part due to me, the company rose to the top five sellers of PCs. I became executive vice president. I got the corner office. I occupied a penthouse suite along the lake, the best place there was. I dated glamorous women. I drove exotic cars.

People looked at me with a special look, and I dug that. Can you imagine what my family and my old neighborhood thought of me? That a kid from the mill district should attend ball games with business leaders, politicians, and athletes? I was a superstar to my mom. I was J. Pierpont Morgan. I was God come down in an Armani suit.

It was at the height of my success that I began using cocaine. Someone offered it to me at a party. At the particular moment in my life, I was feeling invincible—which, if I was really smart, should have been a warning.

But I wasn't really smart. I figured other people got into trouble, but I wouldn't. I would still be me. I would still be fabulously talented and competent. I was so good I could help run a Fortune 500 company and still

It's Not Okay to Be a Cannibal

enjoy a little coke on weekends. Best part was, I could take it or leave it. I was strong inside, like a bull.

But I wasn't a bull inside. More like, I was full of bull inside. I was just a foolish, arrogant young guy. I was playing a dangerous game, riding a business bubble on my own ego. Coke heightened all the dangers. It preyed on my insecurities and delusions of grandeur. Weekend use became daily use. Where I originally was confident I could hide my recreational use, the habit overtook me. Soon I was using in order to keep my "salesman's edge." I would use before giving an important talk. I would duck into the restroom before meetings.

Coke was no longer an amusement that I could handle. It was my wife—a really mean wife. And though she was mean to me, I loved her and swept everything out of the way to be with her. I began giving nutty, convoluted talks to the troops. I began missing meetings. I began failing.

Today I feel some anger toward my colleagues who put up with me. I needed an intervention right there, in the first year of my using. But I was such a powerful, scary guy, people backed off. My mom could see something was wrong, but I waved her away, telling her everything was stupendous, and I was doing terrific.

But I wasn't. I was in a deadly, downward spiral. I was no better than all the old guys from the neighborhood, drinking themselves into a stupor every night in order to face the factory in the morning. I was doing the same thing they were doing, only falling from a greater height. My career stalled. My numbers dropped. There was no joy in work—only blaming, and inappropriate behavior, and revved-up wheel-spinning.

I had lost all my decent friends. The only people who hung out with me were strung out like me. The only thing we cared about was getting and staying high.

I'm going to short-cut this description of hell to give you a description of the final days. I had lost my job. I lost my car. No one famous had come around in a long time. My family kept their distance. I was hanging around exclusively with cannibals like myself. And I was the king of the cannibals.

Here's how bad it was. The light and water in my apartment were shut off. And I peed in coffee cans, because the drain was clogged. I couldn't use the toilet, so I pooped in pizza boxes and took them out once a week, late at night, and stuffed them in the dumpster. Nice work. My apartment maybe looked like a dim shrine to coffee and pizza, if you could ignore the smell.

My number one concern was that my nose was breaking down, making it hard to get the coke up it. The mucous passages were so inflamed, I couldn't use it. So I used things like penny nails and paper clips to poke holes in my passageways so I could snort stuff up there. At one point I attached a vacuum cleaner hose to my nose, hoping to free up some real estate that way.

Cannibal? Damn straight. I was dancing with death, and it was getting very close to the end of the dance. But you know what happened. Thank God for my mom and my brother, who held an intervention for me. They got me to treatment. I have been clean and sober every day since.

Now, we at AIR have been part of hundreds of interventions in the years since we opened our doors. There is a reason why these two tales of cannibalism stand out. It is because the two cannibals are us. The fellow swiping drugs from the emergency ward cabinets was Andrew. The fellow in Chicago with the vacuum cleaner attached to his nose was Bob. And these events were not so long ago—Bob got clean in 1995 and Andrew in 1996.

We met while in early recovery and eventually went into business together. Running an addictions consulting company keeps us close to our recovery and puts us in a position to lend a hand to hundreds of people. We take a firm approach to addiction intervention because we've been there. We know what gets through to people who are lost in their addiction. We were cannibals once ourselves.

WHAT WE KNOW ABOUT CANNIBALS

- They are not the person you love. They are a parasite doing business inside the body of the person you love. Their goal is survival at any expense.
- They do not care about you, your health, your safety, or your financial security. Cannibals are

not sentimental and do not respect the rules of everyday people. They cannot be reached with bribery, compromises, or emotional appeals. Their only goal is to keep getting high.

- They don't care about their own health. In their delusion, they think they are okay. Some don't even realize they are addicted.

- Cannibals are bullies, and they will resort to any trick to get their way. They will threaten, blackmail, shame, lie, manipulate, hide, steal, promise—whatever it takes. They will hug you with one arm and pull a gun on you with the other. Their duplicity knows no bounds.

- It's not the cannibal who is dying, but the person you love who is trapped inside. You and your family are dying, too—because the cannibal is eating you alive.

- A few addicts will get sober on their own or through Twelve Step groups alone. But the solution for most is committing to treatment and follow-up, with all the powers of the family bonded together to drive and keep the cannibal out.

- A cannibal may dwindle, but like a speck of cancer the surgeon couldn't get, he never leaves completely. Know that he is still in there, biding his time, and that he wants to make a comeback, to be bigger and meaner than ever.

- Don't be fooled into thinking your loved one is

It's Not Okay to Be a Cannibal

cured. Recovery requires vigilance. Declaring "mission accomplished" is an invitation to relapse. Learn your lesson in codependency now, so you don't have to repeat it.

4

WHAT DO YOU SAY?

The family knew for many years that this moment was coming. Their son Louis, thirty-three, was grossly overweight, approaching five hundred pounds. Nobody knew for sure what he weighed because he refused to step on a scale.

Louis was in trouble. He hadn't worked in eighteen months. He used to be a clerk for the county records office, but now he spent most of his time in his apartment, eating and watching TV. Judging by his appearance, Louis had gained a lot of weight over the past year.

The family imagined he was eating less because he frequently talked about his forays to Weight Watchers and his promises to cut back on junk food. At family meals, he seemed to eat normally.

One day his sister, Linda, was leaving his apartment after a visit with Louis, when a neighbor stopped her. "You know," he said, "lots of us here in the building are worried about Louis. We've watched him get heavier and heavier this year. The pizza delivery guy is here every single night. We don't know what to do. But we would all like to see him get some help."

Linda passed the information on to her father, John, and he agreed to proceed with an intervention. When he called us, the first words out of his mouth were, "I can't stand it anymore. I think my son is trying to kill himself with food."

James, the client case manager, took the call. After listening to John's situation, he set up a meeting with the clinical staff to discuss the case and assign a clinician, and he scheduled a pre-intervention meeting with the family.

REASONS FOR THE PRE-INTERVENTION MEETING

- **Introduce the interventionist** to the team and have him outline the strategy for the next two days.
- **Unify the family.** Flush all divisive opinions and disabuse the team of myths and other false preconceptions.
- **Plot the possible outcomes** of inaction versus action. What will happen if an intervention does not take place? What would each family member like to see happen as a result of an intervention?
- **Adopt a strategy** for the intervention.
- **Agree on tactics.** Set a precise schedule. Where you will meet? Who else will be invited? Who will be in charge? Who will say what? Who will accompany the addict to treatment?
- **Agree on roles.** Write down and rehearse what each person will say and in what order.

- Go over the do's and don'ts of intervention. Done right, it will be a carefully scripted and managed family meeting
- **Decide,** in advance, how your relationship with the addict will change if he says no.

The Pre-Intervention Process

James scheduled the pre-intervention meeting for 6:30 p.m. He asked John, Louis's father, to serve as point person for the meeting—the person who would make sure everyone else was well-informed about dates, times, locations, expectations, and roles. The meeting was scheduled to last two hours and to take place at John's house.

The team was composed of John, the father; Susan, the mother; Carter, Louis's stepfather; and Linda, the sister. Like Louis, Linda had an obvious weight problem.

It was a cool October evening and despite the difficult two days that lay ahead, there was a newfound sense of hope among the family.

"Good evening," the interventionist began. "My name is Dr. Lessups. I'll be leading you through the pre-intervention meeting today and the family meeting tomorrow that will include Louis. I've been working in the addiction field for twenty years. I've been involved in hundreds of interventions and worked with dozens of clients just like Louis."

Dr. Lessups explained that the agenda for the next day's meeting would focus on three succinct messages:

It's Not Okay to Be a Cannibal

1. "Louis, we love you very much."
2. "We see you struggling in all the areas of your life."
3. "Help is available today."

"That's it. That's all we're going to talk about tomorrow. This is not going to be a family therapy session. Today we're going to do some education and try to come away with a better understanding of why a person overeats. We are going to talk about how this has affected this family as a whole. And, we are going to focus, in a very disciplined way, on helping you all convey those three simple messages. Does everybody understand?"

Everybody did.

"Congratulations to you all," Dr. Lessups continued. "Congratulations on stepping up and taking on the difficult and uncomfortable task in front of you. You have made the decision that the status quo in this family is no longer acceptable and thus something has to change. Even if we stood up from the table and walked away right now, your situation will have improved, because you have admitted there *is* a problem and that doing nothing about it is no longer an option.

"Right off the bat I want to make clear that this is not Louis's meeting. This is a family meeting to discuss issues that are important and affect all of the individual members of this family. One of the main goals of this meeting is to determine what is and is not okay inside this family, starting today. I want us all to be clear about the things this family will support and the things that we will no longer support.

"Before we continue I need to ask, Is anyone at this table in recovery of any kind? Has anyone here been in treatment for chemical dependency or behavioral problems? Has anyone been to an intervention before?"

Susan, the mother, put up her hand. "I'm in AA," she said. "I go to meetings every Wednesday at the Presbyterian church. But I never went to detox or treatment or anything like that."

"Good," Dr. Lessups said. "That experience will be valuable tomorrow. Louis will benefit from the kind of honesty you have learned in the program. At the same time, understand that tomorrow won't be like an AA meeting. It will be a family meeting. We're going to speak our truths to support the idea that Louis has a serious problem. We're going to ask him to be honest with himself and with us in the face of those truths and to come to a decision. We will do our very best to break down his wall of denial."

Linda winced. "But isn't that mean? I mean, won't he feel attacked and betrayed?"

"He may tell us that he feels that way, but just because he says it doesn't mean it's true. We're dealing with a disease that thrives by playing dirty. The Louis you know and love is being held hostage by a disease that doesn't care if it hurts you. We need to get the real Louis to stand up and fight back against the addict Louis. This is hard work. Addicts don't give up without a fight. So we have to build a solid team and create a

It's Not Okay to Be a Cannibal

long-term plan. We have to be tough—his recovery depends upon it."

THE FAMILY'S RESPONSIBILITY

Too often, fear paralyzes a family and keeps members from taking action. Either they back out because they are afraid that the family's secrets will be exposed, or they feel like hypocrites for calling an intervention. ("Where do I get off calling Angela on her drinking when she knows that I smoke marijuana when I am out with my friends?")

Suddenly, the intervention is about them and not their loved one, and this second-guessing can be disruptive. We have two responses:

- **Consider the greater good.** Is it better for all concerned to keep family secrets and withhold help from the individual who is struggling with a disease? Are you obliged to risk the family's reputation to save a family member's life? What would you want if *you* were the individual in trouble? Can you put an emotional, spiritual, or monetary price on an individual's heath and welfare? Do you believe that with great risks come great rewards? Do you believe that with knowledge comes responsibility? These are the questions each family member must ask to consider the greater good.
- **Forget about hypocrisy.** To be human is to be a

hypocrite. None of us lives up to our professed values. We all have feet of clay. The challenge right now is not to be paragons of virtue but to be loving, responsible family members.

Surprising things happen when people start telling the truth to one another. In the honest environment of an intervention, several family issues—in addition to the addiction—are often raised and addressed. As family members see how the addict's life improves with proper treatment, they find the courage to step forward and get help themselves.

Dr. Lessups had another question. "Is there anyone here who wonders if they are a big hypocrite? Who wonders, if Louis decides to make a big deal of your problem, that you might harm the intervention?"

Linda cleared her throat. "I'm not that different from Louis. I've struggled with my weight all my life. It's just that Louis's weight gain has been so dramatic, and we're all so scared about his health. I'm not denying that I have a problem, just that Louis's problem is more severe and immediate."

"So how do you feel about being a part of this effort to help Louis?"

"I want to help my brother."

"Do you think you'll be able to be a part of this effort to get help for your brother today?"

Linda nodded emphatically.

It's Not Okay to Be a Cannibal

"Well, that's what we're concerned about today," Dr. Lessups told her. "The main thing is, we can't have people on the team undermining the goals of the intervention—like a drinking buddy who doesn't think his problem is *so* bad."

Dr. Lessups paused and added this: "You know, Linda, this will be a good thing for you, too."

"I hope so," Linda replied.

CAN ONE ADDICT INTERVENE ON ANOTHER ADDICT?

The answer is almost always yes, provided that individual is there to be supportive of the effort.

If he feels the need to contradict the group or act as coconspirator, the answer is no.

Might the addict find it hypocritical that another addict is taking part in the intervention?

If that happens, explain to the addict that today is his intervention. The other addict will have to wait for another day.

Dr. Lessups emphasized that this meeting was really less for Louis than for the rest of them. "Louis isn't my client. You *all* are my client. One thing we're going to resolve today is what's okay in this family and what's not okay. We're going to develop a livable plan for you all moving forward, independent of what Louis decides to do."

The Conspiracy of Silence

Dr. Lessups explained to the family that an intervention is not an opportunity for a knock-down, drag-out family fight. It's not a chance for everyone to vent, blame, or shame one another. Rather, it's a mechanism for shifting the power in a family so that one sick person no longer controls everyone else. Done right, an intervention changes family dynamics. It exposes the truth and allows every member of the family to make informed decisions moving forward.

The root of most family dysfunction is secrets. There are things no one is allowed to talk about or even to refer to. Addiction is one of the most powerful secrets, and it commands absolute silence in a frightened family. No one mentions it, because that would mean acknowledging it exists, which in turn raises the level of household anxiety and requires people to act.

So families engage in a conspiracy of silence. Everyone in the family knows there is a problem, but by ignoring it, by restricting mealtime conversations to news, weather, and sports, by not saying anything about the addiction in their midst, the family allows it to grow in power and destructiveness. *Silence is the number one way families enable sick individuals.*

By talking, families administer an antidote to this toxic silence. It makes them say the things they have felt forbidden from saying, and it changes the family dynamic forever. By stepping out of "news, weather, and sports," the comfort zone where most of our relationships live, families are showing real love and concern. By doing this, family members will always know they did all they could for Louis. Their goal by the end of this intervention is to be able to say to themselves that they have done 100 percent of the work.

"When you find yourself getting angry, remember that Louis is sick. He's a sick person and we are trying to heal him," Dr. Lessups said. "He's out of control, but he's not a bad person. He is a good person with a bad disease.

"You can hate the cannibal who's taken up residence inside him. But don't hate Louis. With the right amount of love and honesty from us, he has an excellent chance of becoming himself again."

THE ODDS

The biggest question families have at pre-intervention meetings is whether it will work.

The answer is yes, definitely—one way or another:

- Nine out of every ten people we intervene with end up in treatment. Not all go right away.
- About 65 percent go directly from intervention to treatment.
- Another 25 percent go in the weeks that follow.

The Family's Turn to Talk

"I've talked enough for the moment," Dr. Lessups said. "Now it's your turn. I would like to know why you are here today."

Working clockwise around the table, each family member told his or her side of the story.

John: "Louis . . . well, he's my only son. I feel like I have let him down, letting him get so far out of whack. I want to help him get well, if I can. I'm afraid that if we don't do something now, we'll regret it for the rest of our lives. If something happens to him, I need to know that I did all I could to help him."

Susan: "I feel so bad for Louis. He is so alone and in so much pain. And I worry about his health. He was the sweetest baby you ever saw, with the most adorable little smile. I would like him to turn this around. I want to see him smile again."

Carter: "I'm here to support this family and, most of all, my wife, Susan. I don't know Louis very well, but he has gained a tremendous amount of weight this last year, he's unhappy, and it's making Susan upset all the time. I'll do anything you all want me to do. I'll support whatever the family decides."

Linda: "Louis and I used to do everything together. He always looked out for me. If I had a bad day, he always tried to cheer me up. But we have hardly talked the past year. I think now it's my turn to look out for him for a change. I miss my brother. I want my brother back."

Dr. Lessups thanked the family members for their answers. "What I'm hearing you say is that you are all suffering because of Louis. You're worried about him. You wish you could help him, but you don't know what to do. Some of you are mad at him for causing you all

It's Not Okay to Be a Cannibal

this worry. And the worst part is you feel you can't talk about his eating disorder, even though it's tearing you all apart.

"This is the okay part I promised you. And I'm not saying this to be mean to Louis. He sounds like a good guy, deep down. But he has no right to take actions that make everyone in his family feel so miserable. It's not okay to do that to your family. And now, we're going to take this thing to the next level. We're going to tell Louis it isn't okay, and then we're going to ask him to make it okay by making an important decision: to get help. Are you with me?"

Everyone nodded.

"Okay, let's take a short break. I want to have everyone sitting down again in five minutes. When we get back, we'll talk about the how, where, and when of our family meeting tomorrow."

The Three Letters

Dr. Lessups explained that the intervention must maintain a certain emotional tone. That tone arises from love for the addicted family member and deep concern for his well-being.

Being respectful is key as well. The intervention must not become a firing range of accusations, frustrations, and resentments. If that happens, the meeting spirals out of control and the potential for positive results is lost.

Dr. Lessups stressed the importance of using "I" statements. "Begin every sentence not with *you*—which puts the addict on the defensive—but with *I*."

DON'T SAY	DO SAY
"You eat too much, you don't exercise, and you're going to die soon."	"I see you struggling with food issues, and it makes me worried and upset."
"You're selfish and lazy, and it's making Mom and Dad crazy."	"I worry about you all the time. I wish you had a sense of purpose."
"You live off of the kindness of others. You're an embarrassment."	"I loaned you money, and you never paid me back. I know that you're struggling financially."

"Can you hear the difference?" Dr. Lessups asked. "In the 'you' statement, you are dumping judgment and blame on the other person. In the 'I' statement, you are describing what you understand and what you feel. It's more respectful. It's more honest. And, believe me, it will get a better response."

Dr. Lessups continued to outline the plan.

"Each of you is going to speak to Louis in turn. You're going to read from three letters, which you will all write together when you get home tonight. The purpose of these letters is to lay out the truth for Louis, so he knows exactly what the current situation is. These letters are the heart of the intervention because they create emotional pressure. They allow the addict to feel the effects of what his addiction is doing to people.

"The first letter speaks to how you all have seen Louis's life suffer as a result of his disease. Its purpose is to state facts about the addict that the addict can't deny. I want you all to take some time later this evening to write down examples of the things that have happened to Louis as a result of his addiction.

"Write these statements out using full sentences. They must be factual. They should be 'I' based, not 'you' based. And the facts should be recent, not ancient history."

Letter #1: SHOW THE CANNIBAL WHAT HE'S DONE

Be specific, not argumentative or opinionated. The facts you use to describe your loved one's behavior must be beyond dispute. These facts are the evidence that the individual is struggling. Here are some examples:

- "I'm worried about you. Your girlfriend told me that she won't see you anymore because the craziness is too much to handle."
- "I got a call from your school principal. She told me you've skipped so many days that you won't graduate."

- "I got a call at two in the morning from the police saying you had trashed Dad's car and you had an alcohol level of 2.1."

Here is what Louis's father wrote:

"In May I gave you $2,000 for job counseling, and I never heard from you about that again."

"At your Aunt Elsie's seventy-fifth birthday party last year, after turning down dessert at the table, I caught sight of you in the extra bedroom. You were wolfing down chocolate cake and ice cream all by yourself."

The emphasis in these stories is on truthfulness expressed with concern. The main goal of the intervention is to create a "false bottom" for the addict to hit—a way for the truth to break through the denial. Family and friends are not at an intervention to blame or to shame, but rather to show their love.

The second letter follows up on the first. Where the first was about how his addiction has affected *his* life, the second is about how his addiction has affected *your* life. Again, the emphasis is on concern.

Letter #2: TELL THE CANNIBAL
HOW HIS ADDICTION
HAS AFFECTED YOU

This is not a time to "let the addict have it," but to express how his addiction has harmed you. Be truthful, but not hostile. Here are some examples:

- "We went to the bar together and you got drunk. Afterward, you were so mad you kicked my car door in with your foot. I had to pay to have the door fixed."
- "You have lied to me so many times, I can't believe anything you say anymore. I feel angry and betrayed."
- "The brother I used to know has been taken away from me by this disease. That is a huge loss for me. I miss you."

Here is what Louis's mother wrote to tell him:

"I worry about your health. You have type 2 diabetes, and it's out of control when you eat like this. It breaks my heart to see you so sad and angry all the time. I know how cruel people can be, and I know you have suffered. I used to be able to make your problems go away with a kiss. I know I can't do that anymore. I worry that I will have to bury you, and no parent wants to do that."

The third letter is about setting livable boundaries. It's the hardest of the three to write, because it is the tough part of tough love. It asks you to say how your relationship with the addict will change if, at the end of the intervention, the addict decides to say no.

Letter #3: TELL THE CANNIBAL HOW THINGS MUST CHANGE

The addict needs to know you'll still love him—no matter what—but that his behavior is forcing you to set restrictions on how you will interact with him in the future. Here are some examples:

- "I hope you agree to accept the help we have made available today. If you decide not to, you need to know that I will no longer support your addiction by remaining silent and tacitly assenting to your behaviors in the future. I will be vocal about my fears and concerns from this moment forward."
- "I will not loan you any more money. You've lied about what you spend it on, and I will not subsidize your chemical use."
- "I wish you well, but I can't continue to be your friend if you keep involving me in your lies."
- "If we're going to stay married, you'll have to go to treatment. Getting help for your disease constitutes what's okay in our family starting now. Anything less is not okay with me."

It's Not Okay to Be a Cannibal

- "I can't stay in this marriage if you refuse our offer of help today. I'm going to take the kids and build a stable home for them on my own."

Here is how Louis's sister, Linda, put it:

"Louis, you know I love you. And you know that there is nothing I wouldn't do for you. But I'm not going to be your shoulder to cry on if you refuse to get help. I'm not going to take your phone calls late at night and talk against the family. And I'm not going to give you any more of my money. If you really want help, stop crying and get it. This family is holding out the lifeline today. Please accept it. I will always love you. But after today, I am no longer going to be your accomplice in staying sick."

TASKS FOR THE INTERVENTIONIST

It's the interventionist's job to make sure all logistical problems are predicted and addressed:

- A solution is at hand, whether it be a treatment center bed, an assessment scheduled, or a lift to the Salvation Army.
- Transportation is set—airline tickets, driving directions, train schedules, and so on.
- A suitcase is packed.
- The addict has a picture ID.
- The addict is medically stable to travel.

- Contingency and backup plans exist in case any of a hundred things do not go as planned.

The Final Challenge

Dr. Lessups asked if anyone had any final questions.

Linda: "I'm afraid he will think we're ganging up on him."

Dr. Lessups: "Not at all. You are coming together as a family to express your love and concern for someone who is struggling—someone who is not in a position to make great decisions on his own behalf and who desperately needs someone else to make them for him."

John: "I worry he'll never speak to me again. We barely speak as it is."

Dr. Lessups: "Then, realistically, you don't have much to lose, but a lot to gain."

Susan: "I have this voice inside me saying, 'This isn't what a good mother is supposed to do.'"

Dr. Lessups: "That voice is the voice of codependency. And though it often sounds reasonable, it doesn't always tell you the truth. To be a good mom, you have to work against this disease."

Carter: "I think he may be embarrassed that I'm there. I don't know him all that well."

Dr. Lessups: "But he knows you love his mom, and by being there you are saying 'I am willing to show up for you. I am willing to participate as a member of this family.'"

Linda: "I'm afraid that when it's my turn to talk, I won't be able to."

Dr. Lessups: "Linda, don't worry. If you find yourself too choked up, just hand your letters to the person to the right of you, and he or she will read for you."

Dr. Lessups summed up the moment of challenge at the next day's intervention.

"After we've delivered our messages, it's up to Louis to make up his mind. Chances are, he'll come up with reasons why he can't go into treatment just now."

People come up with amazing, urgent things they have to do that are more important than saving their lives and saving their loved ones from worry:

- "I have a trip to Paris planned."
- "I'm indispensable at work."
- "I have an event next week that I just cannot miss."
- "I can't leave my dog alone."

"Each excuse must be answered," Dr. Lessups said. At some point it's okay to stop the addict and say, "Okay, you have lots of objections. But let's be frank. How many of these are insurmountable and how many are manufactured to prevent you from getting the help you need?"

Most addicts will want to know about the following:

- **Money and expenses.** How much will treatment cost? Who will pay for it? Is he insured? Who will pay his bills while he's away?

- **Family and job responsibilities.** Who will look after his children, spouse, elderly parents?
- **Legal obligations.** Is he allowed by law to leave the area? What happens if he misses a child support payment?
- **Transportation.** How will he get to treatment and back again? Will he be able to have a car?

He'll need reassurance and answers on all sorts of logistical considerations. The intervention team needs to anticipate and think through as many details as possible.

"Even at the end of this 'bargaining' phase, addicts still say no," Dr. Lessups said. Families must steel themselves for this possibility. It may be solace that, though the addict is rejecting the family's overtures, the family has done everything possible to show their love and concern."

The addict is saying, in effect: "My disease is still in charge. I am still compelled to make decisions purely based upon *self*. It is more important for me to drink today (or use or eat or not eat or gamble or expose myself or whatever) than it is for me to be a part of this family. You all can move heaven and earth on my behalf, but all I care about is to continue as I am, despite all you have shown me, despite the harm I am causing you, despite the harm I am causing myself, despite the fact that nothing is standing in the way of me going to treatment right now."

STRUCTURING THE INTERVENTION

Many issues are resolved in a pre-intervention meeting:

- **Sequence of speakers.** Someone intriguing to the addict should go first, and whoever has the most consequences to bring should speak last.
- **Transportation.** Be prepared. You can't wait to see what the addict says before buying plane tickets.
- **Time limit.** Conclude the meeting within a reasonable amount of time. An intervention that exceeds two hours is probably too long.
- **Consequences.** What will change if the addict refuses help? What happens in the next thirty seconds? The next hour? Where are you having lunch today? Where is everyone sleeping tonight?

Following Up

The intervention with Louis the next morning was extremely brief, lasting about eight minutes. At 10:15 a.m. Louis answered the door and let his family in. Quietly, they filed into the living room. From the very first moment Louis understood what was happening. He burst into tears, and even before Dr. Lessups had an opportunity to introduce himself, Louis told the family that he would agree to whatever his family wanted. And he apologized for causing them worry and pain.

Louis was flown to the East Coast, where he spent thirty days being assessed and educated about the nature of his disease, compulsive overeating.

He joined a Twelve Step group for overeaters and became a regular participant in a group dealing with issues of anxiety and compulsivity. Over the following nine months, Louis lost 115 pounds. He is no longer housebound. He has a new job, as a phone clerk at a federal housing assistance project, and has gotten good marks for his customer relations skills.

He is deeply grateful to his family for caring enough to confront him that bright October morning. He lives in a new apartment three miles from his mother's home. Every day, for exercise, he walks the distance to see his mother, and eats a giant pile of steamed vegetables.

Not everything turned around overnight for Louis. His weight loss tapered off after the first nine months, and today, a year later, he is working to lose a second hundred pounds. "I hit a wall," he says. "But I've got the attitude now. Even if it takes me a while, I believe I'm going to be okay."

5

CONFRONTING
THE CANNIBAL

In the alcoholic intervention example that follows, the narrator is an AIR interventionist named Mary, a recovering alcoholic and facilitator of more than a hundred interventions. We show the intervention through her eyes to illustrate that, although she says relatively little during the confrontation, she remains in "the driver's seat" the entire time.

This is the story of the intervention of an alcoholic named Joe. Joe is in the hardware business and runs a local store in upstate New York. According to his family, Joe is the kind of addict who "flies under the radar." He never seems particularly drunk. He has never been arrested. He makes a decent living, keeps up appearances, and hasn't gotten cirrhosis. He doesn't wear lampshades at parties. In short, his addictive behavior is largely clandestine. He hasn't hit bottom yet. He's in a kind of cruise control, which is often dangerous because when he finally falls, it will likely be sudden and violent. Nearly all addicts live in some degree of denial, but the deeper that denial is, the more unsettling it is when the truth is finally uncovered. Like being slapped in the face, these addicts are suddenly and painfully shocked by the truth of their own behavior.

In recent months, the signs have been mounting that Joe's life of addiction and denial is about to come crashing down around him. His family is angry at him for distancing himself from them and for his occasional but fierce outbursts of temper. After a decade of wondering what to do, his wife, Sheila, called our national call center, and they arranged for his family and me to meet near Sheila's home in Boston. We met for three hours on a Thursday evening to plan. On hand were Sheila; the two adult sons, David and Stu; Joe's younger brother, Brian; and Thomas, the hardware store manager. Friday morning we held the actual family meeting that included Joe.

ELEMENTS OF AN INTERVENTION MEETING

- **Introductions.** The participants all get settled, and the interventionist introduces himself and describes the agenda for the family meeting.
- **Explanation.** The family speaks to the addict's behavior, how it has changed their lives, and how it has affected their relationship with the addict.
- **Decision.** The addict is asked to choose: recovery or continuing addiction.
- **Action.** The addict leaves for treatment or leaves the family meeting.

It's Not Okay to Be a Cannibal

At 7:45 a.m. I meet the team at a nearby coffee shop. Ten minutes later, our team is knocking on the door of Sheila and Joe's house. Sheila answers the door and lets us in. Joe is in the kitchen putting away the last of the breakfast dishes. I ask the team to sit down in the living room while I step into the kitchen and introduce myself to Joe.

THE WHERE OF INTERVENING

Nine times out of ten, a family intervention is held in the family home. But circumstances sometimes require the family to use what is at hand: a conference room at the office, a hotel suite, a grief room at a hospital, a family room at the jail.

The best place to conduct an intervention is a location that provides the following:

- **Privacy.** This is deeply personal stuff, where people need to feel safe to speak honestly and openly. It's not appropriate to do an intervention in a public place.
- **Quiet.** People need to be able to listen to one another without distraction.
- **Neutrality.** The addict mustn't have an excuse to say that the intervention "deck" is stacked—by holding the meeting in an unfairly advantageous place.
- **An escape route.** This should be accessible if it is not an easy meeting. Addicts should be allowed

> to leave the meeting if they wish. Indeed, this is the very choice they are being offered: to stay with the family, under a revised set of rules, or to leave.

Joe takes one look at me and knows something is up. "Hello, may I help you?" he asks.

I hold out my hand. "Joe, my name is Mary McGregor. We're having a family meeting in the living room. Why don't you come on in and join us?"

NO NEED TO BE POLITE

Politeness is what got the family into this mess—being too nice to put the addict on the spot about his addiction.

The intervention conversation is not something to tiptoe around. The time for tiptoeing around the addict is over. The purpose of interventions is not to spare an addict's feelings but to intensify them—in a way that the addict is able to hear—until the addict is able make a decision.

"Can it wait? I've got to get to the store and get things going today."

"No, I'm afraid not. Joe, your children and your brother are here as well as Thomas, your manager from the hardware store."

It's Not Okay to Be a Cannibal

WHO'S IN CHARGE?

When the addict finally enters the room, it's best if the family is already seated and the interventionist is standing. This posture is direct, and it communicates unmistakably that the interventionist is not there as an observer or interested party. The interventionist is running the meeting—even if he or she sits down and doesn't say another word.

"I'm sorry—who did you say you worked for?"

"Addiction Intervention Resources. We work with families in crisis, Joe. Your family thinks enough of you that they asked me to be here at this meeting. They recognize that you've been struggling lately and want to take some time to talk things through. All they're asking for is about forty-five minutes of your time. Is that okay, Joe?"

Joe nods without saying anything. He quietly acknowledges everyone in the room as he takes a seat next to his wife on the sofa.

"Joe," I quietly inform him, "there is a room reserved for you at a chemical dependency treatment program in California. If after this meeting you decide that treatment is something you're interested in taking advantage of, we can discuss it at greater length then. But before we do that, your family has some things they would like to say. Sound all right so far? Good. Let's begin. Brian, please, go ahead and read."

SEQUENCING THE LETTERS

As a rule, begin with the person who is least threat-ening to the addict—a colleague, a sibling, an out-sider like a minister. And finish with the person who has the most significant changes to discuss. Such a sequence allows the emotional power of the inter-vention to build until the moment of decision and increases the chances of success.

Joe is upset about the intervention, but my sense is that he's not going to stalk out of the room. He's used to using his anger to manage outcomes within this family. My guess is he will try to bully his way out of this confrontation.

"Christ, Sheila, what have you done to me? How could you turn our family business over to this stranger?"

Basic cannibal logic: The intervention is something we are doing *to* Joe, not *for* him. And he positions the in-tervention as if it's not an action of the entire family, as it clearly is. He is trying to separate Sheila from the group and blame her, hoping to splinter the group. It won't work. The family is expecting this tantrum.

TURNING AGAINST THE INTERVENTIONIST

Ideally, the interventionist doesn't have to say much at the intervention, and the family can do the bulk of the talking, as planned.

It's Not Okay to Be a Cannibal

Sometimes this doesn't work. Some families aren't talkers and need more direction.

Addicts often try to turn families against the interventionist:

- "We were doing okay as a family until the suit here showed up."
- "Can't we settle this the way we settle other family business?"
- "I'm uncomfortable airing our laundry in front of a stranger."

The family has to stick to its guns. Without the interventionist there as stage manager, witness, and referee, old family patterns of dysfunction and codependency will scotch the intervention.

"We have a problem, Joe," Sheila answers him, "and we're going to work through this."

"Well, you can do it without me," Joe says, turning to leave. "I'm leaving for work."

I stay seated but speak up before he reaches the door. "Joe," I tell him, "your wife and sons are really worried about you. All they want is forty-five minutes of your time. Is that too much to ask?"

"We want you to get help," Sheila says. "We want you to get well."

Joe pauses, turns, and sits down again. "Listen," he says. "The only help I need right now is for you to end this meeting so I can get to the store. I have a lot of stuff coming at me right now."

I decide to ignore his objections and press on. "Brian, please go ahead and read."

The Naming of the Ships

Brian unfolds his letter and begins to read. "Number one," he says. "Over the past six months, you got two speeding tickets. In the past you've always been a good driver. If you get one more ticket, you lose your license. I was with you when you got the second one, after the Celtics game. You were going like 75 mph in an area posted 55. I know you had been drinking at the game— you were lucky it wasn't a DUI."

"Brian," Joe says, "that cop had it in for me. I sped up to pass some slow traffic. You're supposed to do that!"

Brian presses on. "Number two. Last year you told me you decided not to place a Yellow Pages display ad like you usually do. Then your business went to hell. But the other day you admitted to me that you forgot to send in your ad copy. That isn't like you at all, Joe."

"So you're going to put me in detox over a Yellow Pages display ad? Get real."

"Number three," Brian says. "When I picked you up for the auction in Wakefield last week, you were slurring your speech and you couldn't walk steady. And you smelled like booze. I knew you drank, Joe, but that smell was something else."

Joe now begins to listen in silence. I ask Brian to read his second letter.

"Joe, you're my big brother, and I've always looked

up to you. You've been a good brother, too. But for the past five years, I've hardly known who you are. We haven't spent any real time talking. You always have a reason to be by yourself. So I guess I miss you, and I worry about what will happen. You and I both know that Dad was a closet drinker, just like you, and he died about two years older than you are right now. What I'm saying is, I don't want to lose you. I love you, Joe, and I want to see you stick around with us for a little longer."

Joe sags on the couch and wipes his eye with the back of one hand. Brian's letter has gotten to him. I can tell from his posture that we are doing well. Joe's no longer throwing up a smokescreen. He's listening. We've achieved the number one thing we set out to do—get past his denial.

Without my asking, Brian looks up from his third letter.

"Joe, this part was the hardest for me to write, because I'm saying something against you here, and brothers shouldn't have to do this. But I think it's necessary, so here goes."

He reads: "Joe, you know I love you. But I don't want to be part of your drinking life anymore. If you're drinking, I don't want to be with you. No basketball games, no poker, no boat trips. I'll always be your brother, and I'll always love you, but unless you quit what you've been doing and agree to get help today, I don't want you to be part of my life."

This time it's Brian who starts crying. Sheila rubs his back. Now they're both crying.

"You don't need to cry, brother," Joe says. "It's me who should be crying. I didn't realize how much pressure I was putting you under. I'm really sorry."

We have to sit for a moment before Brian and Joe can collect themselves. Then Joe addresses us.

"I want to hear what you've all written," he says. "Especially after all the trouble you took to put these things down on paper. But I'm gonna take some of the drama out of this. I'll do whatever you guys say. If you want me to go to treatment or to AA, I'll do it. I know I've had a problem, and I've been feeling all kinds of shame and grief about it. But I've just been too scared to admit it to anyone else."

The intervention is not over at this point, but it has peaked. All the important details remain. In most interventions, the critical moment arrives when the last letter by the last person is read, and the addict is asked to decide. I usually say something like this:

"Well, Joe, the one thing I know from working with this family is that they care the world about you. Help is available today, right now. All you have to do is say you want it. What's your decision?"

Then we wait for his answer.

Negotiating the Surrender

Addicts commonly respond to an intervention by testing the participants' resolve—challenging how serious they are—and by trying to diffuse the power of the meeting at the onset. Addicts will seek to weaken the effort by suggesting a compromise agreement that will bring the intervention to a close.

In another intervention, that's what Bill, a crack addict married to Mara, tried to do, just before throwing in the towel. Mara countered by sticking to her promise to cut Bill loose unless he got help.

Bill: Listen . . . all of you . . . what do you want me to do, exactly? Do you want me to spend more time at home? Because I can work less. I don't need to make money—

Mara: It's not about money. It's about the family. We don't want to keep living with you if it's going to be like this. We don't know what's going on, we worry about you, we never know what to believe.

Bill: Okay. Okay. Seriously, what do you want me to do?

Mara: Go with Francisco to the treatment center. Get help. And then come back to us.

Bill: And if I don't?

Mara: If you don't, you can't be part of my life anymore. That's not what I want, Bill, but it's what I have to do. I love you. You're a good father and a good husband. You've been a good provider. But I'm not willing to raise these children in the home of an active crack addict. We miss you and want the old Bill back.

Bill: You'd divorce me?

Mara: Yes, I would, Bill. But I'd be able to tell myself that you left me. You chose the drugs over your role as a father and a husband.

Saying the Unsayable

The hardest part for most family members is breaking the conspiracy of silence that has kept them quiet until now. Reading the letters aloud forces family members to get honest and holds them accountable to their statements.

Scott: Dad, you remember two weeks ago, when I asked you and Mom over to visit Carrie and me and the baby? You said you couldn't because you were working on a restoration project. But when I went out to buy diapers, I saw you coming out of Liquor Village. I was so embarrassed that you would see me; I ducked down in my seat and just drove away.

Al: It's just . . .

Scott: We miss you, Dad. We all do. We're worried about you getting sick or just withdrawing from our lives entirely. We used to do things—scouts, baseball, camping. It's like, I don't even know who you are anymore. I want you to be in the family again. To be my dad and be my kids' grandpa.

Al: I hear you.

Scott: That same day I came down to your office. I wanted to talk to you about this. When I brought it up, you blew your top at me and said I was snooping into your affairs and it was none of my business what you did. You really reamed me out, and it made me feel pretty terrible. I'm mad about that, Dad. I don't deserve to be treated that way.

Al: You're right. I'm sorry about that, Scott.

MILESTONES TO CHANGE

Addiction intervention asks a person to make an enormous change—to put himself in his family's hands and to accept their judgment. It is enormously difficult to do this. At many interventions, we can visibly see the addict move from stage to stage:

- **Shock.** Addicts are astonished that the family is moving in a united fashion to curtail his activities. The visible result of this shock is to freeze in the headlights—to be unable to respond.
- **Anger.** Addicts become frustrated at being outnumbered and lash out at individuals. Everything is somebody else's fault.
- **Denial.** The accusation leveled against them is preposterous. Sure they have a drink every now and then but that doesn't make them an alcoholic!
- **Depression.** As the power of the ultimatum sinks in—to get well or to accept inevitable change—the addict loses energy.
- **Bargaining.** "I'll quit right now if I don't have to go to treatment." "I'll only get high away from the house." "I'll quit starting January 1." Fortunately, having a professional facilitator present short-circuits this phase quickly.

At the other end of these stages is *acceptance*. The addict either accepts that he must continue using without the family's support or that he must go to treatment.

The Moment of Decision, and the Moment After That

As the intervention draws to a close and the choice is put to the addict, he can say one of three things:

1. "Okay, I'll go."

As soon as he says this, everyone in the family can stand up and give him a hug to break the tension. Collect the letters; these will be an important tool during treatment.

Think about packing for the trip. Maybe his wife packed for him in advance. If not, get busy right away. Allow the addict no more than twenty minutes to pack. (If workable, have him packed before the intervention takes place.) The family should stick around for this. No one leaves until the addict is in the car and rolling down the road.

If the addict lives at a different location than the intervention site, arrange to have his stuff delivered to him by the following morning.

2. "Let me think about it."

This is a fleeting position, because within a few minutes it becomes either "I'll go" or "No way, leave me alone."

Give the addict no more than ten minutes to ponder the matter. Rationale: Everyone's time is valuable.

It's important not to bog down. The interventionist must use his judgment about whether to try to talk the addict into going or to let him twist in the wind with the decision. If the interventionist believes the addict is susceptible to convincing, he should allow the family to do the persuading.

The family should be firm in this persuading. If the addict resists, the interventionist should call his bluff and declare this part of the meeting to be over. Ask the family if they have anything else to add. Then stand up, inform the addict that the part of the meeting that requires his presence is over, and announce that the meeting will now continue without him. Escort the addict out of the house.

This tactic is very powerful because it reminds the addict at a pivotal moment that the addiction is not just his problem; it is the entire family's problem, and they will take measures to deal with it if he refuses. Thus, his "I don't know" becomes a "no," with all the negative consequences—financial, emotional, and logistical—that decision entails.

3. "No way, leave me alone."

This is the answer no one wants to hear, but people do say it.

Some interventions don't even get off the ground because the cannibal refuses to open the door and let the family in. Or they pretend they're not home and hope you will give up and leave. Or they leap out the nearest window and run away. This has happened.

One unnerving tactic of committed cannibals is to act out, to trump the intervention with a temper tantrum. A female crack addict locked herself in the bathroom and screamed for us to leave. A man with a history of exposing himself was so ashamed he hid himself in his closet. A heroin addict smiled from inside his picture window and called the cops on us.

There's not much you can do in these kinds of situations. In unmistakable terms the addicts are saying, "I'm not ready for this." They're just being honest.

But most addicts can be reached—provided friends and family speak to them in a language they can understand. That's why interventions are structured the way they are: engaging the addict's curiosity and then leading him to an emotional breakthrough, which is followed by the moment of decision.

But even with all the preparation, people say no. They have a choice. And it's wise for everyone involved to understand this going in. It will help them keep calm in a stressful situation. Understand that the family meeting is structured with "playing the long game" in mind. What happens today is less important than what happens in the next month or three months. Family members should not get into angry accusations during the meeting. Nor should the family "camp out" in the addict's doorway or driveway, hoping to lay siege to him until he relents and changes.

Sometimes, the addict just needs to get away. He

feels overwhelmed, or maybe he really does have an appointment he has to get to.

Do not attempt to tackle the escaping cannibal, or take his car keys, or block his car with yours. Always think of the intervention as a family meeting, not as an action film. Let him go.

When he has gone, return to the group and resume the family meeting. This is, after all, a family meeting at which the addict occupied only one seat; this was not his meeting. Life goes on.

Talk about what happens now. If the addict is choosing to not live within the boundaries that the family has set, what does that mean? It means going through with the measures discussed.

But remember, too, that many people who say no during the intervention come around. The act of confrontation plants seeds that grow in the addict's mind. About 90 percent of addicts who tell us no come back within thirty days and ask to be directed to treatment.

6

THE GOOD INTERVENTIONIST

When we at AIR conduct an intervention, we maintain contact with the family for at least six months after the initial meeting with the addict. During this period we answer questions and provide advice and information. The family's number one concern is the health and progress of the addict in treatment. But the family is often very curious about what happened at the intervention and why we did things the way we did.

Without exception loved ones are grateful to have had an experienced interventionist in the room during such a difficult moment. Family members already under great emotional stress don't need the additional burden of managing a situation that has a high potential for chaos.

This chapter answers the most common questions families ask. What qualities make for a good interventionist? How does he or she know what to say? How much of intervention is a one-size-fits-all process?

This is not a description of the "perfect intervention" or of the "perfect interventionist." Rather, it is knowledge gained by conducting hundreds of interventions where we learned what works with cannibals and what does not.

THE INTERVENTIONIST'S JOB DESCRIPTION

Interventions can be wrenchingly emotional displays of the most genuine kind of love—the love of a family for a sick member. The interventionist is the one person in the room the family can count on to remain calm and rational, even when others have been pushed to the limit emotionally. The interventionist's job includes the following:

- Keeping the addict focused on making a positive decision.
- Getting the addict to accept the help being offered by the family.
- Getting the addict to admit out loud that he doesn't want to change, to have him say, in effect, "Today it's more important for me to be the best addict I can be than it is for me to be a brother or a husband or a father."

What is it like to be an interventionist? A good analogy is the role an FBI interrogator plays. The interrogator meets the suspect and applies pressure until the suspect confesses. The best interrogators apply pressure that is simultaneously empathic yet firm. When the suspect confesses, he feels he is doing it to a friend.

That is the balance the best interventionists maintain: human, but determined—a friend to the human being underneath but no friend to the cannibal.

This is a hard role for most mothers, siblings, or friends to play. But it is from this resolute attitude that interventions succeed.

The choice of an interventionist, then, is one of the most critical decisions a family must make. This chapter describes the qualities of a good interventionist.

An Interventionist Must Be Tough

The job of interventionist is not to provide a warm, supportive, forgiving environment for either the addict or the rest of the family. Rather, this is a formal meeting designed to resolve an important issue that affects all members present.

It calls for toughness. Managing a group of emotionally volatile family members, and asking them to engage in an emotionally taxing conversation with an unpredictable loved one, is no day at the beach.

The first goal of an intervention is to help the family as a whole. But to do that the interventionist must ask family members to speak and act in ways that may be entirely foreign to them. This means no nagging, no shouting, and no blaming. It means abandoning any sympathetic, enabling attitude about the addict that helped deepen and lengthen the period of his addiction.

The interventionist always hopes to catch the cannibal on a "good day," in a moment of relative clarity. It's

It's Not Okay to Be a Cannibal

always tougher when a person is in a rage, is deep in withdrawal, or is in a savage mood. On a good day, the addict will likely be reasonable and compliant. If not, the interventionist must guide the addict to act against his (the cannibal's) own best interest. This is a much taller order, and it is the reason for the careful planning in the pre-intervention stage.

The interventionist must out-think, outsmart, and out-strategize the cannibal. He or she must keep the family's strategy two steps ahead of the cannibal's and maintain a steady emotional siege.

An intervention is an effort to raise the bottom. It is a crisis manufactured according to a timeline that works in the family's favor, not the cannibal's. The purpose of generating this crisis is so that the intervention team can then control the bottom—and create an opportunity for the addict to momentarily see through his wall of denial.

The interventionist controls the intervention. The moment control shifts to the addict, the intervention is in jeopardy.

The biggest initial move in going to war against the disease of addiction is redefining the terms of the debate. Who's in charge? Who's in control? Who has the power to dictate terms and determine outcomes? By definition, addicts do not act in their own best interest; they act in the best interest of their disease. It follows, then, that they do not act in the best interest of their families, their friends, or their employers. Why on earth, then, do we leave them in control?

An intervention is an act of redesigning the power paradigm by defining the terms for moving forward; outlining livable, manageable boundaries; and using every bit of the leverage at hand to put an end to the addiction-related chaos.

An Interventionist Manages the Family

The sickest person in a family—the one most emotionally damaged or incapacitated—is rarely the person you have been hired to intervene on. Very often, it's someone on the intervention team. Sometimes, an interventionist gets glimpses into a family's dynamics that will make the most hardened professional shake his or her head. But unless that dysfunction is relevant to the problem at hand—giving the cannibal an offer of an appropriate level of care—a good interventionist will not focus on it. Yet family members, who are encouraged to speak a truth that has been bottled up for too long, must be reined in when they cross the line into abusiveness. The good interventionist walks the fine line of maintaining the focus on fixing the addict, without letting family members' excesses distract everyone from the main goal of the intervention.

An Interventionist Is Not a "Savior"

The job of interventionist has evolved over recent years. The biggest change has been that interventionists seldom act as "sole practitioners" today. This is not uni-

It's Not Okay to Be a Cannibal

formly true. Some individuals can still be found dashing through airports, presenting the image of a superhero with a cell phone, a one-man rescue committee. These folks are carryovers from the old days, when intervening meant grabbing someone and rushing them off to the nearest detox bed.

Our friend Jamie did interventions in Miami. He was a handsome guy, fluent in Spanish, and very capable. But eventually, after years of working alone, the loneliness of the job and the spiritual vacuum of being his own Higher Power caused him to step back for a time and reassess his career. He came to admit that, for many years, he had an air about him in his work that was superior and grandiose. It seemed to say, "Do not fear, I will take you by the hand and lead you out of your misery." That much grandiosity and self-assumed power eventually made him physically and spiritually sick.

Many families, worn down and confused by years of dealing with their addict members, were grateful when Jamie stepped into their lives, promising a safe way out.

The problem was, Jamie wasn't a savior. He was just a guy with a flamboyant style. He had no better record of success than other interventionists. And when things went badly for him, people were very upset, because he had jacked up their expectations with his heroic flourishes.

"I cringe when I remember the way I used to be," Jamie told us. "At the end of the day, I am still an addict myself. I was caught up in my personal delusions of grandeur, seeing myself as the great rescuer to all the families I worked with. I had no business trying to save people with that attitude."

An Interventionist Is Professional

Another relic of the Wild West mentality is the interventionist who works a little too closely with certain treatment centers—basically acting as a salesperson for their treatment services.

When the family contacts an interventionist, they should make sure that he or she works with a spectrum of treatment facilities. Otherwise, they get a one-size-fits-all service, which may make the family wonder who the real client is: the family or the treatment facility. To truly help a loved one, it's critical to find the right help. Families want to feel secure that their crisis consultant understands their case and is making referrals based on the family's needs, not some internal sales quota system.

The addiction intervention field of today includes large organizations that can provide a full spectrum of service to families: call center support, intake staff, clinical staff, and a large, dependable network of national relationships that serve all parts of the addiction continuum.

Most important, when looking for an interventionist, be sure the organization views intervention as a process for the entire family, not just the addicted individual.

The Interventionist Knows the Intervention Is Not about Him

The philosophy of Twelve Step recovery is that people recover from addiction by telling their stories. All interventionists know this, and most are recovering addicts themselves, so they have exciting, positive stories to tell.

But the intervention is not the place to tell them.

First, the intervention is not about the interventionist—it's about the family as a whole. It's their moment to speak up, to break the conspiracy of silence that has enabled this problem to go on for so long and get as bad as it has. It's about the family's stories.

Second, it's about the addict's recovery. If things go well, this will be a pivotal, defining, life-changing day for the addict.

But it's not about the interventionist. The temptation to "tell all" about one's own addiction, in order to win the addict over, is called self-disclosure. Self-disclosure is a powerful tool in breaking through the armor that the addict has encased himself in. But self-disclosure is an inappropriate technique for the process of intervention.

Why? Because the addict is still very much in cannibal mode—still hungry, still calculating what can be done to keep his addiction fed. Self-disclosure is a form of unilateral disarmament. A clever cannibal will take the interventionist's story and beat him or her over the head with it.

For most interventions, the best strategy is for the

family and interventionist to stay strong, to stay resolute, and to stick to a very simple ultimatum: get help right now or lose the benefits of being in a healthy family.

Every so often, in just the right circumstance, good interventionists break this rule. But their disclosure is a simple sentence of reassurance:

"Hey, I sat right where you were one day—I know it's tough."

The Interventionist Knows When to Stay Quiet

An intervention is not a lecture. Ideally, the interventionist makes only a few comments during the actual meeting. The message of the family is what's most important, and the interventionist is there as moderator and, if necessary, as mediator, making sure that the message is delivered as powerfully as possible.

Sometimes the interventionist is drawn into the conversation. The addict may see the interventionist as a "jury" that he can play to. "Do you think my wife is being reasonable?" "You work in this field. Tell my family that pot is really no big deal." The wise interventionist sees this tactic and is not drawn in.

When things get bogged down, it falls to the interventionist to ask the question that must be asked. "Tom, help is available today. Tell me what you want to do. If you want to accept the family's help, then it's time to get going. If not, and we will honor whatever decision

It's Not Okay to Be a Cannibal

you make, then you understand that all the changes the family talked about go into effect right now. It's your call. Tell me what you want to happen."

The Interventionist Tells the Truth

The single best thing an interventionist can do, sitting across the room from a cannibal, is to tell the cannibal the truth.

In considering the offer you have made to him, the addict will want to know many things. Will he lose his job? Will he have access to a medical detox? Will he still be a member of the family?

Trust is the lifeblood of an intervention. An intervention that serves up deception to the addict is no better than the addict. And trust, once lost, is terribly difficult to recover.

An Interventionist Is Not a Therapist

Marie, a talented interventionist in Ohio, had one bad habit: she ran interventions like family therapy sessions. The problem was, she really wasn't qualified to intervene, and sometimes people found her approach off-putting.

She sometimes summed up what people were saying, translating the family's words for the addict ("What I think your sister is trying to say is, she misses you and wishes you were close again.").

The effect of this "mediating" was often to put

herself in between the family and the addict, and usually that's distracting. The one salutary effect was that the family and the addict, even if they could not agree about anything else, agreed that Marie was annoying.

The task of the interventionist is like that of a stage manager. At the pre-intervention meeting, it is appropriate to give lots and lots of directions. But during the intervention itself, an interventionist should stay in the shadows and let family members do most of the talking, speaking up only when necessary to keep the conversation from getting off topic.

7

THE ECONOMICS
OF INTERVENTION

We at AIR have had the opportunity to work with families from all economic brackets. We have met wonderful people and have had anguished and joyful experiences at every economic level. In the course of these interventions, we have seen the curious ways money, and the lack of it, affects the experiences of families struggling with addiction.

We have done interventions on hip-hop record producers, corporate executives, and long-ball baseball stars. We have intervened on both celebrity addicts and on their offspring and entourages. One general observation—not true in every case—is that, while having money makes it possible to afford interventions, it often serves as a barrier to getting well.

We once worked with a well-known family that was hard driving, talented, and celebrated for achieving great things. This same intensity can get family members into trouble. In this case, it was a son addicted to heroin and pills.

In our years of experience, we have seen that money,

ambition, and power can be enormous obstacles to recovery. The addicted rich can hire lawyers, fix tickets, pay off witnesses, and spend thousands covering up the truth about themselves—and thus never feel the anguish of their own addiction. How does an intervention team create an effective "false bottom" when all the resources of billionaires prevent them from hitting one?

We once intervened with a young woman in Beverly Hills whose situation was made very difficult by her family's financial success that effectively insulated her from economic realities. At age twenty-eight, she had never worked. Her sense of entitlement was great. When we opened the door to meet her, she ignored the assembled group—some of whom had traveled across the country to meet with her—and said to her mother: "Mummy, I need $1,000 for my dry cleaning!"

If the problem with addicts is a feeling of being beyond accountability, that attitude is made worse when the family is able to leverage its power to keep their loved one's name out of the papers.

The codependency of the rich is especially problematic. Recovery programs agree that the first step in getting better requires humility—the understanding that one is helpless in the face of addiction. We are not saying, "Feel sorry for the rich." We are saying that they face special hazards to recovery. Because of their resources, some people believe they are superior to others, putting feelings of humility further out of reach.

In matters of addiction, the "luckiest" demographic group is the upper-middle class. They are accustomed to hiring people in the service industry to take care of their problems. If their pipes leak, they call a plumber. If their kids' teeth are coming in crooked, they find an orthodontist. If they have someone in the next room who is addicted to crack cocaine, they know that the best help they can get is probably someone outside the home.

They can afford to have the work done but can't afford to cover up all the consequences of the addiction. This is an important factor in the high recovery rate of the upper-middle class.

The lower economic levels actually have better access to addiction treatment than many in the middle class. If you can show that you are indigent, that you have no real assets, that you struggle with addiction, and that you really want the help, then many states have services, funding, and treatment available.

Levels of care and access vary widely, but in the United States we generally provide a safety net for those with the least, who often need it most. These programs, often administered through the Department of Health and Human Services, and usually on a local or county level, provide desperately needed help and save thousands of lives.

Here is the story of how one family—in the middle of the middle class—struggled to get addiction help:

"My husband, Gerard, is addicted to Ritalin," the woman on the phone said. "Believe it or not."

We at AIR believed it. Ritalin, the drug school kids take to help them with attention issues, is a stimulant with effects not so very different from methamphetamine. People are drawn to it for performance enhancement but then, before they know it, they're addicted. From that point on, the drug has nothing to do with performance; it's all about staying high.

But the real problem was bigger than Ritalin. In his frequent manic bursts, Gerard had bankrupted the family, spending the family's meager savings on his rapidly escalating habit.

He had lost his job as a carpenter almost a year earlier. The family had two kids in school, one of whom had a disability and required $500 of medication every month. Gerard's wife had just started working as a waitress to try and make ends meet at home. The family bank account was stripped. Indeed, they were $40,000 in debt. They weren't members of any kind of religious organization, and they had no employee health plan they could take advantage of. They desperately needed a professional intervention and quality treatment, but they couldn't afford either.

Every day of the year we have families like Gerard's calling us to intervene with a loved one. In almost every call, we establish the necessity and desirability of immediate action—getting those loved ones into treatment right away. But many people back out. Not because they doubt the need for intervention. They back out because the price tag is more than they can handle.

The theme we have stressed all through this book is that addiction imposes an unjust burden on the family, and because this burden is unjust—"not okay"—it should not be tolerated. The cannibal has all the fun, while the family pays the bills, cleans up the mess, and negotiates bail.

But here is a way in which addiction is especially unfair—the economic hardship it imposes on people without a lot of money.

The United States is the world's leader in addiction treatment. But treatment costs money, a lot of it. A twenty-eight-day inpatient regimen can easily cost $25,000. There are scholarships for people of limited means but not nearly enough.

If treatment is expensive, the intervention that leads to treatment also costs money. Professional interventions can run from $2,500 to $7,500, depending on variables such as travel costs. Just getting plane tickets to and from an appropriate treatment center can cost a lot of money—remember, these are last-minute purchases, when tickets are most expensive. You can see how the cost can add up.

WHAT YOU CAN DO

- **Lobby for insurance coverage.** So-called parity legislation has been stalled on Capitol Hill for years. The legislation calls for insurance companies to treat addiction as the chronic, treatable condition that it is—much like hypertension and diabetes. If passed, it would require insurance companies to cover the cost of addiction treatment.
- **Do research.** Find out what kind of financial help

may be available to you in your situation. Some centers offer "scholarships" and sliding scale fees.

- **Become an activist.** Write your legislator. Sign a petition. Join a group. Send a letter to the editor of your local newspaper.
- **Educate the people you talk to about the high cost of addiction.** As expensive as intervention can be, it is still a bargain compared with continued addiction and early death.

"Why Use an Interventionist?"

Isn't an interventionist just another middle person who can be eliminated? Why don't you—as parent, sibling, child, or colleague of the cannibal—do the intervention yourself? It's like selling your house yourself and not using a real estate agent, right? Think of the bucks you'll save.

It's a valid question, especially if, as we have said, all the best interventionists really do is "stage manage" the intervention event. How hard can *that* be?

If you are up to the challenge, and if you have no alternative, then we support your willingness to conduct an intervention yourself. It's certainly better than maintaining the status quo, which is not okay.

All interventions, as we have said, succeed in the sense of breaking the wall of silence that imprisons the family. But to be really successful—to get your loved one to needed treatment—you will have to undertake several critical tasks:

It's Not Okay to Be a Cannibal

- **Learn the intervention dance.** Families often stumble because they do not yet know what works and what doesn't in an intervention. Families sometimes ache to show love at the very moment when they need to show resolve. They become distracted and lose sight of the intervention's objective. Suddenly, the cannibal is in charge again, and it's the family that is apologizing.
- **Understand and confront cannibal behavior.** Addicts can be very devious. The book *Alcoholics Anonymous* calls this disease "cunning, baffling and powerful." Ask yourself this: If I'm so skilled at dealing with manipulative behavior, why do we need an intervention at all?
- **Detach and distance yourself from outcomes.** Try not to care quite so much. Having someone in the room who is not caught up in the emotional dynamics of the family helps keep things from flying apart when emotional issues arise—as they will.
- **Unite and lead your family** through a difficult experience when all of you are feeling exhausted and (very typically) having divided opinions on the right way to help. This is a lot to take on.
- **Understand the part you play** in your family member's addiction. Remember that this is a family disease—by definition you are co-dependent.

Our sincere advice is, if you can find a way to afford a proper intervention, do it. We know that money can be scarce. But we also know that what is at stake is more precious than money. It is the health of the family, and the very life of the addicted loved one. If your choice is between saving a daughter and building a new deck, we hope you will invest in your daughter. Because treatment works. People get better. Lives get saved every day.

WHO INTERVENES?

If you can't afford a professional interventionist, find someone else to perform the equivalent task. Clergy, teachers, people from Twelve Step recovery groups, social workers, health care providers, employers, colleagues, and friends conduct hundreds of interventions every day—usually for free. The best of these interventionists are successful because they have the requisite knowledge of and attitude toward addiction:

- **Clergy.** Many faith-based leaders have experience with addiction and dependency. Consider whether they're "tough enough" to lay down the law and issue the addict an ultimatum. Some religious groups, like the Salvation Army, bring deep experience with drug and alcohol addiction.
- **Teachers.** A wise and caring teacher who knows

the addict can provide the tone of guidance that helps an intervention to succeed.

- **Social workers and psychologists.** They have a lot of experience dealing with addicts; they understand addiction and its consequences.
- **Police officers and judges.** "Law and order" is a powerful concept even for people living outside the law. Many police officers are trained in conflict resolution. And they know how to speak with manipulators.
- **Professional people.** Lawyers and physicians are one example. A family acquaintance with experience in negotiation, who has reason to be interested in your loved one and who connotes authority, can help referee a confrontation.
- **Employers.** Employers and supervisors can be valuable additions to the intervention team, lending gravity to the discussion. Many companies offer intervention assistance through Employee Assistance Programs.
- **Peers in recovery.** Someone who has been down the same road as the addict—perhaps a member of a Twelve Step recovery group—can provide hope, support, and future direction during a very lonely moment.

When you're looking for a person to lead your intervention, try to find someone who has done it before, if at all possible. And try to include all the steps we have included in this book:

- Meet with the family beforehand to adopt an intervention strategy.
- Have each family member confront the addict individually.
- Explain why the current situation cannot continue.
- Carry this out while communicating a message of love and the promise of support.

Then squarely put the choice to the cannibal: accept the help that is being offered or accept the consequences of refusal.

The Big Problem

The problem with low-budget interventions is what to do after you have intervened. Any offer of help requires that a solution be made available immediately. Just telling someone that a problem exists isn't enough; you have to be willing to help fix it.

The best outcome is an inpatient treatment facility, which gives the addict a chance to clear his head and confront the choices before him.

SOLUTIONS IN A PINCH

If you are uninsured and can't afford to pay for residential treatment, the options are as follows:

It's Not Okay to Be a Cannibal

- **Emergency and urgent care.** Hospitals admit people with addiction problems on an emergency basis either to the detox ward for detoxification or the psych ward for evaluation. At best, detox will hold someone on an involuntary basis until they are medically stable, usually two to three days. The psych ward can hold individuals on a traditional "seventy-two-hour hold" for psychiatric observation. The downside is that just when their head is clearing up enough to learn a new way of living, they are released onto the street.
- **Outpatient programs.** Your family doctor or insurance provider can point you in the direction of a program that will work with the addict. Outpatient programs tend to be most successful for people who are very proactive about taking responsibility for their own recovery.
- **Salvation Army.** One of the missions of this charitable group is to address the suffering of alcoholics and other addicts. They provide food, clothing, shelter, and counseling at no cost.
- **Detox.** Most municipalities support a facility to avoid overcrowding at the local jail and safely medically detox those who enter on their own. The focus is decidedly short term.
- **Cold turkey.** The do-it-yourself way to withdraw. Home, alone, sweating the sheets, and climbing the walls. Intensely painful, often dangerous, and not recommended.

Although people of every income level are susceptible to drug, alcohol, and behavioral addictions, the working poor have the least recourse when they need treatment. If this book does nothing else for you, let it plant the idea that society needs to take addiction seriously. Addiction is pulling energy out of the system at every step. Addiction is destroying families. It is sapping the resources of organizations. It is land-filling our criminal justice system. It is crowding emergency wards with avoidable problems. It is driving up insurance rates and adding to the tax burden of citizens.

In the year 2000, approximately 22 percent of the prison population in the United States was there not for violent crimes but for drugs.* But what kind of society uses prison as the treatment of choice for low-income addicts? Remember that addiction is not a choice, but a disease that if left untreated is terminal. What kind of society puts people with terminal illness in a prison cell, when all the evidence in the world says that treatment works for the majority of addicts?

---

* Paige M. Harrison and Allen J. Beck, "Prisoners in 2001," *Bureau of Justice Statistics Bulletin*, July 2002, http://www.ojp.usdoj.gov/bjs/abstract/p01.htm.

It's Not Okay to Be a Cannibal

8

THE ADDICT'S
PROGRESS

Few areas are subject to as much misunderstanding and misinformation as addiction and recovery. In this chapter we address some of the most common misconceptions people have about what it means to recover. Families need to know what attitude to take during the first weeks and months of recovery. They need to know what helps a newly recovering addict and what doesn't help.

THINGS TO REMEMBER
ABOUT INTERVENTION

- **It's not an event.** What happens during the meeting is less important than what happens in the following twelve months. This is good. It means less pressure on the family.
- **It's a process.** The meeting initiates the process, but it may take many months to yield results.
- **So give it time.** People don't become addicts overnight. Neither do they build a healthy recovery

overnight. Be patient and find encouragement in the small signs of progress.

What a Family Can Do

First, do not think of "intervention" as merely meeting with the addict and talking him into seeking treatment. We may think of that event as "the intervention," but in a larger sense intervention goes on and on—for the entire lives of the addict and family.

The worst thing that can happen is for the intervention event to fade into memory and become an anomaly in the life of the family. What the family needs to do is to change so that intervention, in the most general sense of the word, becomes part of the family culture. In an intervention-minded family

- family members look out for one another. Suspiciousness may be annoying, but it's legitimate in the service of staying sober.
- staying well is more important than extending courtesy. It's okay to remember the way things were and to be determined not to let them be that way again.
- everything is everybody's business. If the addict stops attending AA, the family deserves to know that and to know why.
- "the way things used to be" is gone forever. New rules apply, for the sake of the entire family.

It's Not Okay to Be a Cannibal

- members do not cut one another an infinite amount of slack. If the addict starts acting like a cannibal again, justifying and rationalizing ("One beer is going to kill me?"), the family is obliged to call him on it.
- family members are licensed to go to war the moment the cannibal shows its face again.

These "do's and don'ts" constitute a bill of rights for families fighting addiction. It's not okay to be a cannibal, and it is okay to hurl every weapon at addiction that comes to hand. This kind of fighting may not be pretty, and it may not be polite—but that's the way life is lived in the early stages of recovery. The intervention-minded family accepts the new reality.

FAMILY'S BILL OF RIGHTS (AND RESPONSIBILITIES)

- **You have the right to be left alone.** But you do not have the right to look away when others are in need of your help.
- **You have the right to peace in your own home.** If there is a disrupting force, you have the right to remove it.
- **You have the right to privacy.** But you do not have the right to cover up a family member's crimes.
- **You have the right to your good reputation.** But you do not have the right to harbor or support those who are doing wrong.

Families are welcome to call on us at AIR for six months following an intervention. And people do call. They call when they are worried that their loved one is relapsing, there is tension in the household, or they can feel the bonds of codependency tightening around them again. Their questions are good ones.

Question. A mother in Muskegon, Michigan, called to say her daughter, who had run up thousands of dollars on credit cards, was working again, and doing well—should she be trusted with a credit card?

The answer: "No."

Question. A father in Madison, Wisconsin, wanted to know whether, if his daughter relapsed in her recovery from Valium within the six-month period, he would get a second intervention, free.

The answer: "A second full-dress confrontation isn't what Rosalie needs. What she needs is to be held accountable for managing her chronic illness."

Question. A woman in Fairbanks, Alaska, found a six-pack in her husband's truck cab. The husband, who was a recovering alcoholic, said he was holding it for a friend. What should she do?

The answer: "Make it a big deal."

Question. A Westchester County, New York, man who had quit drinking in December called us every month after his intervention: in January, and again in February, March, April, and May. Each time he had a raft of questions. He truly desired to stay at the top of the staircase and not fall down ever again, and wanted to wring his money's worth from us. "What happens if I call again in a month?" he wanted to know, aware that our six-month contract was about to expire.

The answer: "We will always be glad to hear from you, Larry."

"What Does 'Getting Better' Look Like?"

"Getting better" means the addict stops drinking, drugging, or acting out. It means he gets out of bed and goes to work. It means he shows up for commitments. It means he behaves like a father, a husband, a son. It means change.

Some addicts pull it off. They have the grace and personal power to say to the cannibal, "No thanks. I'm good." They never need to say it twice. They have experienced a genuine conversion. They have hooked their star to a power higher than getting high, and the cannibal never returns.

The fervent wish of every family is that the cannibal that occupied the soul of their loved one will pack his bags, walk out the front door, and never be seen again. But it doesn't always work that way.

Families must understand that relapses do occur, but that they do not necessarily represent defeat. A single "slip" is not a catastrophe. While families hate to see slips occurring, they are often part of a successful pattern of healing.

In cases of tobacco addiction, according to statistics

published in *Time Magazine,* the average smoker quits 10.8 times before kicking the habit for good. It is not uncommon to hear of addicts who relapse twenty or thirty times before achieving abstinence.

Addiction is one of the strongest bonds the human psyche is capable of, right up there with love, parenthood, and religion. Once acquired, the taste for addiction does not want to go away. It preys on anxiety, anger, and resentment. When the addict weakens, it will be there, offering to prop him up again.

Addicts like to say: "While we congratulate ourselves for our recovery, our addiction is out in the parking lot doing push-ups." Addiction does not want to let go of people. Even for people who successfully swear off substances and behaviors, the "itch" never completely leaves. Twelve Step programs teach that this weakness can become part of the recovering addict's strength. Of course, it can also lead him right back into the addicted life.

The cannibal is remarkably like that four-inch red devil in cartoons that pops up on the right shoulder, pitchfork in hand, preying on resentments and envies, urging the character to go for it. To indulge in the old pleasures. To flip the bird to family, to friends, and to God himself—because the devil says so.

Intervention is how we dispatch that little devil.

It's Not Okay to Be a Cannibal

Sometimes the Surprise Is Nice

One of our team members recounted an intervention in Seattle, with a young man named Nate, who was smoking a fair amount of pot. Nate got high every day and was nonresponsive to requests by his parents to obey household rules. So the parents, deciding they had had enough, called us to help them with an intervention.

The intervention seemed to be going well, even though the interventionist was not particularly experienced. From the onset, Nate agreed he had a problem and that he had been unable to get free from it by himself. He agreed to fly with the interventionist to a treatment center in Denver. Here is the clinician's play-by-play:

Nate and I are getting along great. He seems like a good kid. At the Salt Lake City Airport however, just as boarding begins, he excuses himself to go to the restroom. I sit down and wait for him. Minutes tick by, passengers begin to pre-board, and still Nate hasn't returned.

I start to get a sick feeling. This is what I get for trusting that kid. I pictured him dashing to freedom down the main concourse, hailing a cab, and going off to a Ramada Inn to get high.

Finally I grab a counter attendant and say, "I've lost a kid who's in my care. Can you contact airport security for me? Is it possible to postpone the flight? Can we put out an all-points bulletin on him?"

Just as they are getting ready to close the boarding door and I am contemplating calling his parents, I see Nate walking up to me at the gate, holding two double-scoop ice-cream cones—Oreo, my favorite.

"Hi," he says, with an enormous grin. "Eat fast; it's dripping."

A Wish for You

Interventionists can't make guarantees. Our job is to educate families and put choices in front of addicts. About 10 percent say "Thanks, but no thanks."

So we're not in a position to make promises about recovery.

But here's what we can do. We can make a wish—the most sincere wish you've ever heard. It is a wish for peace in your home. It is a wish that the cannibal who lives inside your loved one be driven out. It is a wish that you can all live together the way people are supposed to, feeling your feelings, doing your jobs, and dealing honestly and fairly with one another.

You may have heard of the idea of the "committee" that resides inside us all. Think of a table surrounded by perhaps eight chairs. In addiction, the cannibal has taken up all but one chair and outvotes the individual in the one remaining chair on every matter. ("Shall we paint the house today? No, let's get drunk instead.") The loved one has no chance of prevailing against a committee of cannibals.

But with recovery, the committee math begins to

change. The cannibal dwindles to a single seat at the table, a single voice. The voice of the individual grows stronger and more self-assured as it reclaims seats. Then, surprisingly, other people take their seats in support of the loved one—friends, family, other recovering addicts.

In this wish, almost everything for the addict is better. He will have stopped drinking, drugging, or acting out. With the cannibal relegated to a single seat at the committee table, he'll succeed more often at the things he truly wants to do. He'll show up for work. He'll fulfill his responsibilities. He'll be a father to his kids, a husband to his wife, a son to his folks. He'll be an adult, not a spoiled child. He'll be a human being, not a creature.

It will be different from the cannibal days.

Make no mistake: the cannibal will still be on hand, as long as your loved one lives. His voice will always be audible, singing the siren song of addiction. He will be passionate about his desires, and for this reason he will be persuasive. Most days the loved one will prevail. Some days, the addict may.

But the addict's voice will be just one of several. His power will be diminished as long as the other committee members line up with the individual. His victories will be temporary.

The future of an individual depends on that individual, of course. That's why this is a wish, not a guarantee.

You may not like all the terms of this wish. It involves hard work and changed attitudes—on your part as well as on the addict's. The old way of living is over. Your son Johnny may not be coming home after treatment. Your marriage to Sarah will not be picking up where you left off, before things got bad. Addiction is about comfort, doing the easy thing. Living in recovery is about retraining the brain and body to "do the work" and take responsibility for living with a chronic illness. They will be living at odds with their own intuition. "Whatever I want to do, whenever I want to do it, regardless of the consequences" will no longer be the answer for everything that comes up.

And for the first time in a long time, you will be at peace with yourself, because you did your very best.

It's Not Okay to Be a Cannibal

Epilogue

HOUSE-TO-HOUSE FIGHTING

We are sometimes asked, "So how do you feel about the War on Drugs?"

Part of our answer is that we are soldiers in a war on drugs. We have dedicated our lives to helping families through the difficulties of addiction in the home. We find nothing cute or fashionable about drugs and alcohol. We absolutely take a very tough line on getting people free of substances that don't enlighten, entertain, or improve a human being—they only fool us into thinking they do these things and then they kill us instead.

Having said all this, we have serious issues with the official, government-driven War on Drugs.

The War on Drugs is into its fourth decade now, having begun in the Nixon administration. Over that time it has used the power of government in just about every way to stem the flow of drugs into our country and into our loved ones and ourselves:

- We have poisoned marijuana fields in Mexico, blighted the cocaine plantations of Colombia and Bolivia, and set fire to the poppy fields of Afghanistan.
- We have focused the combined power and intelligence of local, state, federal, and international criminal justice systems on stopping the importation, sale, and use of drugs.
- We have spent hundreds of millions of dollars on public awareness programs, using TV, radio, the print media, and in-school programs to stress the dangers posed by drugs.
- We have imprisoned tens of thousands of our citizens—with the idea that there will be no access to drugs in the penal system. Back in 1980, almost 600,000 Americans were arrested for drug use. By 2003, that figure was almost triple, 1,678,200. We arrest more people for drugs than for murder, manslaughter, rape, and assault combined.*
- A generation of kids has grown up with one or both parents in jail for drugs.

After all this effort, what has been the effect on drug use here and in other countries?

It's gone up.

We believe that the War on Drugs, fully capitalized,

* Norm Stamper, "Legalize Drugs—All of Them," *Seattle Times,* December 4, 2005, http://archives.seattletimes.nwsource.com/cgi-bin/texis.cgi/web/vortex/display?slug=sunstamper04&date=20051204&query=legalize+drugs.

It's Not Okay to Be a Cannibal

is itself a form of addictive behavior—in which we *quest for something unattainable,* endlessly *repeat a behavior* known to be extremely *injurious,* and ultimately *never get what we want.*

Recovering addicts talk frequently about the definition of insanity when describing addiction. "This time if I use cocaine, it will be like that first hit. It will feel great, and I won't have any consequences, even though the past one hundred times I have said this it has not been the case." Is this wishful thinking or pure insanity? If you know that something doesn't work but keep repeating the behavior, that's *insanity.*

Likewise, a War on Drugs that seriously harms thousands of families but, for the most part, doesn't succeed in discouraging drug use is, as addicts use the word, *insane.*

This war is not hard to critique. You are most likely reading this because you have a loved one who is an addict. What effect would you say the government's War on Drugs has had in discouraging your loved one's use? Chances are it has made him cynical. Telling an addict to "Just say no" is asking for scorn. If addicts could stop on their own, they certainly would. No one wants to grow up to disappoint their parents, lie, cheat, steal, and become the best addict they can be, but it happens all the time. By definition, active addicts aren't able to *not* use drugs. Has interdiction abroad caused the inflow of drugs to significantly diminish? Has the threat of jail helped the addict overcome desire? Have all the public service announcements combined caused your addicted loved one to stop using? Too often the answer is no. Prevention is a useful and necessary component in the effort to minimize the effects of addiction on our society. You are reading this book, however, so you already know that prevention does little for those who are already addicted. Compare these two sets of approaches, one that we know doesn't work well and one that we know *does* work:

THE WAR ON DRUGS	INTERVENTION
Approaches the problem from afar	Approaches the problem person by person
Does not have a clear outcome	Forces the addict to make a choice
Coercive and impersonal in character	Family-based and loving
No specified deadline for progress	Deadline is today
Costs billions of dollars with no way to evaluate outcomes	Modest cost with immediate, measurable results

The War on Drugs simply doesn't work because it is a creature of bureaucracy, a million light years from where drugs are consumed and harm actually occurs, in the bedrooms and basements of ordinary families.

Instead of a B-1 bomber approach to addiction, flying 30,000 feet above the action, the need is for something much smaller in scale, more personal, more focused.

It's Not Okay to Be a Cannibal

Think of a different kind of war, one that is fought entirely on the ground. One that consists of hand-to-hand combat, house-to-house fighting in which families confront their loved ones, eyeball to eyeball, tell them the truth that everyone has been too afraid to utter, and require the cannibals to change.

Where the War on Drugs is wholesale, this kind of fighting is retail. Where the government's war is distant and remote, this war is as close as the sofa in your living room, so close you can count the tears.

We suspect that we as a society indulge in the wholesale, B-1 bomber approach out of cowardice. It's psychically easier to confront drug addiction on a high-altitude, impersonal basis. It's scary as hell to look your son or daughter or spouse in the eye and say: "I won't tolerate your addiction anymore. Things are going to change."

We are so deep into addiction as a people that we can no longer think straight. Like the cannibals we live with, it has made us a little crazy, deluded. We live in wishful thinking:

- "Mary was in a good mood today."
- "Maybe Harold isn't really doing that much crack."
- "If I don't say the wrong thing, we'll be all right."
- "I'm going to make the most wonderful pie. George loves my pies."

We have had to make room for insanity in our lives and to pretend that the natural response to life's difficulties is to get high, to escape, to create little shrines to our specialness. After a while, it's hard to tell who's nuttier, the cannibal or his keeper.

Our world is so insane that tens of millions of people feel safer and more like themselves when they are living criminal, cannibal existences in which they turn their backs on the humble values that have held human society together over the last hundred thousand years:

- **Trust** and the act of being trustworthy to one another, the ability to take part in healthy relationships.
- **Respect** for one another, and the simple decency that springs naturally from that.
- **Gratitude** for the everyday blessings that our lives abound in—we haven't got everything, but we've got a lot.
- **Joy in living life** without dosing ourselves with artificial additives.
- **Perspective** on who we are and what our place is in this world—wisdom.

All these things, the cannibal laughs at. How hilarious. How insipid. How uncool.

In the place of these simple values, the addict substitutes alcohol, speed, pot, and frantic compulsivity.

They think addiction is just a lifestyle choice and that they are existential heroes, swashbuckling Errol

Flynns, laughing at danger. Only instead of swinging from chandeliers and tree branches, they are taking their risks with alcohol, drugs, and compulsive, self-destructive behaviors.

Cannibals are so gone into themselves that they aren't even aware of the misery they are causing the people who put up with them.

They think it's okay to be that way.

It's not.

It all has to go, starting in your house, and moving from family to family, supporting one another, until you drive these monsters out and get your loved ones back.

How do you do it? By ending the conspiracy of silence. By telling the truth. And by doing for these people what they would want us to do if they could think straight.

Speak out. Get involved. Work for change.

It doesn't matter whether you are a mother, father, daughter, son, grandparent, uncle, or roommate's cousin.

If you care, you must lead.

We know it's scary. Things can go wrong. But things are already very, very wrong. It's up to you to show courage.

The downside of doing nothing is death.

The upside of intervening is the possibility of possibility: joy, restoration, and a deeper love than you even thought existed.

INDEX

A

abstinence, false, 57

accountability, 21, 41–42, 50, 143

achievement addiction, 31

activity addiction, 31

addiction

  categories of addictive behaviors, 31

  conspiracy of silence and, 45, 86–87

  controls addict, 5–7, 146

  definition of, 30, 32

  denial by families of, 24–25, 37, 155–56

  family obligation and, 14

  is disease, 5, 11, 48, 87

  is not socially acceptable, 25–26

  legal, 14

  myths of, 10, 38–40

  physical signs of, 4, 32–33

  relationship to mental illness of, 29, 30

  See also specific types

addiction interventions. *See* interventions

addicts

  behaviors of, 15, 62, 65, 101

  characteristics of, 75–77

  choices made by, 13–14, 17, 42, 53–54

  communication after interventions with, 8–9

  deceptions used by, 55–58, 59, 60, 66

  denial of addiction by, 11, 58, 113, 156–57

  family behaviors toward, 7, 21, 45

  feelings of, 104

  harmless, 21–22

  interventions change power within family of, 19–20, 52–54, 61, 94–95, 148–49

  manipulation of families by, 6–7, 44, 47–48, 52–53

  mental health of, 27–28, 29, 30

in recovery as interventionists, 85, 137
response to interventions
of, 43–44, 114–17
addicts at interventions
acceptance by, 114
anger of, 113
bargaining by, 97–98,
110–11, 113
bullying by, 106–7
denial by, 113
excuses made by, 97–98
aggressive misdirection, 66
alcoholics
are not socially acceptable,
25–26
description of intervention
with, 101–3, 104–6,
107–10
detoxification dangers for,
33–34
harmless, 22
physical signs of, 4
secret lives of, 62, 101
anger at interventions, 113
appearance obsessions, 31
appearances
can be explained away by
addicts, 62
keeping up, 56

B

balance of power within families, 19–20, 52–54, 61,
94–95, 148–49

bargaining by addicts at interventions, 97–98, 110–11,
113
behaviors
of addicts, 15, 62, 65, 101
of addicts at interventions,
97–98, 106–7, 110–11,
113–114
enabling, 20, 21, 45, 64, 96
of families during inter-
ventions, 7, 79, 106–7
War on Drugs as example
of addictive, 152–53
benzodiazepines, 4, 35
blame shifting, 58
bluffing, 58
boundary setting, 94–95

C

cannibal characteristics,
75–77
cannibal creed, 5–7
cannibal twist, 66
care facilities, types of, 29–30
choices
made by addicts, 13–14, 17,
42, 53–54
made by families, 62–63
clergy, 136
cocaine addiction, 72–73
codependency
definition of, 64
denial and, 25
lies enabling, 96
wealthy and, 130

cold turkey, 35, 139
communication
    with addicts after interventions, 8-9
    conspiracy of silence
        addiction thrives in, 45
        families engage in, 86-87
        interventions break, 8, 9-10, 86-87, 112
compromise agreements. *See* bargaining by addicts at interventions
conflict training, 137
confrontations, avoiding, 66
conspiracy of silence
    addiction thrives in, 45
    families engage in, 86-87
    interventions break, 8, 9-10, 86-87, 112
co-occurring disorders, 29, 30
costs, 133-34, 138-39
crack addiction, physical signs of, 3, 4

D
death
    from detoxification among alcoholics, 33
    from eating disorders, 35
    hitting bottom and, 10
    preventing, 39
    rate for heroin addicts, 32
    from suicide, 46
deceptions by addicts, 55-58, 59, 60, 66

decisions
    made by addicts, 13-14, 17, 42, 53-54
    made by families, 62-63
denial of addiction
    by addicts, 11, 58, 113, 156-57
    codependency and, 25
    by family, 24-25, 37, 155-56
depression, 57, 113
destructive social patterns, 31
detoxification
    alcoholics and, 33-34
    facilities for uninsured, 138-39
    supervision of, 35
doctors, 137
driving under the influence (DUI), 41
drug production, 41-42

E
eating disorders, 31, 35-36, 62
emergency care centers, 139
emotional blackmail, 44, 47-48
employers, 137
enabling behaviors, 20, 21, 45, 64, 96
enmeshment, 64-65
escape routes, 103-4
evidence, 55-56
excuses, 57

heroin addiction, physical
    signs of, 32–33
hitting bottom, 10, 38–40
homelessness, 14, 42
hospital emergency care, 139
humility, 130
hypocrisy, 83–84

I
indigent, 131
insurance coverage, 133
intellectual addictions, 31
interventionists
    addicts and, 106–7
    alternatives to professional,
        136–37
    characteristics of good,
        105, 119–22
    characteristics of poor,
        123–24
    family members as, 134–35
    job description of, 95–96,
        119
    peer, 85, 137
    reasons to use professional,
        134–36
    self-disclosure by, 125–26
    skills of, 126–27, 128
    sole practitioners, 122–23
    treatment center connec-
        tions and, 124
    truth and, 127
interventions
    addicts at
        acceptance by, 114

anger of, 113
bargaining by, 97–98,
    110–11, 113
bullying by, 106–7
denial by, 113
excuses made by, 97–98
are manufactured crisis,
    121
are not therapy sessions,
    127–28
are process, 141
best time for, 3
common questions after,
    144–45
compared to War on
    Drugs, 154
cost of, 133
elements of, 17–18, 102
follow-up, 99–100
letters for
    breaking conspiracy of
        silence with, 112
    preparing, 90–95
    reading, 108–10
    sequencing, 106
    using during treatment,
        114
location of, 103–4
obstacles to, 10, 37, 38–40,
    155–56
pain is part of, 43
by peers, 85, 137
planning meetings for
    concerns of partici-
        pants, 96–97

letters, 90–95
process, 80–83, 84–89
purpose of, 79–80
realign balance of power,
19–20, 52–54, 61, 94–95,
148–49
results of
addicts response, 114–17
conspiracy of silence
broken, 8, 9–10,
86–87, 112
success rate, 11, 13, 24,
87, 117, 130–31
sequencing letters during,
106
short-term vs. long-term,
19
truth is essential in, 84
See also families
"I" statements, 90

J
job loss, 6, 60
Johnson, Vernon, 10–11
Johnson Model. *See* interventions
judges, 137
jumping-off point, 18
Just say no, 153

L
lawyers, 137
legal addiction, 14
long-term interventions, 19
lower classes, access to treatment, 131
lying, 58

M
manipulation, 44, 47–48, 58
mental health
of addicts, 27–28, 29, 30
of families, 6
mental illness
interventions and, 28–29
relationship to addiction
of, 27–28, 29, 30
social acceptability of,
25–26
used by addicts as excuse,
57
methamphetamine, 34
middle class recovery rate,
130–31
misdirection, 56, 58, 66
money compulsions, 31, 36
municipal detoxification
facilities, 139
myths of addiction, 10, 38–40

N
noncompliance, terms of,
53–54

O
outpatient programs, 139
overeaters, 62

P
pain
is part of intervention, 43
as motivator, 40
suicide and conscious, 46
parents. *See* families
peers in recovery, 85, 137

phone calls, 18
physicians, 137
police officers
    calling, 41–42
    as interventionists, 137
politeness, 104
pre-intervention meetings
    concerns of participants,
        96–97
    letters, 90–95
    process, 80–83, 84–89
    purpose of, 79–80
prison population, 140, 152
psychologists, 137

R
recovery
    characteristics of, 145–46
    family culture and, 142–43
    life during, 149–50
    obstacles to, 129–30
    rates of, 11, 130–31
    vigilance is necessary to
        maintain, 70, 77
relapses, 145–46
relationship addictions, 31
religious addictions, 31
reputations, 6, 18
respect, 89
responsibility, 21, 41–42, 50, 143
Ritalin addiction, 131–32
rock bottom, 10, 38–40

S
Salvation Army, 136, 139
secrecy. See conspiracy of
    silence

self-disclosure, 125–26
sexual addictions, 31, 62
shock of addicts during inter-
    ventions, 113
short-term interventions, 19
silence, conspiracy of. See con-
    spiracy of silence
social workers, 137
spit-back methadone, 69
status quo, accepting, 63
stealing, 58, 60
suicide
    conscious pain and, 46
    gambling and, 36
    threats of, 44, 46–48, 57
support groups, 45

T
teachers, 136–37
temper tantrums, 116
theft, 58, 60
therapy, interventions are not,
    127–28
thinking patterns, successful,
    15
tobacco addiction, 145–46
tough love
    is necessary, 12
    setting boundaries, 94–95
treatment
    consequences of refusal to
        go for, 53–54
    costs of, 133–34, 138–39
    indigent and, 131
    interventionists connected
        with specific centers for,
        124

intervention letters used
during, 114
options for, 29–30, 76
rate after interventions,
11, 13, 24, 87, 117,
130–31
refusal to go for, 98
truth
ability to tell, 10
interventionists and, 127
at interventions, 84
turning the tables, 58, 66
Twelve Step programs, 76, 146

U

upper-middle class recovery
rate, 130–31
urgent care centers, 139

V

vigilance, recovery requires,
70, 77

W

War on Drugs, 12, 151–55
wet brain, 33–34
withdrawal
by alcoholics, 33
facilities for uninsured,
138–39
supervision of, 35
workaholism, 31
working poor, treatment for,
140

Y

"You" statements, 90

ABOUT THE AUTHORS

Andrew T. Wainwright and Robert Poznanovich founded Addiction Intervention Resources Inc. (AIR) in 2001 and established a new model for dealing with the problems of alcohol, drug, and other addictions. AIR has become the nation's leading addiction consulting company. A clinically based, independent organization, AIR provides solutions for families and organizations struggling with addiction around the globe.

Andrew T. Wainwright is a nationally recognized expert on addictions and intervention. He has been involved with thousands of interventions both in the United States and abroad. Andrew was the leading interventionist for National Counseling Intervention Services and was trained by Dr. James Fearing, a pioneer in this field.

Robert Poznanovich is a nationally recognized speaker on treatment and addictions. Also known as "Chicago Bob," he has helped thousands of people come to terms with the consequences of addiction and the promise and possibility of recovery.

The authors may be contacted at www.Intervene .com/Cannibal.

Other titles that may interest you:

Codepependent No More
Melody Beattie
Through personal examples and exercises, readers are shown how controlling others forces them to lose sight of their own needs. Softcover, 264 pp.
Order No. 5014

Boundaries
Anne Katherine
This book offers help for strengthening relationships and presents real-life stories that illustrate the ill effects of not setting limits. Softcover, 144 pp.
Order No. 7803

The Addictive Personality
Craig Nakken
The author examines how addictions begin and progress, as well as how our society encourages addictive behavior. Softcover, 144 pp.
Order No. 5221

Hazelden books are available at fine bookstores everywhere. To order directly from Hazelden, call 1-800-328-9000 or visit www.hazelden.org/bookstore.

CORNERED!

There were Indians riding circles out on the plain, and I knew there were others crawling closer through the sagebrush.

I hunkered in the buffalo wallow, holding my horse down. This time I couldn't run.

I had to get out of that hole alive, not just for me, but for my brother Orrin. The frontier was crawling with men who wanted to kill Orrin, and he needed me. Me and my gun.

My horse pricked his ear, and I turned just in time. Four Utes were sneaking up the slope in back of me.

I snapped off a shot . . .

BENDIGO SHAFTER
BORDEN CHANTRY
BOWDRIE
BOWDRIE'S LAW
BRIONNE
THE BROKEN GUN
BUCKSKIN RUN
THE BURNING HILLS
THE CALIFORNIOS
CALLAGHEN
CATLOW
CHANCY
THE CHEROKEE TRAIL
COMSTOCK LODE
CONAGHER
CROSSFIRE TRAIL
DARK CANYON
DOWN THE LONG HILLS
THE EMPTY LAND
FAIR BLOWS THE WIND
FALLON
THE FERGUSON RIFLE
THE FIRST FAST DRAW
FLINT
FRONTIER
GUNS OF THE TIMBERLANDS
HANGING WOMAN CREEK
HELLER WITH A GUN
THE HIGH GRADERS
HIGH LONESOME
THE HILLS OF HOMICIDE
HONDO
HOW THE WEST WAS WON
THE IRON MARSHAL
THE KEY-LOCK MAN
KID RODELO
KILKENNY
KILLOE
KILRONE
KIOWA TRAIL
LAW OF THE DESERT BORN
THE LONESOME GODS
THE MAN CALLED NOON
THE MAN FROM SKIBBEREEN
MATAGORDA
MILO TALON
THE MOUNTAIN VALLEY WAR
NORTH TO THE RAILS
OVER ON THE DRY SIDE
THE PROVING TRAIL

THE QUICK AND THE DEAD
RADIGAN
REILLY'S LUCK
THE RIDER OF LOST CREEK
RIVERS WEST
THE SHADOW RIDERS
SHALAKO
SHOWDOWN AT YELLOW
   BUTTE
SILVER CANYON
SITKA
SON OF A WANTED MAN
THE STRONG SHALL LIVE
TAGGART
TO TAME A LAND
TUCKER
UNDER THE SWEET-
   WATER RIM
UTAH BLAINE
THE WALKING DRUM
WAR PARTY
WESTWARD THE TIDE
WHERE THE LONG GRASS
   BLOWS
YONDERING

Sackett Titles by
Louis L'Amour

1. SACKETT'S LAND
2. TO THE FAR BLUE
   MOUNTAINS
3. THE DAYBREAKERS
4. SACKETT
5. LANDO
6. MOJAVE CROSSING
7. THE SACKETT BRAND
8. THE LONELY MEN
9. TREASURE MOUNTAIN
10. MUSTANG MAN
11. GALLOWAY
12. THE SKY-LINERS
13. THE MAN FROM THE
    BROKEN HILLS
14. RIDE THE DARK TRAIL
15. THE WARRIOR'S PATH
16. LONELY ON THE
    MOUNTAIN
17. RIDE THE RIVER

LOUIS L'AMOUR
THE DAYBREAKERS

BANTAM BOOKS
TORONTO • NEW YORK • LONDON • SYDNEY • AUCKLAND

THE DAYBREAKERS

A Bantam Book / February 1960

2nd printing . December 1971	14th printing .. January 1979
81d printing .... April 1972	15th printing ..... July 1979
4th printing . September 1972	16th printing . December 1979
5th printing ... August 1973	17th printing .... May 1980
6th printing . September 1974	18th printing . December 1980
7th printing . September 1975	19th printing ..... June 1981
8th printing . December 1975	20th printing ... March 1982
9th printing .. January 1977	21st printing ... August 1982
10th printing .... July 1977	22nd printing .. March 1983
11th printing . November 1977	23rd printing .... July 1983
12th printing . November 1978	24th printing .... May 1984
13th printing .. January 1979	25th printing .... April 1985

ISBN 0-553-25275-5

Published simultaneously in the United States and Canada

Bantam Books are published by Bantam Books, Inc. Its trade-
mark, consisting of the words "Bantam Books" and the por-
trayal of a rooster, is Registered in U.S. Patent and Trademark
Office and in other countries. Marca Registrada. Bantam
Books, Inc., 666 Fifth Avenue, New York, New York 10103.

PRINTED IN THE UNITED STATES OF AMERICA

H   34 33 32 31 30 29

CHAPTER I

My Brother, Orrin Sackett, was big enough to fight
bears with a switch. Me, I was the skinny one, tall as
Orrin, but no meat to my bones except around the
shoulders and arms. Orrin could sing like an angel, or
like a true Welshman which was better than any
angel. Far away back and on three sides of the family, we were Welsh. Orrin was a strapping big man,
but for such a big man he was surprising quick.

Folks said I was the quiet one, and in the high-up
hills where we grew up as boys, folks fought shy of
me come fighting time. Orrin was bigger than me, fit
to wrassle a bull, but he lacked a streak of something
I had.

Maybe you recall the Sackett-Higgins feud? Time I
tell about, we Sacketts were just fresh out of Higginses.

Long Higgins, the mean one, was also the last one.
He came hunting Sackett hide with an old squirrel
rifle. It was Orrin he was hunting, being mighty brave
because he knew Orrin wouldn't be packing anything
in the way of sidearms at a wedding.

Orrin was doing no thinking about Higginses this
day with Mary Tripp there to greet him and his mind
set on marrying, so I figured it was my place to meet
Long Higgins down there in the road. Just as I was
fixing to call him to a stand, Preacher Myrick drove
his rig between us, and by the time I got around it
Long Higgins was standing spraddlelegged in the road
with a bead on Orrin.

Folks started to scream and Long Higgins shot and
Mary who saw him first pushed Orrin to save him.
Only she fell off balance and fell right into the bullet
intended for Orrin.

"Long!"

He turned sharp around, knowing my voice, and he had that rifle waist-high and aimed for me, his lips drawed down hard.

Long Higgins was a good hip shot with a rifle and he shot quick ... maybe too quick.

That old hog-leg of mine went back into the holster and Long Higgins lay there in the dust and when I turned around, that walk up into the trees was the longest I ever did take except one I took a long time later.

Ollie Shaddock might have been down there and I knew if Ollie called I'd have to turn around, for Ollie was the Law in those mountains and away back somewheres we were kin.

When Ma saw me cutting up through the woods she knew something was cross-ways. Took me only a minute to tell her. She sat in that old rocker and looked me right in the eye while I told it. "Tye," she was almighty stern, "was Long Higgins looking at you when you fetched him?"

"Right in the eye."

"Take the dapple," Ma said, "he's the runningest horse on the mountain. You go west, and when you find a place with deep, rich soil and a mite of game in the hills, you get somebody to write a letter and we'll come down there, the boys an' me."

She looked around at the place, which was mighty rundown. Work as we would, and us Sacketts were workers, we still hadn't anything extra, and scarcely a poor living, so Ma had been talking up the west ever since Pa died.

Most of it she got from Pa, for he was a wandering and a knowing man, never to home long, but Ma loved him for all of that, and so did we younguns. He had a Welshman's tongue, Pa did, a tongue that could twist a fine sound from a word and he could bring a singing to your blood so you could just see that far land yonder, waiting for folks to come and crop it.

Those old blue eyes of Ma's were harder to face

than was Long Higgins, and him with a gun to hand. "Tye, do you reckon you could kill Ollie?"

To nobody else would I have said it, but to Ma I told the truth. "I'd never want to, Ma, because we're kin but I could fetch him. I think maybe I can draw a gun faster and shoot straighter than anybody, anywhere."

She took the pipe from her lips. "Eighteen years now I've seen you growing up, Tyrel Sackett, and for twelve of them you've been drawing and shooting. Pa told me when you was fifteen that he'd never seen the like. Ride with the law, Tye, never against it." She drew the shawl tighter about her knees. "If the Lord wills we will meet again in the western lands."

The way I took led across the state line and south, then west. Ollie Shaddock would not follow beyond the line of the state, so I put Tennessee behind me before the hills had a shadow.

It was wild land through which the trail led, west out of Tennessee, into Arkansas, the Ozarks, and by lonely trails into Kansas. When I rode at last into the street at Baxter Springs folks figured me for one more mountain renegade coming to help keep tick-infected Texas cattle out of the country, but I was of no such mind.

It was eight miles to where the Texas men held their cattle, so there I rode, expecting no warm welcome for a stranger. Riding clear of the circling riders I rode up to the fire, the smell of grub turning my insides over. Two days I'd been without eating, with no money left, and too proud to ask for that for which I could not pay.

A short, square man with a square face and a mustache called out to me. "You there! On the gray! What do you want?"

"A job if one's to be had, and a meal if you've grub to spare. My name is Tyrel Sackett and I'm bound westward from Tennessee toward the Rockies, but if there's a job I'll ride straight up to it."

He looked me over, mighty sharp, and then he said, "Get down, man, and come to the fire. No man was ever turned from my fire without a meal inside him. I'm Belden."

When I'd tied Dapple I walked up to the fire, and there was a big, handsome man lying on the ground by the fire, a man with a golden beard like one of those Vikings Pa used to tell of. "Hell," he said agreeably, "it's a farmer!"

"What's wrong with farming?" I asked him. "You wouldn't have your belly full of beans right now if they'd not been farmed by somebody."

"We've had our troubles with farmers, Mr. Sackett," Belden said, "there's been shooting, the farmers killed a man for me."

"So," said a voice alongside, "so maybe we should kill a farmer."

He had an itch for trouble and his kind I'd met before. He was a medium-tall man with a low hanging shoulder on his gun side. His black brows met over his nose and his face was thin and narrow. If it was trouble he was hunting he was following the right trail to get it.

"Mister," I told him, "any time you think you can kill this farmer, you just have at it."

He looked across the fire at me, surprised I think, because he had expected fear. My clothes showed I was from the hills, a patched, old homespun shirt, jeans stuffed into clumsy boots. It was sure that I looked like nothing at all, only if a man looked at the pistol I wore he could see there'd been a sight of lead shot out of that barrel.

"That's enough, Carney!" Mr. Belden said sharply. "This man is a guest at our fire!"

The cook brought me a plate of grub and it smelled so good I didn't even look up until I'd emptied that plate and another, and swallowed three cups of hot black coffee. Up in the hills we like our coffee strong but this here would make bobwire grow on a man's chest in the place of hair.

The man with the golden beard watched me and he said to Mr. Belden, "Boss, you better hire this man. If he can work like he can eat, you've got yourself a hand."

"Question is," Carney broke in, "can he fight?"

It was mighty quiet around that fire when I put my plate aside and got up. "Mister, I didn't kill you before because when I left home I promised Ma I'd go careful with a gun, but you're a mighty tryin' man."

Carney had the itch, all right, and as he looked across the fire at me I knew that sooner or later I was going to have to kill this man.

"You promised Ma, did you?" he scoffed. "We'll see about that!" He brought his right foot forward about an inch and I durned near laughed at him, but then from behind me came a warm, rich voice and it spoke clear and plain. "Mister, you just back up an' set down. I ain't aimin' to let Tyrel hang up your hide right now, so you just set down an' cool off."

It was Orrin, and knowing Orrin I knew his rifle covered Carney.

"Thanks, Orrin. Ma made me promise to go careful."

"She told me . . . an' lucky for this gent."

He stepped down from the saddle, a fine, big, handsome man with shoulders wide enough for two strong men. He wore a belt gun, too, and I knew he could use it.

"Are you two brothers?" Belden asked.

"Brothers from the hills," Orrin said, "bound west for the new lands."

"You're hired," Mr. Belden said, "I like men who work together."

So that was how it began, but more had begun that day than any of us could guess, least of all the fine-looking man with the beard who was Tom Sunday, our foreman on the drive. From the moment he had spoken up all our lives were pointed down a trail together, but no man could read the sign.

From the first Orrin was a well-loved man. With that big, easy way of his, a wide smile, as well as courage and humor enough for three men, he was a man to ride the trail with. He did his share of the work and more, and at night around the fire he would sing or tell yarns. When he sang to the cows in that fine Welsh baritone of his, everybody listened.

Nobody paid me much mind. Right off they saw I could do my work and they let me do it. When Orrin told them I was the tough one of the two they just laughed. Only there was one or two of them who didn't laugh and of these one was Tom Sunday, the other Cap Rountree, a thin, wiry old man with a walrus mustache who looked to have ridden a lot of trails.

The third day out, Tom Sunday fetched up alongside me and asked, "Tye, what would you have done if Reed Carney had grabbed his gun?"

"Why, Mr. Sunday," I said, "I'd have killed him." He glanced at me. "Yes, I expect you would have."

He swung off then, only turned in his saddle. "Call me Tom. I'm not much on long-handled names."

Have you seen those Kansas plains? Have you seen the grass stretch away from you to the horizon? Grass and nothing but grass except for flowers here and there and maybe the white of buffalo bones, but grass moving gentle under the long wind, moving like a restless sea with the hand of God upon it.

On the fifth day when I was riding point by myself, and well out from the herd a dozen men came riding out of a ravine, all bunched up. Right off I had a smell of trouble, so instead of waiting for them to come up, I rode right to meet them.

It was a mighty pleasant day and the air was balmy with summer. Overhead the sky was blue and only a mite of cloud drifting like a lost white buffalo over the plain of the sky.

When they were close I drew up and waited, my Spencer .56 cradled on my saddle, my right hand over the trigger guard.

They drew up, a dirty, rough-looking bunch—their leader mean enough to sour cream.

"We're cuttin' your herd," he was a mighty abrupt man, "we're cuttin' it now. You come through the settlements an' swept up a lot of our cattle, an' they've et our grass."

Well, I looked at him and I said, "I reckon not."

Sort of aimlesslike I'd switched that Spencer to cover his belt buckle, my right finger on the trigger.

"Look here, boy," he started in to bluster.

"Mister," I said, "this here Spencer ain't no boy, an' I'm just after makin' a bet with a fellow. He says one of those big belt buckles like you got would stop a bullet. Me, I figure a chunk of lead, .56 caliber, would drive that buckle right back into your belly. Mister, if you want to be a sport we can settle that bet."

He was white around the eyes, and if one of the others made a wrong move I was going to drop the bull of the herd and as many others as time would allow.

"Back," it was one of the men behind the leader, "I know this boy. This here is one of them Sacketts I been tellin' you about."

It was one of those no-account Aikens from Turkey Flat, who'd been run out of the mountains for hog stealing.

"Oh?" Back smiled, kind of sickly. "Had no idea you was friends. Boy," he said, "you folks just ride on through."

"Thanks. That there's just what we figured to do."

They turned tail around and rode off and a couple of minutes later hoofs drummed on the sod and here came Mr. Belden, Tom Sunday, Cap Rountree, and Reed Carney, all a-sweat an' expecting trouble. When they saw those herd cutters ride off they were mighty surprised.

"Tye," Mr. Belden asked, "what did those men want?"

"They figured to cut your herd."

"What happened?"

"They decided not to."

He looked at me, mighty sharp. Kneeing Dapple around I started back to the herd.

"Now what do you make of that?" I could hear Belden saying. "I'd have sworn that was Back Rand."

"It was," Rountree commented dryly, "but that there's quite a boy."

When Orrin asked me about it at the fire that night, I just said, "Aiken was there. From Turkey Flat."

Carney was listening. "Aiken who? Who's Aiken?"

"He's from the mountains," Orrin said, "he knows the kid."

Reed Carney said nothing more but a couple of times I noticed him sizing me up like he hadn't seen me before.

There would be trouble enough, but man is born to trouble, and it is best to meet it when it comes and not lose sleep until it does. Only there was more than trouble, for beyond the long grass plains were the mountains, the high and lonely mountains where someday I would ride, and where someday, the Good Lord willing, I would find a home.

How many trails? How much dust and loneliness? How long a time until then?

CHAPTER II

There was nothing but prairie and sky, the sun by day and the stars by night, and the cattle moving westward. If I live to be a thousand years old I shall not forget the wonder and the beauty of those big longhorns, the sun glinting on their horns; most of them six or seven feet from tip to tip. Some there were like old brindle, our lead steer, whose horns measured a fair nine feet from point to point, and who stood near to seventeen hands high.

It was a sea of horns above the red, brown, brindle, and white-splashed backs of the steers. They were big, wild, and fierce, ready to fight anything that walked the earth, and we who rode their flanks or the drag, we loved them and we hated them, we cussed and reviled them, but we moved them westward toward what destination we knew not.

Sometimes at night when my horse walked a slow circle around the bedded herd, I'd look at the stars and think of Ma and wonder how things were at home. And sometimes I'd dream great dreams of a girl I'd know someday.

Suddenly something had happened to me, and it happened to Orrin too. The world had burst wide open, and where our narrow valleys had been, our hog-backed ridges, our huddled towns and villages, there was now a world without end or limit. Where our world had been one of a few mountain valleys, it was now as wide as the earth itself, and wider, for where the land ended there was sky, and no end at all to that.

We saw no one. The Plains were empty. No cattle had been before us, only the buffalo and war parties of Indians crossing. No trees, only the far and endless

9

grass, always whispering its own soft stories. Here ran the antelope, and by night the coyotes called their plaintive songs to the silent stars.

Mostly a man rode by himself, but sometimes I'd ride along with Tom Sunday or Cap Rountree, and I learned about cattle from them. Sunday knew cows, all right, but he was a sight better educated than the rest of us, although not one for showing it.

Sometimes when we rode along he would recite poetry or tell me stories from the history of ancient times, and it was mighty rich stuff. Those old Greeks he was always talking about, they reminded me of mountain folk I'd known, and it fair made me ache to know how to read myself.

Rountree talked mighty little, but whatever he said made a sight of sense. He knew buffalo . . . although there was always something to learn about them. He was a mighty hard old man, rode as many hours as any of us, although he was a mighty lot older. I never did know how old he was, but those hard old gray eyes of his had looked on a sight of strange things.

"Man could make some money," Rountree said one day, "over in the breaks of western Kansas and Colorado. Lots of cows over there, belongin' to nobody, stuff drifted up from the Spanish settlements to the south."

When Rountree spoke up it was because there was an idea behind it. Right then I figured something was stirring in that coot's skull, but nothing more was said at the time.

Orrin and me, we talked it over. Each of us wanted a place of our own, and we wanted a place for Ma and the boys. A lot of cattle belonging to no man . . . it sounded good to us.

"It would take an outfit," Orrin said.

Tom Sunday, I was sure, would be for it. From things he'd said on night herd I knew he was an ambitious man, and he had plans for himself out west. Educated the way he was, there was no telling how far he would go. Time to time he talked a good deal about politics . . . out west a man could be whatever he was man enough to be, and Tom Sunday was smart.

"Orrin and me," I said to Rountree, "we've been talking about what you said. About those wild cows. We discussed the three of us and maybe Tom Sunday, if you're willing and he wants to come in."

"Why, now. That there's about what I had in mind. Fact is, I talked to Tom. He likes it."

Mr. Belden drove his herd away from the Kansas-Missouri border, right out into the grassy plains, he figured he'd let his cows graze until they were good and fat, then sell them in Abilene; there were cattle buyers buying and shipping cattle from there because of the railroad.

Anybody expecting Abilene to be a metropolis would have been some put out, but to Orrin and me, who had never seen anything bigger than Baxter Springs, it looked right smart of a town. Why, Abilene was quite a place, even if you did have to look mighty fast to see what there was of it.

Main thing was that railroad. I'd heard tell of railroads before, but had never come right up to one. Wasn't much to see: just two rails of steel running off into the distance, bedded down on crossties of hewn logs. There were some stock pens built there and about a dozen log houses. There was a saloon in a log house, and across the tracks there was a spanking-new hotel three stories high and a porch along the side fronting the rails. Folks had told me there were buildings that tall, but I never figured to see one.

There was another hotel, too. Place called Bratton's, with six rooms to let. East of the hotel there was a saloon run by a fat man called Jones. There was a stage station ... that was two stories ... a blacksmith shop and the Frontier Store.

At the Drovers' Cottage there was a woman cooking there and some rooms were let, and there were three, four cattle buyers loafing around.

We bunched our cows on the grass outside of town and Mr. Belden rode in to see if he could make a deal, although he didn't much like the look of things. Abilene was too new, it looked like a put-up job and Kansas hadn't shown us no welcome signs up to now.

Then Mr. Belden came back and durned if he hadn't hired several men to guard the herd so's we could have a night in town ... not that she was much of a place, like I said. But we went in.

Orrin and me rode down alongside the track, and Orrin was singing in that big, fine-sounding voice of his, and when we came abreast of the Drovers' Cottage there was a girl a-setting on the porch.

She had a kind of pale blond hair and skin like it never saw daylight, and blue eyes that made a man think she was the prettiest thing he ever did see. Only second glance she reminded me somehow of a hammer-headed roan we used to have, the one with the one blue eye ... a mighty ornery horse, too narrow between the ears and eyes. On that second glance I figured that blonde had more than a passing likeness to that bronc.

But when she looked at Orrin I knew we were in for trouble, for if ever I saw a man-catching look in a woman's eyes it was in hers, then.

"Orrin," I said, "if you want to run maverick a few more years, if you want to find that western land, then you stay off that porch."

"Boy," he put a big hand on my shoulder, "look at that yaller hair!"

"Reminds me of that hammer-headed, no-account roan we used to have. Pa he used to say, 'size up a woman the way you would a horse if you were in a horse trade; and Orrin, you better remember that."

Orrin laughed. "Stand aside, youngster," he tells me, "and watch how it's done."

With that Orrin rides right up to the porch and standing up in his stirrups he said, "Howdy, ma'am! A mighty fine evening! Might I come up an' set with you a spell?"

Mayhap he needed a shave and a bath like we all did, but there was something in him that always made a woman stop and look twice.

Before she could answer a tall man stepped out. "Young man," he spoke mighty sharp, "I will thank you not to annoy my daughter. She does not consort with hired hands."

Orrin smiled that big, wide smile of his. "Sorry, sir, I did not mean to offend. I was riding by, and such beauty, sir, such beauty deserves its tribute, sir."

Then he flashed that girl a smile, then reined his horse around and we rode on to the saloon.

The saloon wasn't much, but it took little to please us. There was about ten feet of bar, sawdust on the floor, and not more than a half-dozen bottles behind the bar. There was a barrel of mighty poor whiskey. Any farmer back in our country could make better whiskey out of branch water and corn, but we had our drinks and then Orrin and me hunted the barrels out back.

Those days, in a lot of places a man might get to, barrels were the only place a man could bathe. You stripped off and you got into a barrel and somebody poured water over you, then after soaping down and washing as best you could you'd have more water to rinse off the soap, and you'd had yourself a bath.

"You watch yo'se'f," the saloon keeper warned, "feller out there yestiddy shot himself a rattler whilst he was in the barrel."

Orrin bathed in one barrel, Tom Sunday in another, while I shaved in a piece of broken mirror tacked to the back wall of the saloon. When they finished bathing I stripped off and got into the barrel and Orrin and Tom, they took off. Just when I was wet all over, Reed Carney came out of the saloon.

My gun was close by but my shirt had fallen over it and there was no chance to get a hand on it in a hurry.

So there I was, naked as a jaybird, standing in a barrel two-thirds full of water, and there was that trouble-hunting Reed Carney with two or three drinks under his belt and a grudge under his hat.

It was my move, but it had to be the right move at the right time, and to reach for that gun would be the wrong thing to do. Somehow I had to get out of that tub and there I was with soap all over me, in my hair and on my face and dribbling toward my eyes.

The rinse water was in a bucket close to the barrel so acting mighty unconcerned I reached down, picked it up, sloshing it over me to wash off that soap.

"Orrin," Carney said, grinning at me, "went to the *ho*-tel and it don't seem hardly right, you in trouble and him not here to stand in front of you."

"Orrin handles his business. I handle mine."

He walked up to within three or four feet of the barrel and there was something in his eyes I'd not seen before. I knew then he meant to kill me.

"I've been wonderin' about that. I'm curious to see if you can handle your own affairs without that big brother standing by to pull you out."

The bucket was still about a third full of water and I lifted it to slosh it over me.

There was a kind of nasty, wet look to his eyes and he took a step nearer. "I don't like you," he said, "and I—" His hand dropped to his gun and I let him have the rest of that water in the face.

He jumped back and I half-jumped, half-fell out of the barrel just as he blinked the water away and grabbed iron. His gun was coming up when the bucket's edge caught him alongside the skull and I felt the *whiff* of that bullet past my ear. But that bucket was oak and it was heavy and it laid him out cold.

Inside the saloon there was a scramble of boots, and picking up the flour-sack towel I began drying off, but I was standing right beside my gun and I had the shirt pulled away from it and easy to my hand it was. If any friends of Carney's wanted to call the tune I was ready for the dance.

The first man out was a tall, blond man with a narrow, tough face and a twisted look to his mouth caused by an old scar. He wore his gun tied to his leg and low down the way some of these fancy gunmen wear them. Cap Rountree was only a step behind and right off he pulled over to one side and hung a hand near his gun butt. Tom Sunday fanned out on the other side. Two others ranged up along the man with the scarred lip.

"What happened?"

"Carney here," I said, "bought himself more than he could pay for."

That blond puncher had been ready to buy himself a piece of any fight there was left and he was just squaring away when Cap Rountree put in his two-bit's worth. "We figured you might be troubled, Tye," Cap said in that dry, hard old voice, "so Tom an' me, we came out to see the sides were even up."

You could feel the change in the air. That blond with the scarred lip—later I found out his name was Fetterson—he didn't like the situation even a little. Here I was dead center in front of him, but he and his two partners, they were framed by Tom Sunday and Cap Rountree.

Fetterson glanced one way and then the other and you could just see his horns pull in. He'd come through that door sure enough on the prod an' pawin' dust, but suddenly he was so peaceful it worried me.

"You better hunt yourself a hole before he comes out of it," Fetterson said. "He'll stretch your hide."

By that time I had my pants on and was stamping into my boots. Believe me, I sure hate to face up to trouble with no pants on, and no boots.

So I slung my gun belt and settled my holster into place. "You tell him to draw his pay and rattle his hocks out of here. I ain't hunting trouble, but he's pushing, mighty pushing."

The three of us walked across to the Drovers' Cottage for a meal, and the first thing we saw was Orrin setting down close to that blond girl and she was looking at him like he was money from home. But that was the least of it. Her father was setting there listening himself ... leave it to Orrin and that Welsh-talking tongue of his. He could talk a squirrel right out of a walnut tree ... I never saw the like.

The three of us sat down to a good meal and we talked up a storm about that country to the west, and the wild cattle, and how much a man could make if he could keep Comanches, Kiowas, or Utes from lifting his hair.

Seemed strange to be sitting at a table. We were all so used to setting on the ground that we felt awkward with a white cloth and all. Out on the range a man ate with his hunting knife and what he could swab up with a chunk of bread.

That night Mr. Belden paid us off in the hotel office, and one by one we stepped up for our money. You've got to remember that neither Orrin or me had ever had twenty-five dollars of cash money in our lives before. In the mountains a man mostly swapped for what he needed, and clothes were homespun.

Our wages were twenty-five dollars a month and Orrin and me had two months and part of a third coming.

Only when he came to me, Mr. Belden put down his pen and sat back in his chair.

"Tye," he said, "there's a prisoner here who is being held for the United States Marshal. Brought in this morning. His name is Aiken, and he was riding with Back Rand the day you met them out on the prairie."

"Yes, sir."

"I had a talk with Aiken, and he told me that if it hadn't been for you Back Rand would have taken my herd . . . or tried to. It seems, from what he said, that you saved my herd or saved us a nasty fight and a stampede where I was sure to lose cattle. It seems this Aiken knew all about you Sacketts and he told Rand enough so that Rand didn't want to call your bluff. I'm not an ungrateful man, Tye, so I'm adding two hundred dollars to your wages."

Two hundred dollars was a sight of money, those days, cash money being a shy thing.

When we walked out on the porch of the Drovers' Cottage, there were three wagons coming up the trail, and three more behind them. The first three were army ambulances surrounded by a dozen Mexicans in fringed buckskin suits and wide Mexican sombreros. There were another dozen riding around the three freight wagons following, and we'd never seen the like.

Their jackets were short, only to the waist, and their pants flared out at the bottom and fitted like a glove along the thighs. Their spurs had rowels like mill wheels on them, and they all had spanking-new rifles and pistols. They wore colored silk sashes like some of those Texas cowhands wore, and they were all slicked out like some kind of a show.

Horses? Mister, you should see such horses! Every one clean-limbed and quick, and every one showing he'd been curried and fussed over. Every man Jack of that crowd was well set-up, and if ever I saw a fighting crowd, it was this lot.

The first carriage drew up before the Drovers' Cottage and a tall, fine-looking old man with pure white hair and white mustaches got down from the wagon, then helped a girl down. Now I couldn't rightly say how old she was, not being any judge of years on a woman, but I'd guess she was fifteen or sixteen, and the prettiest thing I ever put an eye to.

Pa had told us a time or two about those Spanish *dons* and the *señoritas* who lived around Santa Fe, and these folks must be heading that direction.

Right then I had me an idea. In Indian country the more rifles the better, and this here outfit must muster forty rifles if there was one, and no Indian was going to tackle that bunch for the small amount of loot those wagons promised. The four of us would make their party that much stronger, and would put us right in the country we were headed for.

Saying nothing to Sunday or Rountree, I went into the dining room. The grub there was passing fine. Situated on the rails they could get about what they wanted and the Drovers' Cottage was all set up to cater to cattlemen and cattle buyers with money to spend. Later on folks from back east told me some of the finest meals they ever set down to were in some of those western hotels ... and some of the worst, too.

The don was sitting at a table with that pretty girl, but right away I could see this was no setup to buck if a man was hunting trouble. There were buckskin-clad riders setting at tables around them and when I approached the don, four of them came out of their chairs like they had springs in their pants, and they stood as if awaiting a signal.

"Sir," I said, "from the look of your outfit you'll be headed for Santa Fe. My partners and me ... there are four of us ... we're headed west. If we could ride along with your party we'd add four rifles to your strength and it would be safer for us."

He looked at me out of cold eyes from a still face. His mustache was beautifully white, his skin a pale tan, his eyes brown and steady. He started to speak, but the girl interrupted and seemed to be explaining something to him, but there was no doubt about his answer.

She looked up at me. "I am sorry, sir, but my grandfather says it will be impossible."

"I'm sorry, too," I said, "but if he would like to check up on our character he could ask Mr. Belden over there."

She explained, and the old man glanced at Mr. Belden across the room. There was a moment when I thought he might change his mind, but he shook his head.

"I am sorry." She looked like she really was sorry. "My grandfather is a very positive man." She hesitated and then she said, "We have been warned that we may be attacked by some of your people."

I bowed . . . more than likely it was mighty awkward, it was the first time I ever bowed to anybody, but it seemed the thing to do.

"My name is Tyrel Sackett, and if ever we can be of help, my friends and I are at your service." I meant it, too, although that speech was right out of a book I'd heard read one time, and it made quite an impression on me. "I mean, I'll sure come a-foggin' it if you're in trouble."

She smiled at me, mighty pretty, and I turned away from that table with my head whirling like somebody had hit me with a whiffletree.

Orrin had come in, and he was setting up to a table with that blond girl and her father, but the way those two glared at me you'd have sworn I'd robbed a hen roost.

Coming down off the steps I got a glimpse into that wagon the girl had been riding in. You never seen the like. It was all plush and pretty, fixed up like nothing you ever saw, a regular little room for her. The second wagon was the old man's, and later I learned that the third carted supplies for them, fine food and such, with extra rifles, ammunition, and clothing. The three freight wagons were heavy-loaded for their rancho in New Mexico.

Orrin followed me outside. "How'd you get to know Don Luis?"

"That his name? I just up an' talked to him."

"Pritts tells me he's not well thought of by his neighbors." Orrin lowered his voice. "Fact is, Tyrel, they're getting an outfit together to drive him out."

"Is that Pritts? That feller you've been talking to?"

"Jonathan Pritts and his daughter Laura. Mighty fine New England people. He's a town-site developer. She wasn't pleased to come west and leave their fine home behind and all their fine friends, but her Pa felt it his duty to come west and open up the country for the right people."

Now something about that didn't sound right to me, nor did it sound like Orrin. Remembering how my own skull was buzzing over that Spanish girl I figured he must have it the same way over that narrow-between-the-eyes blond girl.

"Seems to me, Orrin, that most folks don't leave home unless they figure to gain by it. We are going west because we can't make a living out of no side-hill farm. I reckon you'll find Jonathan Pritts ain't much different."

Orrin was shocked. "Oh, no. Nothing like that. He was a big man where he came from. If he had stayed there he would be running for the Senate right now."

"Seems to me," I said, "that somebody has told you a mighty lot about her fine friends and her fine home.

If he does any developin' it won't be from goodness of his heart but because there's money to be had."

"You don't understand, Tyrel. These are fine people. You should get acquainted."

"We'll have little time for people out west rounding up cows."

Orrin looked mighty uncomfortable. "Mr. Pritts has offered me a job, running his outfit. Plans to develop town sites and the like; there's a lot of old Spanish grants that will be opened to settlement."

"He's got some men?"

"A dozen now, more later. I met one of them, Fetterson."

"With a scarred lip?"

"Why, sure!" Orrin looked at me mighty curious. "Do you know him?"

For the first time then I told Orrin about the shindig back of the saloon when I belted Reed Carney with the bucket.

"Why, then," Orrin said quietly, "I won't take the job. I'll tell Mr. Pritts about Fetterson, too." He paused. "Although I'd like to keep track of Laura."

"Since when have you started chasing girls? Seems to me they always chased after you."

"Laura's different ... I never knew a city girl before, and she's mighty fine. Manners and all." Right then it seemed to me that if he never saw them again it would be too soon ... all those fancy city manners and city fixings had turned Orrin's head.

Another thing. Jonathan Pritts was talking about those Spanish land grants that would be opened to settlement. It set me to wondering just what would happen to those Spanish folks who owned the grants?

Sizing up those riders of the don's I figured no rawhide outfit made up of the likes of Fetterson would have much chance shaking the dons loose from their land. But that was no business of ours. Starting tomorrow we were wild-cow hunters.

Anyway, Orrin was six years older than me and he had always had luck with girls and no girl ever paid

me much mind, so I was sure in no position to tell
him.

This Laura Pritts was a pretty thing ... no taking
that away from her. Nonetheless I couldn't get that
contrary hammerheaded roan out of mind. They surely did favor.

Orrin had gone back into the cottage and I walked
to the edge of the street. Several of the don's riders
were loafing near their wagons and it was mighty
quiet.

Rountree spoke from the street. "Watch yourself,
Tye."

Turning, I looked around.

Reed Carney was coming up the street.

CHAPTER III

Back in the hills Orrin was the well-liked brother, nor did I ever begrudge him that. Not that folks disliked me or that I ever went around being mean, but folks never did get close to me and it was most likely my fault. There was always something standoffish about me. I liked folks, but I liked the wild animals, the lonely trails, and the mountains better.

Pa told me once, "Tyrel, you're different. Don't you ever regret it. Folks won't cotton to you much, but the friends you will make will be good friends and they'll stand by you."

Those days I thought he was wrong. I never felt any different than anybody else, far as I could see, only now when I saw Reed Carney coming up the street, and knowing it was me he was coming to kill, something came up in me that I'd never felt before, not even when Long Higgins started for Orrin.

It was something fierce and terrible that came up and liked to choke me, and then it was gone and I was very quiet inside. The moments seemed to plod, every detail stood out in sharp focus, clear and strong. Every sense, every emotion was caught and held, concentrated on that man coming up the street.

He was not alone.

Fetterson was with him, and the two who had come from the saloon when I laid Carney low with the bucket. They were a little behind him and spread out.

Orrin was inside somewhere and only that dry, harsh old man with his wolf eyes was there. He would know what was to be done, for nobody needed to tell him how to play his cards in a situation like this ... and no one needed to tell me. Suddenly, with a queer wave of sadness and fatality, I realized that it was for moments such as this that I had been born.

Some men are gifted to paint, some to write, and some to lead men. For me it was always to be this, not to kill men, although in the years to come I was to kill more than I liked, but to command such situations as this.

Reed was coming up the street and he was thinking what folks would say when they told the story in the cow camps and around the chuck wagons. He was thinking of how they would tell of him walking up the street to kill Tyrel Sackett.

Me, I wasn't thinking. I was just standing there. I was just me, and I knew some things were inevitable.

On my right a door closed and I knew Don Luis had come out on the porch. I even heard, it was that still, the scratch of the match when he lit his cigar.

When Reed started at me he was more than a hundred yards off, but when he had covered half the distance, I started to meet him.

He stopped.

Seems like he didn't expect me to come hunting it. Seems like he figured he was the hunter and that I would try to avoid a shoot out. Seems like something had happened to him in that fifty yards, for fifty yards can be a lifetime.

Suddenly, I knew I didn't have to kill him. Mayhap that was the moment when I changed from a boy into a man. Somewhere I'd begun to learn things about myself and about gunfights and gunfighters. Reading men is the biggest part; drawing fast, even shooting straight, they come later. And some of the fastest drawing men with guns were among the first to die. That fast draw didn't mean a thing . . . not a thing.

The first thing I was learning was there are times when a man had to kill and times when he had no need to.

Reed Carney wanted a shoot out and he wanted to win, but me, I'm more than average contrary.

Watching Reed come up the street, I knew I didn't need a gun for him; suddenly it came over me that

Reed Carney was nothing but a tinhorn. He fancied himself as a tough man and a gunfighter, but he didn't really want anybody shooting at him. The trouble with having a reputation as a tough man is that the time always comes when you have to be a tough man. It's a whole lot different.

Nothing exciting or thrilling about a gunfight. She's a mighty cold proposition for both parties. One or t'other is to be killed or hurt bad, maybe both.

Some folks take chances because they've got it in their minds they're somebody special, that something will protect them. It is always, they figure, somebody else who dies.

Only it ain't thataway. *You* can die. You can be snuffed out like you never existed at all and a few minutes after you're buried nobody will care except maybe your wife or your mother. You stick your finger in the water and you pull it out, and that's how much of a hole you leave when you're gone.

Reed Carney had been thinking of himself as a mighty dangerous man and he had talked himself into a shoot out.

Maybe it was something in his walk or the way he looked or in the fact that he stopped when I started toward him. Mayhap it was something sensed rather than seen, that something within me that made me different than other men. Only suddenly I knew that by the time he had taken ten steps toward me the fight had begun to peter out of him, that for the first time he was realizing that I was going to be shooting at him to kill.

Panic can hit a man. You never really know. You can have a man bluffed and then something wild hits him and you're in a real honest-to-warchief shooting.

Those others were going to wait for Reed, but I'd leave them to Cap. Reed was my problem and I knew he wanted to kill me. Or rather, he wanted it known around that he'd killed me.

As I walked toward him I knew Reed knew he should draw, and he felt sure he was going to draw, but he just stood there. Then he knew that if he didn't draw it would be too late.

The sweat was streaming down his cheeks although it wasn't a hot evening. Only I just kept walking up on him, closing in. He took a step back and his lips parted like he was having trouble breathing, and he knew that if he didn't draw on me then he would never be the same man again as long as he lived.

When I stopped I was within arm's length of him and he was breathing like he'd run a long way uphill.

"I'd kill you, Reed."

It was the first time I'd ever called him by his first name and his eyes looked right into mine, startled, like a youngster's.

"You want to be a big man, Reed, but you'll never make it with a gun. You just ain't trimmed right for it. If you'd moved for that gun you'd be dead now ... cold and dead in the dust down there with only the memory of a gnawing rat of pain in your belly.

"Now you reach down mighty careful, Reed, and you unbuckle your belt and let it fall. Then you turn around and walk away."

It was still. A tiny puff of wind stirred dust, then died out. Somewhere on the porch of the Drovers' Cottage a board creaked as somebody shifted weight. Out on the prairie a meadow lark sang.

"Unbuckle the belt!"

His eyes were fastened on mine, large and open. Sweat trickled down his cheeks in rivulets. His tongue fumbled at his lips and then his fingers reached for his belt buckle. As he let the belt fall there was a gasp from somewhere, and for a split second everything hung by a hair. There was a moment then when he might have grabbed for a gun but my eyes had him and he let the belt go.

"Was I you I'd straddle my bronc and light a shuck out of here. You got lots of country to choose from."

He backed off, then turned and started to walk away, and then as he realized what he'd done he walked faster and faster. He stumbled once, caught himself, and kept going.

After a moment I scooped up the gun belt with my left hand and turned back toward the Drovers' Cottage.

They were all on the porch. Orrin, Laura Pritts and her Pa, and Don Luis ... even his granddaughter.

Fetterson stood there, mad clear through. He had come itching for trouble and he was stopped cold. He had no mind to tackle Cap Rountree for fun ... nobody wanted any part of that old wolf. But he had a look in those gun-metal eyes of his that would frighten a body.

"I'll buy the drinks," I said.

"Just coffee for me," Cap replied.

My eyes were on Fetterson. "That includes you," I said.

He started to say something mean, and then he said, "Be damned if I won't. That took guts, mister."

Don Luis took the cigar from his lips and brushed away the long ash that had collected there during the moments just past. He looked at me and spoke in Spanish.

"He says we can travel west with him if we like," Cap translated, "he says you are a brave man ... and what is more important, a wise one."

"*Gracias,*" I said, and it was about the only Spanish word I knew.

In 1867, the Santa Fe Trail was an old trail, cut deep with the ruts of the heavy wagons carrying freight over the trail from Independence, Missouri. It was no road, only a wide area whose many ruts showed the way the wagons had gone through the fifty-odd years the trail had been used. Cap Rountree had come over it first in 1836, he said.

Orrin and me, we had an ache inside us for new country, and a longing to see the mountains show up on the horizon.

We had to find a place for Ma, and if we had luck out west, then we could start looking for a place.

Back home we had two younger brothers and one

older, but it had been a long time since we'd seen
Tell, the oldest of our brothers who was still alive and
should be coming home from the wars soon. When
the War between the States started he joined up and
then stayed on to fight the Sioux in the Dakotas.

We rode west. Of a night we camped together and
it sure was fine to set around the fire and listen to
those Spanish men sing, and they did a lot of it, one
time or another.

Meantime I was listening to Rountree. That old
man had learned a lot in his lifetime, living with the
Sioux like he did, and with the Nez Perce. First off he
taught me to say that name right, and he said it
Nay-Persay. He taught me a lot about their customs,
how they lived, and told me all about those fine
horses they raised, the appaloosas.

My clothes had give out so I bought me an outfit
from one of the Spanish men, so I was all fixed out
like they were, in a buckskin suit with fringe and all.
In the three months since I'd left home I'd put on
nearly fifteen pounds and all of it muscle. I sure
wished Ma could see me. Only thing that was the
same was my gun.

The first few days out I'd seen nothing of the don
or his granddaughter, except once when I dropped an
antelope with a running shot at three hundred yards.
The don happened to see that and spoke of it . . .

Sometimes his granddaughter would mount her
horse and ride alongside the wagons, and one day
when we'd been out for about a week, she cantered
up on a ridge where I was looking over the country
ahead of us.

A man couldn't take anything for safe in this country. From the top of a low hill that country was open
grass as far as you could see. There might be a
half-dozen shallow valleys out there or ditches, there
might be a canyon or a hollow, and any one of them
might be chock full of Indians.

This time that Spanish girl joined me on the ridge,
I was sizing up the country. She had beautiful big dark

eyes and long lashes and she was about the prettiest thing I ever did see.

"Do you mind if I ride with you, Mr. Sackett?"

"I sure don't mind, but what about Don Luis? I don't expect he'd like his granddaughter riding with a Tennessee drifter."

"He said I could come, but that I must ask your permission. He said you would not let me ride with you if it was not safe."

On the hill where we sat the wind was cool and there was no dust. The train of wagons and pack horses was a half mile away to the southeast. The first Spanish I learned I started learning that day from her.

"Are you going to Santa Fe?"

"No, ma'am, we're going wild-cow hunting along the Purgatoire."

Her name it turned out was Drusilla, and her grandmother had been Irish. The *vaqueros* were not Mexicans but Basques, and like I'd figured, they were picked fighting men. There was always a *vaquero* close by as we rode in case of trouble.

After that first time Drusilla often rode with me, and I noticed the *vaqueros* were watching their back trail as carefully as they watched out for Indians, and some times five or six of them would take off and ride back along the way we had come.

"Grandfather thinks we may be followed and attacked. He has been warned."

That made me think of what Jonathan Pritts had told Orrin, and not knowing if it mattered or not, I told her to tell the don. It seemed to me that land that had been granted a family long ago belonged to that family, and no latecomer like Pritts had a right to move in and drive them off.

The next day she thanked me for her grandfather. Jonathan Pritts had been to Santa Fe before this, and he was working through political means to get their grant revoked so the land could be thrown open to settlement.

Rountree was restless. "By this time we should have met up with Injuns. Keep those rides closer in, Tye, d' you hear?"

He rode in silence for a few minutes, then he said, "Folks back east do a sight of talkin' about the noble red man. Well, he's a mighty fine fighter, I give him that, but ain't no Injun, unless a Nez Perce, who wouldn't ride a couple hundred miles for a fight. Folks talk about takin' land from the Injuns. No Injun ever *owned* land, no way. He hunted over the country and he was always fightin' other Injuns just for the right to hunt there.

"I fought Injuns and I lived with Injuns. If you walked into an Injun village of your own will they'd feed you an' let you be as long as you stayed ... that was their way, but the same Injun in whose tipi you slept might follow you when you left an' murder you.

"They hadn't the same upbringin' a white man has. There was none of this talk of mercy, kindness and suchlike which we get from the time we're youngsters. We get it even though most folks don't foller the teachin'. An Injun is loyal to nobody but his own tribe ... an' any stranger is apt to be an enemy.

"You fight an Injun an' whup him, after that maybe you can trade with him. He'll deal with a fightin' man, but a man who can't protect hisself, well, most Injuns have no respect for him, so they just kill him an' forget him."

Around the fires at night there was talk and laughter. Orrin sang his old Welsh and Irish ballads for them. From Pa he'd picked up some Spanish songs, and when he sang them you should have heard them Spanish men yell! And from the far hills the coyotes answered.

Old Rountree would find a spot well back from the flames and set there watching the outer darkness and listening. A man who stares into flames is blind when he looks into outer darkness, and he won't shoot straight ... Pa had taught us that, back in Tennessee.

This was Indian country and you have to figure, understanding Indians, that his whole standing in his tribe comes from how many coups he's counted, which means to strike an enemy, a living emeny, or to be the first one to strike a man who has fallen ... they figure that mighty daring because the fallen man may be playing possum.

An Indian who was a good horse thief, he could have the pick of the girls in the tribe. Mostly because marriage was on the barter system, and an Indian could have all the wives he could afford to buy ... usually that wasn't more than two or three, and mostly one.

Orrin hadn't forgotten that Laura girl. He was upset with me, too, for leading him off again when he was half a mind to tie up with Pritts.

"He's paying top wages," Orrin said, one night.

"Fighting wages," I said.

"Could be, Tyrel," Orrin said, and no friendly sound to his voice, "that you're holding something against Mr. Pritts. And against Laura, too."

Go easy, boy, I told myself, this is dangerous ground. "I don't know them. Only from what you've said he's planning to horn in on land that doesn't belong to him."

Orrin started to speak but Tom Sunday got up. "Time to turn in," he spoke abruptly, "gettin'-up time comes early."

We turned in, both of us with words we were itching to say that were better unsaid.

It rankled, however. There was truth about me having a holding against Pritts and his daughter. That I had ... she didn't look right to me, and I've always been suspicious of those too-sanctimonious men like Jonathan Pritts.

The way he looked down that thin New England nose of his didn't promise any good for those who didn't agree with him. And what I said to Orrin that time, I'd believed. If Pritts had been so much back home, what was he doing out here?

We filled our canteens at daybreak with no certain water ahead of us. A hot wind searched the grass. At Mud Creek there was enough water in the creek bottom for the horses, but when we left it it was bone dry. It was seven miles to the Water Holes, and if there was no water there it was a dry day's travel to the Little Arkansas.

The sun was hot. Dust lifted from the feet of the horses and mules, and we left a trail of dust in the air. If any Indians were around, they'd not miss us.

"A man would have to prime himself to spit in country like this," Tom Sunday remarked. "How about the country we're heading toward, Cap?"

"Worse ... unless a man knows the land. Only saving thing, there's no travel up thataway except for Comanches. What water there is we'll likely have to ourselves."

Every day then, Drusilla was riding with me. And every day I felt myself looking for her sooner than before. Sometimes we were only out for a half hour, at most an hour, but I got so I welcomed her coming and dreaded her going.

Back in the mountains I'd known few girls. Mostly I fought shy of them, not figuring to put my neck in any loops I couldn't pull out of ... only I had a feeling I was getting bogged down with Drusilla.

She was shy of sixteen, but Spanish girls marry that young and younger, and in the mountains they did also. Me, I had nothing but a dapple horse, a partnership in some mules, and my old Spencer and a Colt pistol. It didn't count up to much.

Meanwhile, I'd been getting to know the *vaqueros*. I'd never known anybody before who wasn't straight-out American, and back in the hills we held ourselves suspicious of such folk. Riding with them, I was finding they were good, solid men.

Miguel was a slim, wiry man who was the finest rider I ever knew, and maybe a couple of years older than me. He was a handsome man with a quick laugh, and like me he was always ready to ride far afield.

Juan Torres was the boss of the lot, a compact man of forty-three or four, who rarely smiled but was always friendly. Maybe he was the finest rifle shot I ever saw ... he had worked for Don Luis Alvarado since he, Torres, was a boy, and thought of him like he was a god.

There was Pete Romero, and a slim, tough young devil called Antonio Baca ... the only one who didn't have the Basque blood. It seemed to me he thought he was a better man than Torres, and there was something else I figured was just my thinking until Cap mentioned it.

"Did you ever notice how young Baca looks at you when you ride with the *senorita*?"

"He doesn't seem to like it. I noticed that."

"You watch yourself. That boy's got a streak of meanness."

That was all Cap said, but I took it to mind. Stories I'd heard made out these Spanish men to be mighty jealous, although no girl was going to look serious at me when there were men around like Orrin and Tom Sunday.

There's no accounting for the notions men get, and it seems to me the most serious trouble between men comes not so much from money, horses, or women, but from notions. A man takes a dislike to another man for no reason at all but they rub each other wrong, and then something, a horse or a woman or a drink sets it off and they go to shooting or cutting or walloping with sticks.

Like Reed Carney. Only a notion. And it could have got him killed.

At the Little Arkansas we camped where a little branch flowed from a spring in the bluff and ran down to the river. It was good water, maybe a mite brackish.

After night guard was set I slipped out of camp with a rifle and canteen and went down to the Little Arkansas. Dark was coming on but a man could see. Moving down to the river's edge ... there was more sand than water ... I stood listening.

A man should trust his senses and they'll grow sharper from use. I never took it for granted that the country was safe. Not only listening and watching as I moved, but testing the air for smells. Out on the prairie where the air is fresh a man can smell more than around people, and after awhile he learns to smell an Indian, a white man, a horse, or even a bear.

Off in the distance there was heat lightning, and a far-off rumble of thunder.

Waiting in the silence after the thunder a stone rattled across the river and a column of riders emerged from the brush and rode down into the river bed.

There might have been a dozen, or even twenty, and although I could not make them out I could see white streaks on their faces that meant they were painted for war.

Crossing the stream sixty, seventy yards below me they rode out across the prairie. They would not be moving this late unless there was a camp not far off, and that meant more Indians and a possible source of trouble.

When they had gone I went back to camp and got Cap Rountree. Together, we talked to Torres and made what plans we could.

Daylight came, and on the advice of Torres, Drusilla remained with the wagons. We moved slowly, trying to keep our dust down.

It was dry ... the grass was brown, parched and sun-hot when we fetched up to Owl Creek and found it bone-dry. Little and Big Cow Creeks, also dry.

This last was twenty miles from our last night's camp and no sign of water, with another twenty to go before we reached the Bend of the Arkansas.

"There'll be water," Rountree said in his rasping voice, "there's always water in the Arkansas."

By that time I wasn't sure if there was any water left in Kansas. We took a breather at Big Cow Creek and I rinsed out Dapple's mouth with my handkerchief a couple of times. My lips were cracked and even Dapple seemed to have lost his bounce. That heat and the dry air, with no water, it was enough to take the spry out of a camel.

Dust lifted from the brown grass ... white buffalo bones bleached in the sun. We passed the wrecks of some burned-out wagons and the skull of a horse. In the distance clouds piled up enormous towers and battlements, building dream castles in the sky. Along the prairie, heat waves danced and rippled in the sun, and far off a mirage lake showed the blue of its dream water to taunt our eyes.

From the top of a low hill I looked around at miles of brown emptiness with a vast sweep of sky overhead where the sun seemed to have grown enormously until it swept the sky. From my canteen I soaked my handkerchief and sponged out the Dapple's mouth, again. It was so dry I couldn't spit.

Far below the wagons made a thin trail ... the hill on which I sat was low, but there was a four-mile-long slope leading gradually up to it.

The horizon was nowhere, for there was only a haze of heat around us, our horses slogging onward without hope, going because their riders knew no better.

The sky was empty, the land was still ... the dust hung in the empty air. It was very hot.

CHAPTER IV

Rountree humped his old shoulders under his thin shirt and looked ready to fall any minute but the chances were he would outlast us all. There was iron and rawhide in that old man.

Glancing back I saw a distant plume of dust, and pointed it out to Orrin who gave an arm signal to Torres. We got down from our horses, Orrin and I, and walked along to spell our mounts.

"We got to get that place for Ma," I said to Orrin, "she ain't got many years. Be nice if she could live them in comfort, in her own home, with her own fixin's."

"We'll find it."

Dust puffed from each step. Pausing to look back, he squinted his eyes against the glare and the sting of sweat. "We got to learn something, Tye," he said suddenly, "we're both ignorant, and it ain't a way to be. Listening to Tom makes a man think. If a body had an education like that, no telling how far he'd go."

"Tom's got the right idea. In this western land a man could make something of himself."

"The country makes a man think of it. It's a big country with lots of room to spread out ... it gives a man big ideas."

When we got back into the saddle the leather was so hot on my bottom I durned near yelled when I settled down into my seat.

After awhile, country like that, you just keep moving, putting one foot ahead of the other like a man in a trance. It was dark with the stars out when we smelled green trees, grass, and the cool sweetness of water running. We came up to the Arkansas by star-

light and I'd still a cup of brackish water in my
canteen. Right away, never knowing what will happen, I dumped it out, rinsed the canteen and filled it up
again.

Taking that canteen to Drusilla's wagon I noticed
Baca watching me with a hard look in his eyes. She
was too good for either of us.

The four of us built our own fire away from the
others because we had business to talk.

"The don has quite a place, Torres tells me. Big
grant of land. Mountains, meadows, forest . . . and lots
of cattle." Cap had been talking to Torres for some
time. "Runs sheep, too. And a couple of mines, a
sawmill."

"I hear he's a land hog," Orrin commented. "Lots of
folks would like to build homes there, if he'd let 'em."

"Would you, Orrin, if you owned the land?" Tom
asked mildly.

"Nobody has a right to all that. Anyway, he ain't
an American," Orrin insisted.

Rountree was no hand to argue but he was a just
old man. "He's owned that land forty years, and he got
it from his father who moved into that country back
in 1794. Seems they should have an idea of who it
belongs to."

"Maybe I was mistaken," Orrin replied. "That was
what I'd heard."

"Don Luis is no pilgrim," Rountree told us, "I heard
about him when I first come west. He and his pappy,
they fought Utes, Navajo, and Comanches. They
worked that land, brought sheep and cattle clear from
Mexico, and they opened the mines, built the sawmill. I reckon anybody wants to take their land is
goin' to have to dig in an' scratch."

"It doesn't seem to me that Jonathan Pritts would
do anything that isn't right," Orrin argued. "Not if he
knows the facts."

Pawnee Rock was next . . . Torres came over to our
fire to tell us Don Luis had decided to fight shy of it.

Orrin wanted to see it and so did I, so the four of

us decided to ride that way while the wagons cut wide around it.

Forty or fifty men were camped near the Rock, a tough, noisy, drunken crowd, well supplied with whiskey.

"Looks like a war party," Rountree commented.

Suddenly I had a bad feeling that this was the Pritts crowd, for I could think of no reason why a bunch of that size should be camping here without wagons or women. And I saw one of them who had been with the Back Rand crowd the other side of Abilene.

When they saw us riding up, several got up from where they'd been loafing. "Howdy! Where you from?"

"Passing through." Tom Sunday glanced past the few men who had come to greet us at their camp, which was no decent camp, but dirty, untidy and casual. "We're headed for the upper Cimarron," he added.

"Why don't you step down? We got a proposition for you."

"We're behind time," Orrin told him, and he was looking at their faces as if he wanted to remember them.

Several others had strolled toward us, sort of circling casually around as if they wanted to get behind us, so I let the dapple turn to face them.

They didn't take to that, not a little bit, and one redhead among them took it up. "What's the matter? You afraid of something?"

When a man faces up to trouble with an outfit like that you get nowhere either talking or running, so I started the dapple toward him, not saying a word, but walking the horse right at him. My right hand was on my thigh within inches of my six-shooter, and it sized up to me like they figured to see what would happen if Red crowded me.

Red started to side-step but the dapple was a cutting horse Pa had used working stock, and once you pointed that horse at anything, man or animal, he knew what his job was.

Red backed off, and long ago I'd learned that when you get a man to backing up it's hard for him to stop and start coming at you. Every move he made the dapple shifted and went for him, and all of a sudden Red got desperate and grabbed for his gun and just as he grabbed I spurred the dapple into him. The dapple hit him with a shoulder and Red went down hard. He lost grip on the pistol which fell several feet away.

Red lay on the ground on his back with the dapple right over him, and I hadn't said a word.

While everybody was watching the show Red and the dapple were putting on, Orrin had his pistol lying there in his lap. Both Tom Sunday and Cap Rountree had their rifles ready and Cap spoke up. "Like I said, we're just passing through."

Red started to get up and the dapple shifted his weight and Red relaxed. "You get up when we're gone, Red. You're in too much of a sweat to get killed."

Several of the others had seen what was going on and started toward us.

"All right, Tye?" Orrin asked.

"Let's go," I said, and we dusted out of there.

One thing Cap had in mind and I knew it was what he was thinking. If they were watching us they wouldn't have noticed the passing of the wagons, and they didn't. We watered at Coon Creek and headed for Fort Dodge.

The Barlow, Sanderson Company stage came in while we were in Fort Dodge. Seems a mighty fine way to travel, sitting back against the cushions with nice folks around you.

We were standing there watching when we heard the stage driver talking to a sergeant. "Looks like a fight shaping up over squatters trying to move in on the Spanish grants," he said.

Orrin turned away. "Good thing we're straying shut

of that fight," he said. "We'll be better off hunting cows."

When we rode back to camp everything was a-bustle with packing and loading up.

Torres came to us. "We go, *señores*. There is word of trouble from home. We take the dry route south from here. You will not come with us?"

"We're going to the Purgatoire."

"Then it will be *adios*." Torres glanced at me. "I know that Don Luis will wish to say good-by to you, *señor*."

At the wagons Don Luis was nowhere in sight, but Drusilla was. When she saw me she came quickly forward. "Oh, Tye! We're going! Will I ever see you again?"

"I'll be coming to Santa Fe. Shall I call on you then?"

"Please do."

We stood together in the darkness with all the hurry around us of people packing and getting ready to move, the jingle of trace chains, the movement and the shouts.

Only I felt like something was going right out from my insides, and I'd never felt this way before. Right then I didn't want to hunt wild cows. I wanted to go to Santa Fe. Was this the way Orrin felt about Laura Pritts?

But how could I feel any way at all about her? I was a mountain boy who could scarcely read printing and who could not write more than his name.

"Will you write to me, Tyrel?"

How could I tell her I didn't know how? "I'll write," I said, and swore to myself that I'd learn. I'd get Tom to teach me.

Orrin was right. We would have to get an education, some way, somehow.

"I'll miss you."

Me, like a damned fool I stood there twisting my hat. If I'd only had some of Orrin's easy talk! But I'd never talked much to any girl or even womenfolks, and I'd no idea what a man said to them.

"It was mighty fine," I told her, "riding out on the plains with you."

She moved closer to me and I wanted to kiss her the worst way, but what right had a Tennessee boy to kiss the daughter of a Spanish don?

"I'll miss the riding," I said, grasping at something to say. "I'll sure miss it."

She stood on her tiptoes suddenly and kissed me, and then she ran. I turned right around and walked right into a tree. I backed off and started again and just then Antonio Baca came out of the darkness and he had a knife held low down in his hand. He didn't say anything, just lunged at me.

Talking to girls was one thing, cutting scrapes was something else. Pa had brought me up right one way, at least. It was without thinking, what I did. My left palm slapped his knife wrist over to my right to get the blade out of line with my body, and my right hand dropped on his wrist as my left leg came across in front of him, and then I just spilled him over my leg and threw him hard against a tree trunk.

He was in the air when he hit it, and the knife fell free. Scooping it up, I just walked on and never even looked back. One time there, I figured I heard him groan, but I was sure he was alive all right. Just shook up.

Tom Sunday was in the saddle with my dapple beside him. "Orrin and Cap went on. They'll meet us at the Fort."

"All right," I said.

"I figured you'd want to say good-by. Mighty hard to leave a girl as pretty as that."

I looked at him. "First girl ever paid me any mind," I said. "Girls don't cotton to me much."

"As long as girls like that one like you, you've nothing to worry about," he said quietly. "She's a real lady. You've a right to be proud."

Then he saw the knife in my hand. Everybody knew that knife who had been with the wagons. Baca was always flashing it around.

"Collecting souvenirs?" Tom asked dryly.

"Wasn't planning on it." I shoved the knife down in my belt. "Sort of fell into it."

We rode on a few steps and he said, "Did you kill him?"

"No."

"You should have," he said, "because you'll have it to do."

Seems I never had a difficulty with a man that made so little impression. All I could think of was Drusilla Alvarado, and the fact that we were riding away from her. All the time I kept telling myself I was a fool, that she was not for me. But it didn't make a mite of difference, and from that day on I understood Orrin a lot better and felt sorry for him.

Nothing changed my mind about that narrow-between-the-ears blonde, though. That roan horse never had been any account, and miserable, contrary and ornery it was, too.

We could see the lights of the Fort up ahead and behind me the rumble of those wagon wheels as the train moved out, the rattle of trace chains, and the Mexicans calling to each other.

"Tom," I said, "I got to learn to write. I really got to learn."

"You should learn," he told me seriously, "I'll be glad to teach you."

"And to read writing?"

"All right."

We rode in silence for a little while and then Tom Sunday said, "Tye, this is a big country out here and it takes big men to live in it, but it gives every man an equal opportunity. You're just as big or small as your vision is, and if you've a mind to work and make something of yourself, you can do it."

He was telling me that I could be important enough for even a don's daughter, I knew that. He was telling me that and suddenly I did not need to be told. He was right, of course, and all the time I'd known it. This was a country to grow up in, a land where a man had a chance.

The stars were bright. The camp lay far behind.

Somebody in the settlement ahead laughed and somebody else dropped a bucket and it rolled down some steps.

A faint breeze stirred, cool and pleasant. We were making the first step. We were going after wild cows.

We were bound for the Purgatoire.

CHAPTER V

Cap Rountree had trapped beaver all over the country we were riding toward. He had been there with Kit Carson, Uncle Dick Wootton, Jim Bridger, and the Bents. He knew the country like an Indian would know it.

Tom Sunday ... I often wondered about Tom. He was a Texan, he said, and that was good enough. He knew more about cattle than any of us.

Orrin and me, well, most of what we'd had all our lives came from our own planting or hunting, and we grew up with a knowledge of the herbs a man can eat and how to get along in the forest.

The country we were riding toward was Indian country. It was a place where the Comanches, Utes, Arapahos, and Kiowas raided and fought, and there were Cheyennes about, too. And sometimes the Apaches raiding north. In this country the price for a few lazy minutes might be the death of every man in the party. It was no place for a loafer or one lacking responsibility.

Always and forever we were conscious of the sky. City folks almost never look at the sky or the stars but with us there was no choice. They were always with us.

Tom Sunday was a man who knew a sight of poetry, and riding across the country thataway, he'd recite it for us. It was a lonely life, you know, and I expect what Sunday missed most was the reading. Books were rare and treasured things, hard to come by and often fought over. Newspapers the same.

A man couldn't walk down to the corner and buy a paper. Nor did he have a postman to deliver it to him. I've known cowhands to memorize the labels off canned fruit and vegetables for lack of reading.

Cap knew that country, knew every creek and every fork. There were no maps except what a man had in his skull, and nobody of whom to ask directions, so a body remembered what he saw. Cap knew a thousand miles of country like a man might know his kitchen, to home.

These mornings the air was fresher. There was a faint chill in the air, a sign we were getting higher. We were riding along in the early hours when we saw the wagons.

Seven wagons, burned and charred. We moved in carefully, rifles up and ready; edged over to them, holding to a shallow dip in the prairie until we were close up.

Folks back east have a sight to say about the poor Indian but they never fought him. He was a fighter by trade, and because he naturally loved it, mercy never entered his head.

Mercy is a taught thing. Nobody comes by it natural. Indians grew up thinking the tribe was all there was and anybody else was an enemy.

It wasn't a fault, simply that nobody had ever suggested such a thing to him. An enemy was to be killed, and then cut up so if you met him in the afterlife he wouldn't have the use of his limbs to attack you again. Some Indians believed a mutilated man would never get into the hereafter.

Two of the men in this outfit had been spread-eagled on wagon wheels, shot full of arrows, and scalped. The women lay scattered about, their clothing ripped off, blood all over. One man had got into a buffalo wallow with his woman and had made a stand there.

"No marks on them," I said, "they must have died after the Indians left."

"No," Cap indicated the tracks of moccasins near the bodies. "They killed themselves when their ammunition gave out." He showed us powder burns on the woman's dress and the man's temple. "Killed her and then himself."

The man who made the stand there in the wallow had accounted for some Indians. We found spots of blood on the grass that gave reason to believe he'd killed four or five, but Indians always carry their dead away.

"They aren't mutilated because the man fought well. Indians respect a fighter and they respect almost nobody else. But sometimes they cut them up, too."

We buried the two where they lay in the wallow, and the others we buried in a common grave nearby, using a shovel found near one of the wagons.

Cap found several letters that hadn't burned and put them in his pocket. "Least we can do," he said, "the folks back home will want to know."

Sunday was standing off sizing up those wagons and looking puzzled. "Cap," he said, "come over here a minute."

The wagons had been set afire but some had burned hardly at all before the fire went out. They were charred all over, and the canvas tops were burned, of course.

"See what you mean," Orrin said, "seems to be a mighty thick bottom on that wagon."

"Too thick," Sunday said, "I think there's a false bottom."

Using the shovel he pried a board until we could get enough grip to pull it loose. There was a compartment there, and in it a flat iron box, which we broke open.

Inside were several sacks of gold money and a little silver, coming to more than a thousand dollars. There were also a few letters in that box.

"This is better than hunting cows," Sunday said. "We've got us a nice piece of money here."

"Maybe somebody needs that money," Orrin suggested. "We'd better read those letters and see if we can find the owner."

Tom Sunday looked at him, smiling, but something

in his smile made a body think he didn't feel like smiling. "You aren't serious? The owner's dead."

"Ma would need that money mighty bad if it had been sent to her by Tyrel and me," Orrin said, "and it could be somebody needs this money right bad."

First off, I'd thought he was joking, but he was dead serious, and the way he looked at it made me back up and take another look myself. The thing to do was to find who the money rightfully belonged to and send it to them ... if we found nobody then it would be all right to keep it.

Cap Rountree just stood there stoking that old pipe and studying Orrin with care, like he seen something mighty interesting.

There wasn't five dollars amongst us now. We'd had to buy pack animals and our outfit, and we had broke ourselves, what with Orrin and me sending a little money to Ma from Abilene. Now we were about to start four or five months of hard work, and risk our hair into the bargain, for no more than this.

"These people are dead, Orrin," Tom Sunday said irritably, "and if we hadn't found it years might pass before anybody else did, and by that time any letter would have fallen to pieces."

Standing there watching the two of them I'd no idea what was happening to us, and that the feelings from that dispute would affect all our lives, and for many years. At the time it seemed such a little thing.

"Not in this life will any of us ever find a thousand dollars in gold. Not again. And you suggest we try to find the owner."

"Whatever we do we'd better decide somewheres else," I commented. "There might be Indians around."

Come dusk we camped in some trees near the Arkansas, bringing all the stock in close and watering them well. Nobody did any talking. This was no place to have trouble but when it came to that, Orrin was my brother ... and he was in the right.

Now personally, I'm not sure I'd have thought of it. Mayhap I wouldn't have mentioned it if I did think of it ... a man never knows about things like that. Rountree hadn't done anything but listen and smoke that old pipe of his.

It was when we were sitting over coffee that Tom brought it up again. "We'd be fools not to keep that money, Orrin. How do we know who we'd be sending it to? Maybe some relative who hated him. Certainly, nobody needs it more than we do."

Orrin, he just sat there studying those letters. "Those folks had a daughter back home," Orrin said, finally, "an' she's barely sixteen. She's living with friends until they send for her, and when those friends find out she isn't going to be sent for, and they can expect no more money, then what happens to that girl?"

The question bothered Tom, and it made him mad. His face got red and set in stubborn lines, and he said, "You send your share. I'll take a quarter of it ... right now. If I hadn't noticed that wagon the money would never have been found."

"You're right about that, Tom," Orrin said reasonably, "but that money just ain't ours."

Slowly, Tom Sunday got to his feet. He was mad clear through and pushing for a fight. So I got up, too.

"Kid," he said angrily, "you stay out of this. This is between Orrin and me."

"We're all in this together, Cap an' me as much as Orrin and you. We started out to round up wild cattle, and if we start it with trouble there's no way we can win."

Orrin said, "Now if that money belonged to a man, maybe I'd never have thought of returning it, but with a girl as young as that, no telling what she'll come to, turned loose on the world at that age. This money could make a lot of difference."

Tom was a prideful and stubborn man, ready to take on the two of us. Then Rountree settled matters.

"Tom," he said mildly, "you're wrong, an' what's more, you know it. This here outfit is four-sided and

I vote with the Sackett boys. You ain't agin democracy, are you, Tom?"

"You know darned well I'm not, and as long as you put it that way, I'll sit down. Only I think we're damned fools."

"Tom, you're probably right, but that's the kind of a damned fool I am," said Orrin. "When the cows are rounded up if you don't feel different about it you can have my share of the cows."

Tom Sunday just looked at Orrin. "You damned fool. Next thing we know you'll be singing hymns in a church."

"I know a couple," Orrin said. "You all set down and while Tyrel gets supper, I'll sing you a couple."

And that was the end of it ... or we thought it was. Sometimes I wonder if anything is ever ended. The words a man speaks today live on in his thoughts or the memories of others, and the shot fired, the blow struck, the thing done today is like a stone tossed into a pool and the ripples keep widening out until they touch lives far from ours.

So Orrin sang his hymns, and followed them with *Black, Black, Black, Lord Randall, Barbara Allan* and *Sweet Betsy*. When Orrin finished the last one Tom reached over and held out his hand and Orrin grinned at him and shook it.

No more was said about the gold money and it was put away in the bottom of a pack and to all intents it was forgotten. If that amount of gold is ever forgotten.

We were getting into the country of the wild cattle now. Cap Rountree as well as others had noticed these wild cattle, some of them escaped from Spanish settlements to the south, and some escaped or stampeded by Indians from wagon trains bound for California.

No doubt Indians had killed a few, but Indians preferred buffalo, and many of these cattle had come south with buffalo herds. There was no shortage of buffalo in 1867, and the Indians only killed the wild cattle when there was nothing else.

The country we were going to work lay south of the Mountain Branch of the Santa Fe Trail, between the Purgatoire and Two Buttes Creek, and south to the Mal Pais. It was big country and it was rough country. We rode south through sage plains with some mesquite, with juniper and piñon on the hills.

Cap had in his mind a hidden place, a canyon near the base of a mountain where a cold spring of sweet water came out of the rocks. There was maybe two hundred acres of good grass in the bottom, grass belly-high to a horse, and from the look of it nobody had seen it since Cap Rountree stumbled on it twenty years back.

First off, we forted up. Behind us the cliffs lifted sheer with an overhang that provided shelter from above. Right out in front there was four or five acres of meadow with good grass, edged on the far side by trees and rocks. Beyond that was the bowl with the big pasture as we called it, and in an adjoining canyon was a still larger area where we figured to trap the wild cattle and hold them.

We spent that first day gathering fuel, adding a few rocks to our fort, and generally scouting the country close around our hide-out. Also, I killed a deer and Cap got a buffalo. We brought the meat into camp and started jerking it.

Next morning at daybreak we started out to scout the country. Within an hour's riding we'd seen sixty or seventy head. A man never saw such cattle. There was a longhorn bull in that crowd that must have stood seven feet and would have weighed sixteen hundred pounds. And horns? Needle sharp.

By nightfall we had a good bunch of cattle in the bowl or drifted toward it. By the third day we had more than a hundred head in that bowl and we were beginning to count our money.

It was slow, patient work. Push them too fast and they would stampede clear out of the country, so we tried to move them without them guessing what we planned.

We had two things to accomplish: to catch our-

selves some wild cattle and to stay alive while doing
it. And it wasn't only Indians we had to think about,
but the cattle themselves, for some of those tough old
bulls showed fight, and the cows could be just as
mean if they caught a man afoot. Of a night we
yarned around the fire or belly-ached about somebody's cooking. We took turn about on that job.

We kept our fires small, used the driest wood, and
we moved around only when we had to. We daren't
set any patterns of work so's Indians could lay for us.
We never took the same trail back that we used on
the way out, and we kept our eyes open all the time.

We gathered cattle. We sweated, we swore, and we
ate dust, but we gathered them up, six one day,
twelve another, nineteen, then only three. There was
no telling how it would be. We got them into the
bowl where there was grass and plenty of water and
we watched them get fat. Also, it gave them time to
settle down.

Then trouble hit us. Orrin was riding a sorrel we
had picked up in Dodge. He was off by himself and
he started down a steep hillside and the sorrel fell.
That little sorrel got up fast with Orrin's foot caught
in the stirrup and he buckled down to run. There was
only one way Orrin could keep from being dragged to
death, and that was one reason cowhands always
carried pistols. He shot the sorrel.

Come nightfall there was no sign of Orrin. We had
taken to coming in early so if anything went wrong
with any of us there would be time to do something
before night.

We set out to look. Tom went south, swinging back
toward the east, Cap went west, and I followed up a
canyon to the north before topping out on the rim. It
was me found him, walking along, packing his saddle
and his Winchester.

When he put down the saddle on seeing me, I rode
up to him. "You took long enough," he grumbled, but
there was no grumble in his eyes, "I was fixing to
cache my saddle."

"You could have fired a shot."

"There were Indians closer than you," he said.

Orrin told us about it around the fire. He had shucked his saddle off the dead sorrel and started for camp, but being a sly one, he was not about to leave a direct trail to our hide-out, so he went downhill first and stumbled on a rocky ledge which he followed sixty or seventy yards.

There had been nine or ten Indians in the party and he saw them before they saw him, so he just laid right down where he was and let them pass by. They were all warriors, and the way they were riding they might miss his dead horse.

"They'll find it," Cap told us, "it's nigh to dark now, so they won't get far tonight. Likely they'll camp somewhere down the creek. At daybreak they'll see the buzzards."

"So?"

"That's a shod horse. It isn't likely they'd pass up a chance to get one man afoot and alone."

Any other time we could have high-tailed it out of the country and left them nothing but tracks, but now we were men of property and property ties a man down.

"Think they'll find us?"

"Likely," Cap said. "Reckon we better hold to camp a day or two. Horses need the rest, anyway."

We all sat there feeling mighty glum, knowing the chances were that if the Indians didn't find us they would stay around the country, looking for us. That meant that our chance of rounding up more cattle was coming down to nothing.

"You know what I think?" They waited for me to speak up. "I think we should cash in our chips. I think we should take what we've got and hit the trail for Santa Fe, sell what we've got, and get us a proper outfit. We need three or four horses per man for this kind of work."

Tom Sunday flipped his bowie knife into the sand, retrieved it and studied the light on the blade while he gave it thought. "Not a bad idea," he said.

"Cap?"

"If Orrin's willin'." Cap hesitated. "I figure we should dust out of here, come daybreak."

"Wasn't what I had in mind," I said, "I meant to leave right now ... before those Indians find that sorrel."

The reason I hadn't waited for Orrin to speak was because I knew he was pining to see that yellow-haired girl and I had some visiting in mind my own self.

Only it wasn't that ... it was the plain, common-sense notion that once those Indians knew we were here, starting a herd might be tough to do. It might take them a day or two to work out our trail. Chances were by the time they found we were gone we'd be miles down the trail.

So I just picked up my saddle and headed for my horse. There is a time that calls for action and when debate makes no sense. Starting a herd in the middle of the night isn't the best thing to do, but handling cattle we'd be scattered out and easy picking for Indians, and I wanted to get started.

We just packed up and lit out. Those cattle were heavy with water and grass and not in the mood for travel but we started them anyhow. We put the north star at our backs and started for Santa Fe.

When the first sun broke the gray sky we had six miles behind us.

CHAPTER VI

We had our troubles. When that bunch began to realize what was happening they didn't like it. We wore our horses to a frazzle but we kept that herd on the trail right up to dusk to tire them out as much as to get distance behind us. We kept a sharp lookout, but we saw no Indians.

Santa Fe was a smaller town than we expected, and it sure didn't shape up to more than a huddle of adobe houses built around a sunbaked plaza, but it was the most town I'd ever seen, or Orrin.

Folks stood in the doorways and shaded their eyes at us as we bunched our cows, and then three riders, Spanish men, started up the trail toward us. They were cantering their horses and staring at us, then they broke into a gallop and came charging up with shrill yells that almost started our herd again. It was Miguel, Pete Romero, and a rider named Abreu.

"Ho!" Miguel was smiling. "It is good to see you, *amigo*. We have been watching for you. Don Luis has asked that you be his guests for dinner."

"Does he know we're here?" Orrin was surprised.

Miguel glanced at him. "Don Luis knows most things, *señor*. A rider brought news from the Vegas."

They remained with the herd while we rode into town.

We walked over to the La Fonda and left our horses in the shade. It was cool inside, and quiet. It was shadowed there like a cathedral, only this here was no cathedral. It was a drinking place, and a hotel, too, I guess.

Mostly they were Spanish men sitting around, talking it soft in that soft-sounding tongue of theirs, and it gave me a wonderful feeling of being a travelled man, of being in foreign parts. A couple of them spoke to us, most polite.

We sat down and dug deep for the little we had. Wasn't much, but enough for a few glasses of wine and mayhap something to eat. I liked hearing the soft murmur of voices, the clink of glasses, and the click of heels on the floor. Somewhere out back a woman laughed, and it was a mighty fine sound.

While we sat there an Army officer came in. Tall man, thirtyish with a clean uniform and a stiff way of walking like those Army men have. He had mighty fancy mustaches.

"Are you the men who own those cattle on the edge of town?"

"Are you in the market?" Orrin said.

"That depends on the price."

He sat down with us and ordered a glass of wine.

"I will be frank, gentlemen, there has been a drought here and a lot of cattle have been lost. Most of the stock is very thin. Yours is the first fat beef we've seen."

Tom Sunday glanced up and smiled. "We will want twenty-five dollars per head."

The captain merely glanced at him. "Of course not," he said, then he smiled at us and lifted his glass. "Your health—"

"What about Don Luis Alvarado?" Orrin asked suddenly.

The captain's expression stiffened a little and he asked, "Are you one of the Pritts crowd?"

"No," Tom Sunday said, "we met the don out on the Plains. Came west from Abilene with him, as a matter of fact."

"He's one of those who welcomed us in New Mexico. Before we took over the Territory the Mexican government was in no position to send troops to protect these colonies from the Indians. Also, most of the trade was between Santa Fe and the States, rather than between Santa Fe and Mexico. The don appreciated this, and most of the people here welcomed us."

"Jonathan Pritts is bringing in settlers," Orrin said.

"Mr. Pritts is a forceful and energetic man," the captain said, "but he is under the false impression that because New Mexico has become a possession of the United States ... I should say, a part of the United States ... that the property rights of all Spanish-speaking people will be tossed out the window."

There was a pause. "The settlers—if one wishes to call them that—that Jonathan Pritts is bringing in are all men who bring their guns instead of families."

I had me another glass of wine and sat back and listened to the captain talking with Tom Sunday. Seems the captain was out of that Army school, West Point, but he was a man who had read a sight of books. A man never realizes how little he knows until he listens to folks like that talk. Up where I was born we had the Bible, and once in awhile somebody would bring a newspaper but it was a rare thing when we saw any other kind of reading.

Politics was a high card up in the hills. A political speech would bring out the whole country. Folks would pack their picnic lunches and you'd see people at a speech you'd never see elsewhere. Back in those days' most every boy grew up knowing as much about local politics as about coon dogs, which was about equal as to interest.

Orrin and me, we just set and listened. A man can learn a lot if he listens, and if I didn't learn anything else I was learning how much I didn't know. It made me hungry to know it all, and mad because I was getting so late a start.

We'd picked up a few more head of cattle coming south and the way it was going to figure out, each of us would have more than a thousand dollars of his own when we'd settled up. Next day Orrin and Cap went to the stage office and arranged to ship east the gold we'd found in the wagon.

The itch to see the town got the best of me so I walked outside. Those black-eyed señoritas was enough to turn a man's good sense. If Orrin would look at some of these girls he'd forget all about Laura.

It was no wonder he fell for her. After a man has been surrounded for months by a lot of hard-handed, hairy-chested men even the doggiest kind of female looks mighty good.

Most of all right now I wanted a bath and a shave. Cap, he followed me.

"Seems to me there's things around town need seeing to," I suggested.

"You look here, Tyrel, if you're thinkin' of what I think you're thinkin' you'd better scout the country and study the sign before you make your move. If you figure to court a Spanish gal you'd also better figure to fight her man."

"Seems like it might be worth it."

This was siesta time. A dog opened one eye and wagged a tail to show that if I didn't bother him he'd be pleased. Me, I wasn't of a mind to bother anybody.

Taking it slow, I walked down the dusty street. The town was quiet. A wide door opened into a long, barnlike building with a lot of tubs and water running through in a ditch. There was homemade soap there and nobody around. There was a pump there, too. It was the first time I ever saw a pump inside a house. Folks are sure getting lazy ... won't even go outside the house to pump.

This here must be a public bathhouse, but there was nobody around to take my money. I filled a tub with water, stripped off and got in and when I'd covered with soap, head to foot, three women came in with bundles of clothes on their heads.

First off I stared and they stared and then I yelled. All of a sudden I realized this here was no bathhouse but a place to wash clothes.

Those Spanish girls had taken one look and then they began to shriek, and first off I figured they were scared, but they weren't running, they were just standing there laughing at me.

Laughing!

Grabbing a bucket of water I doused myself with it and grabbed up a towel. Then they ran outside and

I could hear screams and I never crawled into my clothes so fast in all my born days. Slinging gun belt around me at a dead run I beat it for my horse.

It must have been a sight, me all soapy in that tub. Red around the gills. I started Dapple out of town on a run and the last thing I could hear was laughter. Women sure do beat all.

Anyway, I'd had a bath.

Morning was bright and beautiful like nine mornings out of ten in the high desert country. We met the captain and turned the cattle over to him. We'd finally settled on twenty dollars a head, which was a very good price at the time and place.

First off, as we rode into town, a girl spotted me. She pointed her finger at me, gasped, and spoke excitedly to the girl with her, and then they both began to look at me and laugh.

Orrin was puzzled because the girls always noticed him first and paid me no mind. "Do you know those girls?"

"Me? I never saw them before in my life." But it gave me a tip-off as to what it was going to be like. That story must be all over Santa Fe by now.

Before we reached the La Fonda we'd passed a dozen girls and they all laughed or smiled at me. Tom Sunday and Orrin, they hadn't an idea of what was going on.

The La Fonda was cool and pleasant again, so we ordered wine and a meal. The girl who took our order realized all of a sudden who I was and she began to giggle. When she went out with our order, two or three girls came from the kitchen to look at me.

Picking up a glass of wine, I tried to appear worldly and mighty smug about it all. Fact was, I felt pretty foolish.

Orrin was getting sore. He couldn't understand this sudden interest the girls were taking in me. He was curious, interested and kind of jealous all to once. Only thing I could do was stand my ground and wear it out or high-tail it for the brush.

Santa Fe was a small town, but it was a friendly

town. Folks here all wanted the good time that strangers brought. Those years, it was a town at the end of things, although it was old enough to have been a center of everything. And the girls loved a fandango and enjoyed the presence of the Americans.

There was a cute little button of a Mexican girl and every time I'd see her she'd give me a flashing glance out of those big dark eyes, and believe me, I'd get flustered.

This one had a shape to take a man's eye. Every time she'd pass me on the streets she'd give a little more swish to her skirts and I figured we could get acquainted if I just knew how to go about it. Her name was Tina Fernandez.

Night of the second day, there was a knock at the door and when I opened it Fetterson was standing there.

"Mr. Pritts wants to see you, all of you. He wants to talk business."

We looked at each other, then Orrin got up to go. The rest of us followed him and a Mexican standing at the bar turned his back on us. Anybody who was friendly to Jonathan Pritts would find few friends in Santa Fe.

It wasn't just that which worried me. It was Orrin.

Jonathan Pritts had four men outside the adobe where he lived and a few others loafing near the corral. Through the bunkhouse door I could see several men, all armed.

One thing you've got to watch, Tyrel, I told myself, is a man with so many fighters around. He wouldn't have all those men unless he figured he'd need them.

Rountree glanced at me. He was badger tough and coon smart. Sunday paused on the porch and took out a cigar; when he reached back and struck the match on his pants three chairs creaked as men put their hands to their guns. Tom didn't let on he noticed but there was a sly smile around his mouth.

Laura came to meet us in a blue dress that brought out the blue in her eyes, so she looked like an angel.

The way she offered both hands to Orrin and the way she looked at him ... it was enough to make a man gag. Only Orrin wasn't gagging. He was looking like somebody had hit him with a fence post.

Cap was uncommon sour but Sunday—always a hand with the ladies—gave her a wide smile. Sometimes I thought it irritated him that Laura had chosen to fall for Orrin and not him.

Her eyes looked past Orrin at me and our minds were hitched to the same idea. We simply did not like each other.

Jonathan Pritts entered wearing a preacher's coat and a collar that made you wonder whether he was going to offer prayer or sell you a gold brick.

He passed around a box of cigars and I was glad I didn't smoke. Orrin accepted a cigar, and after the slightest hesitation, Tom did too.

"I don't smoke," I said.

"Will you have a drink?"

"I don't drink," I said.

Orrin looked at me, because while I don't care for the stuff I sometimes drink with friends.

"You boys have done well with your cattle," Pritts said, "and I like men with business minds. However, I am wondering what you plan to do with the proceeds of your success. I can use men who want to invest business brains and capital, men who can start something and carry it through."

Nobody said anything and he brushed the ash from his cigar and studied the glowing end for a minute.

"There may be a little trouble at first. The people on the land are not Americans and may resent our moving in."

Orrin spoke slowly. "Tyrel and me came west hunting land. We're looking for a home."

"Good! New Nexico is now a part of the United States, and it's time that we American citizens had the benefits."

He drew deep on his cigar. "The first comers will be first served."

"The way it sounds," I said, "you plan to shove out the first comers and move in yourself."

Pritts was mad. He was not accustomed to straight talk—least of all from men like us. He said nothing for a moment and Laura sat down near Orrin and I got a whiff of her perfume.

"The Mexicans have no rights," Pritts replied. "The land belongs to us freeborn Americans, and if you come in with us now you will have shares in the company we are forming."

"We need a home for Ma," Orrin said, "we do need land."

"If we get it this way, there'll be blood on it," I said, "but first we should get Mr. Pritts' proposition in writing, just what he has in mind, and how he aims to settle up." That was Pa talking. Pa always said, "Get it in writing, boy."

"A gentleman's word," Pritts replied stiffly, "should be enough."

I got up. I'd no idea what the others figured to do and didn't much care. This sanctimonious old goat was figuring to steal land from folks who'd lived on it for years.

"A man who is talking of stealing land with guns," I said, "is in no position to talk about himself as being a gentleman. Those people are American citizens now as much as you or me."

Turning around, I started for the door, and Cap Rountree was only a step behind me. Tom Sunday hesitated, being a polite man, but the four of us were four who worked and travelled together, so he followed us. Orrin lagged a little, but he came.

Pritts yelled after us, his voice trembling he was so mad. "Remember this! Those who aren't with me are against me! Ride out of town and don't come back!"

None of us were greenhorns and we knew those men on the porch weren't knitting so when we stopped, the four of us faced out in four directions. "Mr. Pritts," I said, "you've got mighty big ideas for such a small head. Don't you make trouble for us or we'll run you back to the country they run you out of."

He was coming after us and he stopped in mid-stride, stopped as though I'd hit him with my fist. Right then I knew what I'd said was true ... somebody had run him out of somewhere.

He was an arrogant man who fancied himself important, and mostly he carried it off, but now he was mad. "We'll see about that!" he shouted. "Wilson, *take them!*"

Rountree was facing the first man who started to get out of a chair, which was Wilson, and there was no mercy in old Cap. He just laid a gun barrel alongside of Wilson's head and Wilson folded right back into his chair.

The man facing Orrin had a six-shooter in his stomach and I was looking across a gun barrel at Pritts himself.

"Mr. Pritts," I said, "you're a man who wants to move in on folks with guns. Now you just tell them to go ahead with what they've started and you'll be dead on the floor by the time you've said it."

Laura stared at me with such hatred as I've ever seen on a woman's face. There was a girl with a mighty big picture of her pa and anybody who didn't see her pa the way she did couldn't be anything but evil. And whoever she married was always going to play second fiddle to Jonathan Pritts.

Pritts looked like he'd swallowed something that wasn't good for him. He looked at that Navy Colt and he knew I was not fooling. And so did I.

"All right." He almost choked on it. "You can go."

We walked to our horses with nobody talking and when we were in our saddles Orrin turned on me. "Damn you, Tye, you played hell. You the same as called him a thief."

"That land belongs to Alvarado. We killed a lot of Higginses for less."

That night I slept mighty little, trying to figure out if I'd done right. Anyway I looked at it, I thought I'd done the right thing, and I didn't believe my liking for Drusilla had a thing to do with it. And believe me, I thought about that.

Next morning I saw Fetterson riding out of town with a pack of about forty men, and Wilson was with him. Only Wilson's hat wasn't setting right because of the lump on his skull. They rode out of town, headed northeast.

About the time they cleared the last house a Mexican boy mounted on a speedy looking sorrel took off for the hills, riding like the devil was on his tail.

Looked to me like Don Luis had his own warning system and would be ready for Fetterson before he got there. Riding that fast he wouldn't be riding far, so chances were a relay of horses was waiting to carry the word. Don Luis had a lot of men, lots of horses, and a good many friends.

Orrin came out, stuffing his shirt into his pants. He looked mean as a bear with a sore tooth. "You had no call to jump Mr. Pritts like that."

"If he was an honest man, I'd have nothing to say."

Orrin sat down. One thing a body could say for Orrin, he was a fair man. "Tyrel," he said at last, "you ought to think before you talk. I like that girl."

Well ... I felt mighty mean and low down. I set store by Orrin. Most ways he was smarter than me, but about this Pritts affair, I figured he was wrong.

"Orrin, I'm sorry. We never had much, you and me. But what we had, we had honest. We want a home for Ma. But it wouldn't be the home she wants if it was bought with blood."

"Well ... damn it, Tyrel, you're right, of course. I just wish you hadn't been so rough on Mr. Pritts."

"I'm sorry. It was me, not you. You ain't accountable for the brother you've got."

"Tyrel, don't you talk thataway. Without you that day back home in Tennessee I'd be buried and nobody knows it better than me."

CHAPTER VII

This was raw, open country, rugged country, and it bred a different kind of man. The cattle that went wild in Texas became the longhorn, and ran mostly to horns and legs because the country needed a big animal that could fight and one who could walk three days to get water. Just so it bred the kind of man with guts and toughness no eastern man could use.

Most men never discover what they've got inside. A man has to face up to trouble before he knows. The kind of conniving a man could get away with back east wouldn't go out here. Not in those early years. You can hide that sort of behavior in a crowd, but not in a country where there's so few people. Not that we didn't have our own kinds of trickery and cheating.

Jonathan Pritts was one of those who mistook liberty for license and he figured he could get away with anything. Worst of all, he had an exaggerated idea of how big a man he was ... trouble was, he wasn't a big man, just a mean one.

We banked our money with the Express Company in Santa Fe, and then we saddled up and started back to Purgatoire after more cattle. We had us an outfit this time. Dapple was still my horse, and a better no man was likely to have, but each of us now had four extra mounts and I'd felt I'd done myself proud.

The first was a *grulla*, a mouse-colored mustang who, judging by disposition, was sired out of a Missouri mule by a mountain lion with a sore tooth. That *grulla* was the most irritating, cantankerous bit of horseflesh I ever saw, and he could buck like a sidewinder on a red-ant hill. On the other hand he could go all day and night over any kind of country on less grass and water than one of Beale's camels. My name for him was Sate, short for Satan.

There was a buckskin, a desert horse used to rough going, but steady. In many ways the most reliable horse I had. His name was Buck, like you might expect.

Kelly was a big red horse with lots of bottom. Each horse I paid for out of my own money, although Sate they almost gave me, glad to be rid of him, I expect.

First time I straddled Sate we had us a mite of a go-around. When I came off him I was shook up inside and had a nosebleed, but I got off when I was good and ready and from that time on Sate knew who was wearing the pants.

My fourth horse I bought from an Indian.

We'd spent most of the day dickering with Spanish men, and this Indian sat off to one side, watching. He was a big-framed Nez Perce from up Idaho, Montana way.

He was at the corral at sunup and by noontime I'd not seen him have a bite to eat.

"You're a long way from home," I said, slicing off a chunk of beef I'd had fixed for a lunch and handed it to him.

He looked at me, a long, careful look, then he accepted it. He ate slow like a starving man who can't eat a lot at first because his stomach shrinks up.

"You speak English?"

"I speak."

Splitting my grub down the middle, I gave him half, and we ate together. When we'd finished he got up. "Come—you see horse."

The horse was a handsome animal, a roan with a splash of white with red spots on the white, the kind of horse they call an Appaloosa. Gaunt as his owner he stood a good sixteen hands. Looked like this Indian had come a long way on short rations.

So I swapped him my old rifle (I'd bought a .44 Henry the day before) and some grub. I threw in my old blanket.

We were a week out of Santa Fe when we found a

spot in the bend of a creek among some rocks. When we'd forted up they left it to me to scare up some fresh meat as we planned to live off the country and stretch our store-bought rations.

That Montana horse could move. He could get out and go, lickety-brindle, and he was smart. We passed up antelope because no matter what folks tell you it's the worst kind of Rocky Mountain meat. Old-timers will tell you that cougar meat is best. Lewis and Clark said that, and Jim Bridger, Kit Carson, Uncle Dick Wootton, Jim Baker ... they all agreed.

Morning, with a bright sun over far hills, shadows lying in the folds and creases of the country, sunlight on cottonwood leaves and sparkling on the river water ... a meadow lark calling. Montana horse and me, we sure loved it. We took off along an old deer trail. This was higher country than before, the plateaus giving way to long ridges crested with pines and slopes dotted with juniper or piñon.

Suddenlike, I saw a deer ... and then another. Tethering Montana horse I moved up with my rifle.

Feeding deer are easy to stalk if a man is careful on his feet and doesn't let them get wind of him. When deer put their heads down to graze, you can move up on them, and you can keep moving, very quiet. When their tails start to switch they're going to look up, so you freeze in position. He may be looking right at you when he looks up, and he might look a long time, but if you stand right still, after awhile he will decide you're a harmless tree or stump and go back to feeding.

I worked my way up to within fifty yards of a good big buck and then I lifted my rifle and put a bullet behind the left foreleg. There was another deer no further off and on my left, and as I fired at the first one I swung the rifle just as he was taking his first jump and my bullet broke his neck as he hit ground.

Working fast, I butchered those deer, loaded the choice cuts into their hides and mounted Montana horse. When I came out of the trees a couple of miles further on a half-dozen buffalo were running across the wind. Now no buffalo runs without reason.

Pulling up on the edge of the trees I knew we'd be hard to see, for that roan and me with my buckskin outfit fitted into the country like part of it. No man in this country ever skylines himself if he can help it.

Sometimes the first man to move is the first to die, so I waited. The sun was bright on the hillside. My horse stamped a foot and switched his tail. A bee hummed around some leaves on a bush nearby.

They came in a single file, nine of them in a row. Utes, from the description I'd heard from Cap. They came out of the trees and angled along the slope in front of me.

Now most times I prefer to stand my ground and fight it out for running can make your back a broad target, but there are times to fight and times to run and the wise man is one who can choose the right time for each.

First off, I sat still, but they were riding closer and closer to me, and if they didn't see me their horses would. If I tried to go back into the trees they'd hear me.

Sliding my rifle across my saddle I said a prayer to the guardian angel of fools and covered maybe thirty yards before they saw me. One of them must have spoken because they all looked.

Indians can make mistakes like anybody. If they had all turned and come at me I'd have had to break for the brush and I'd have been fairly caught. But one Indian got too anxious and threw up his rifle and fired.

Seeing that rifle come up, I hit the spurs to Montana horse and went away from there, but in the split seconds before I hit him with the spurs, I fired. As I'd been timing my horse's steps I'd shot at the right time and I didn't miss.

My shot took out, not the Indian shooting at me but the one who seemed to be riding the best horse. My shot was a hair ahead of his and he missed when Montana horse jumped.

We took out ... and I mean we really lit a shuck. There was nothing around there I wanted and what I wanted most was distance from where I was.

With that first Indian down I'd cut my sign right across their trail and now they wanted me mighty bad, but that horse didn't like Utes any better than I did. He put his ears back and stretched out his tail and left there like a scared rabbit.

My next shot was a miss. With Montana horse travelling like he'd forgot something in Santa Fe, there wasn't much chance of a hit. They had all come right at me with the shooting and I saw unless I did something drastic they had me so I swung and charged right at the nearest Indian. He was fifty yards ahead of the nearest Ute and which shot got his horse I don't know, but I fired three or four shots at him.

Dust jumped from the horse's side and the horse went down throwing his rider over his head into the grass, and when I went by at a dead run I shot into that Indian as I rode.

They were all messed up for a minute or two, switching directions and running into each other, but meanwhile I rode through a small creek and was out on the open prairie beyond.

We were eight to ten miles from camp and I wasn't about to lead these Utes full tilt into my friends. And then I saw a buffalo wallow.

Slowing Montana horse we slid into that wallow and I hit ground and threw my shoulder into the horse and grabbed his off foreleg, hoping to throw him, but Montana horse seemed to know just what I wanted and he went down and rolled on his side like he had been trained for it ... which he probably had, the Nez Perce using Appaloosas for war horses.

Dropping to one knee, the other leg stretched out ahead of me, I drew a careful bead on the chest of the nearest Ute and squeezed off my shot.

There was a minute when I believed I'd missed, and him coming right into my sights, then his horse swung wide and dumped a dead Ute into the grass.

There was a bright stain of blood on the horse's side as he swung away.

It was warm and still. Patting Montana horse I told him, "You rest yourself, boy, we'll make out."

He rolled his eyes at me like he understood every word.

You would never have believed that a moment ago there was shooting and killing going on, because suddenly everything was still. The hillside was empty, those Indians had gone into the ground faster than you would believe. Lying there, knowing any moment might be my last, I liked the feel of the warm sun on my back, the smell of parched brown grass and of dust.

Three of the Utes were down in the grass and there were six left. Six to one might seem long odds but if a man has nerve enough and if he thinks in terms of combat, the advantage is often against sheer numbers. Sheer numbers rob a man of something and he begins to depend . . . and in a fighting matter no man should depend. He should do what has to be done himself.

My canteen was full and I'd some jerked meat in my saddlebag, lots of fresh meat, and plenty of ammunition.

They would try to come over the rise behind me. That crest, only a couple of feet away, masked my view of the far slope. So I had out my bowie knife and began cutting a trench. That was a nine-inch blade, sharp enough to shave with, and I worked faster than ever in my born days.

It took me only minutes to have a trench that gave me a view of the back slope, and I looked around just in time. Four of them were coming up the slope toward me on foot and running bent over. My shot was a miss . . . too quick. But they hit dirt. Where there had been running Indians there was only grass stirring in the wind.

They would be creeping on their bellies now, getting closer. Taking a chance, I leaped up. Instantly, I spotted a crawling Indian and fired, then dropped into my hole with bullets spearing the air where I'd been. That was something I couldn't try again, for now they'd be expecting.

Overhead there were high streamers of white clouds. Turning around I crawled into my trench, and just in time. An Indian was coming up that back slope, bent over and coming fast and I let him come. It was high time I shortened the odds against me, so I put my rifle in position, reached down to ease my Colt for fast work in case the others closed in at the same time. That Ute was going to reach me with his next rush.

Some were down, but I doubted if more than one was actually dead. I wasn't counting any scalps until I had them.

Minutes loitered. Sweat trickled down my cheeks and my neck. I could smell the sweat of my own body and the hot dust. Somewhere an eagle cried. Sweat and dust made my skin itch, and when a big horsefly lit on Montana, my slap sounded loud in the hot stillness.

Eastern folks might call this adventure, but it is one thing to read of adventure sitting in an easy chair with a cool drink at hand, and quite another thing to be belly down in the hot dust with four, five Indians coming up the slope at you with killing on their minds.

A grasshopper flew into the grass maybe fifteen yards down slope, then took off at once, quick and sharp. That was warning enough. Lifting the rifle I steadied it on that spot for a quick shot, then chanced a glance over my shoulder. Just as I looked back that Ute charged out of the grass like he was bee-stung.

My guess had been right, and he came up where that grasshopper had lit. My sights were on the middle of his chest when I squeezed off my shot and he fell in plain sight.

Behind me their feet made a whisper in the dry grass and rolling over I palmed my Colt and had two shots off before I felt the slam of the bullet. The Utes vanished and then I was alone but for a creeping numbness in my left shoulder and the slow welling of blood.

Sliding back from the trench I felt sickish faint and plugged the hole with a handkerchief. The bullet had gone through and I was already soaked with blood on my left side. With bits of handkerchief I plugged the bullet hole on both sides and knew I was in real trouble.

Blinking against the heat and sudden dizziness I fed shells into my guns. Then I took the plug from my canteen and rinsed my mouth. It was lukewarm and brackish.

My head started to throb heavily and it was an effort to move my eyebrows. The smell of sweat and dried grass grew stronger and overhead the sky was yellow and hot as brass. From out of an immeasurable distance a buzzard came.

Suddenly I hated the smells, hated the heat, hated the buzzard circling and patient—as it could be patient—knowing that most things die.

Crawling to the rim of the buffalo wallow my eyes searched the terrain before me, dancing with heat waves. I tried to swallow and could not, and Tennessee and its cool hills seemed very far away.

Through something like delirium I saw my mother rocking in her old chair, and Orrin coming up from the spring with a wooden bucket full of the coldest water a man could find.

Lying in a dusty hole on a hot Colorado hillside with a bullet hole in me and Utes waiting to finish the job, I suddenly remembered what day it was.

It had been an hour ... or had it been more? It had been at least an hour since the last attack. Like the buzzards, all those Utes needed was time, and what is time to an Indian?

Today was my birthday ... today I was nineteen years old.

CHAPTER VIII

Long fingers of shadow reached out from the senti-
nel pines before I took my next swallow of water.
Twice I'd sponged out the mouth of that Montana
horse, who was growing restless and harder to keep
down.

No chance to take a cat nap, or even take my eyes
off the country for more than a minute because I
knew they were still out there and they probably
knew I was hurt. My shoulder was giving me billy-
hell. Even if I'd had a chance to run for it Montana
horse would be stiff from lying so long.

About that time I saw the outfit coming up the
slope. They rode right up to that buffalo wallow bold
as brass and sat their horses grinning at me, and I was
never so glad to see anybody.

"You're just in time for tea," I said, "you all just pull
up your chairs. I've got the water on and she'll be
ready any minute."

"He's delirious," Tom Sunday grinned like a big
ape. "He's gone off his rocker."

"It's the heat," Orrin agreed. "The way he's dug in
you'd think he'd been fighting Indians."

"Hallucinations," Rountree added, "a plain case of
prairie sickness."

"If one of you will get off his horse," I suggested,
"I'll plain whip him till his hair falls out, one-handed
at that. Where've you been? Yarning it in the shade?"

"He asks us where we've been?" Sunday exclaimed.
"And him sitting in a nice cool hole in the ground
while we work our fool heads off."

Rountree, he cut out and scouted around, and
when he rode back he said, "Looks like you had

71

yourself a party. By the blood on the grass you got two, anyway."

"You should backtrack me." I was feeling ornery as a stepped-on baby. "If I didn't score on five out of nine Utes, I'll put up money for the drinks."

"Only three took off when we showed up," Sunday agreed.

Grabbing my saddle horn I pulled myself into the leather; for the first time since I'd sighted those Utes I could count on another day of living.

For the next three days I was cook which comes of having a bum wing on a cow outfit. Cap was a fair hand at patching up wounds and he made a poultice of herbs of some kind which he packed on my shoulder. He cleaned the wound by running an arrow shaft through with a cloth soaked in whiskey, and if you think that's entertainment, you just try it on for size.

On the fifth day I was back in the saddle but I fought shy of Sate, reckoning he'd be too much for me, feeling like I was. So I worked Dapple and Buck to a frazzle, and ended up riding Montana horse who was turning into a real cow horse.

This was rougher country than before. We combed the breaks and drifted the cattle into a rough corral. It was hot, rough, cussing work, believe you me. Here and there we found some branded stock, stuff that had stampeded from trail herds further east, or been driven off by Indians.

"Maybe we should try Abilene this time," I suggested to the others. "The price would be better. We just happened to be lucky in Santa Fe."

Seven hundred head of cattle was what we started out with, and seven hundred head can be handled by four men if they work like dogs and are passing lucky.

As before, we let them graze as they moved. What we wanted was fat cattle at selling time. In that box canyon they had steadied down a good bit with plenty of water and grass and nothing much to do but eat and lie around.

First night out from the Purgatoire we bedded

down after a long drive with the cattle mighty tired. After awhile Orrin stopped near me.

"Tyrel, I sure wish you and Laura cottoned to each other more'n you do."

"If you like her, Orrin, that's what matters. I can't be no different than I am, and something about her doesn't ring true. Orrin, the way I see it, you'd always play second fiddle to her old man."

"That's not true," he said, but there wasn't much force in it.

After awhile we met again and stopped together. "Ma's not getting younger," he said, "and we've been gone a year."

A coyote made talk to the stars, but nothing else seemed to be stirring.

"If we sell this herd we'll have more money than any Sackett ever heard of, and I figure we should buy ourselves an outfit and start ranching. Then we ought to get some book learning. Especially you, Orrin. You could make a name for yourself."

Orrin's thoughts were afar off for a minute or two, gathering dreams somewhere along tomorrow's road.

"I've had it in mind," he said finally.

"You've a talking way with you, Orrin. You could be governor."

"I haven't the book learning."

"Davy Crockett went to Congress. Andrew Johnson was taught to read and write by his wife. I figure we can get the book learning. Hell, man, if youngsters can learn we should be able to throw it and hog-tie it. I figure you should study law. You've got a winning way with that Welsh tongue of yours."

We drove through Dodge on to Abilene, and that town had spread itself all over the prairie, with saloons side by each, all of them going twenty-four hours to the day, and packed most of the time.

Everywhere a man looked around the town there were herds of Texas cattle. "We came to the wrong market," Cap said dourly, "we should have sold out in Dodge."

We swung the herd into a tight circle and saw

several riders coming toward us. Two of them looked like buyers and the other two looked like trouble. Orrin did his talking to the first two, Charlie English and Rosie Rosenbaum. Rosenbaum was a stocky man with mild blue eyes, and I could tell by the way he was sizing up our cattle that he knew beef.

"How many head have you got?" he asked Orrin.

"Seven hundred and forty, as of last night," Orrin said, "and we want a fast deal."

The other two had been studying our herd and sizing us up.

"I should think you would," one of them said, "those are stolen cattle."

Orrin just looked at him. "My name is Orrin Sackett, and I never stole anything in my life." He paused. "And I never had anything stolen from me, either."

The man's face shadowed. "You've got Two-Bar cattle in that herd," he said, "and I'm Ernie Webb, foreman of the Two-Bar."

"There are Two-Bar cows in that herd, and we rounded them up in the Colorado country along with a lot of wild cattle. If you want to claim them get your boss and we'll talk a deal, but he'll pay for the rounding up and driving."

"I don't need the boss," Webb replied, "I handle my own trouble."

"Now see here," Rosenbaum interfered quietly. "There's no need for this. Sackett is reasonable enough. Get your boss and when the matter is settled, I'll buy."

"You stay out of this." Webb was staring at Orrin, a trouble-hunting look on his face. "This is a rustled herd and we're taking it over."

Several rough-looking riders had been drifting closer, very casually. I knew a box play when I saw one.

Where I was sitting Webb and his partner couldn't see me because Sunday was between us. They'd never seen Orrin before but they'd both seen me that day on the plains of east Kansas.

"Cap," I said, "if they want it, let's let them have it."

"Tom," I wheeled my horse around Sunday which allowed me to flank Webb and his partner, "this man may have been foreman for Two-Bar once, but he also rode with Back Rand."

Cap had stepped down from his saddle and had his horse between himself and the oncoming riders, his rifle across his saddle. "You boys can buy the herd," Cap said, "but you'll buy it the hard way."

The riders drew up.

Rosenbaum was waiting right in the middle of where a lot of lead could be flying but there wasn't a quiver in him. For a man with no stake in the deal, he had nerve.

Webb had turned to look at me, and Orrin went on like he hadn't been interrupted. "Mr. Rosenbaum, you buy these cattle and keep track of any odd brands you find. I think they'll check with those in our tally books, and we'll post bond for their value and settle with any legitimate claimant but nobody is taking any cattle from us."

Ernie Webb had it all laid out for him nice and pretty, and it was his turn to call the tune. If he wanted to sashay around a bit he had picked himself four men who could step to the music.

"It's that loudmouth kid," Webb said, "somebody will beat it out of him someday, and then rub his nose in it."

"You try," Orrin invited. "You can have any one of us, but that kid will blow you loose from your saddle."

We sold out for thirty-two dollars a head, and Rosenbaum admitted it was some of the fattest stock brought into Abilene that year. Our herd had grazed over country no other herds travelled and with plenty of water. We'd made our second lucky drive and each of us had a notion we'd played out our luck.

When we got our cash we slicked out in black broadcloth suits, white shirts, and new hats. We were more than satisfied and didn't figure to do any better than what we had.

Big John Ryan showed up to talk cattle. "This the Sackett outfit?"

"We're it."

"Hear you had Tumblin' R stock in your herd?"

"Yes, sir. Sit down, will you?" Orrin told him about it. "Seven head, including a brindle steer with a busted horn."

"That old devil still alive? Nigh cost me the herd a few times and if I'd caught him I'd have shot him. Stampede at the drop of a hat and take a herd with him."

"You've got money coming, Mr. Ryan. At thirty-two dollars a head we figure—"

"Forget it. Hell . . . anybody with gumption enough to round up those cows and drive them over here from Colorado is entitled to them. Besides, I just sold two herds of nearly six thousand head . . . seven head aren't going to break me."

He ordered a drink. "Fact is, I'd like to talk to you boys about handling my herd across the Bozeman Trail."

Orrin looked at me. "Tom Sunday is the best cattleman among us. Orrin and me, we want to find a place of our own."

"I can't argue with that. My drive will start on the Neuces and drive to the Musselshell in Montana. How about it, Sunday?"

"I think not. I'll trail along with the boys."

There I sat with almost six thousand dollars belonging to me and about a thousand more back in Santa Fe, and I was scared. It was the first time in my life I'd ever had anything to lose.

The way I saw it unless a man knows where he's going he isn't going anywhere at all. We wanted a home for Ma, and a ranch, and we also wanted enough education to face the changing times. It was time to do some serious thinking.

A voice interrupted. "Aren't you Tyrel Sackett?"

It was the manager of the Drovers' Cottage. "There's a letter for you."

"A letter?" I looked at him stupidly. Nobody had ever written me a letter.

Maybe Ma ... I was scared. Who would write to me?

It looked like a woman's handwriting. I carefully unfolded the letter. It scared me all hollow.

Worst of it was, the words were handwritten and the letters were all which-way and I had a time making them out. But I wet my lips, dug in my heels, and went to work—figuring a man who could drive cattle could read a letter if he put his mind to it.

First off there was the town: Santa Fe. And the date. It was written only a week or so after we left Santa Fe.

Dear Mr. Sackett:

Well, now! Who was calling me mister? Mostly they called me Tyrel, or Tye, or Sackett.

The letter was signed *Drusilla.*

Right about then I started to get hot around the neck and ears, and took a quick look to see if anybody noticed. You never saw so many people paying less attention to anybody.

They heard I was in Santa Fe and wondered why I did not visit them. There had been trouble when some men had tried to take part of the ranch but the men had gone away. All but four, which they buried. And then her grandfather had gone to town to see Jonathan Pritts. In my mind's eyes I could see those two old men facing each other, and it must have been something to see, but my money was on the don. She ended with an invitation to visit them when I was next in Santa Fe.

Time has a way of running out from under a man. Looked like a man would never amount to much without book learning and every day folks were talking of what they read, of what was happening, but none of it made sense to me who had to learn by listening. When a man learns by listening he is never sure whether he is getting the straight of things or not.

There was a newspaper that belonged to nobody and I took that; it took me three days to work my way through its four pages.

There was a man in town with gear to sell, and figuring on buying an extra pistol, I went to see him. The gun I bought, and some boxes of shells, but when I saw some books in his wagon I bought them without looking.

"You don't want to know what they are?"

"Mister, I don't see that's your business, but the fact is, I wouldn't know one from the other. I figured if I studied out those books I'd learn. I'd work it out."

He had the look of a man who knew about writing and printing. "These aren't the books I'd recommend for a beginner, but you may get something out of them."

He sold me six books and I took them away.

Night after night I sat by the campfire plugging away at those books, and Tom Sunday sure helped a lot in telling me what words were about. First off, I got a surprise by learning that a man could learn something about his own way of living from a book. This book by an Army man, Captain Randolph Marcy, was written for a guide to parties traveling west by wagon. He told a lot of things I knew, and a good many I didn't.

Cap Rountree made out like he was sour about the books. "Need an extry pack horse for all that printed truck. First time I ever heard of a man packin' books on the trail."

CHAPTER IX

Santa Fe lay lazy in the sun when we rode into town. Nothing seemed to have changed, yet there was a feeling of change in me. And Drusilla was here, and this time I would call at her home. I'd never called on a girl before.

My letter from Drusilla was my own secret and I had no idea of telling anyone about it. Not even Orrin.

When Drusilla wrote I didn't answer because I couldn't write and if I'd traced the letters out—well, it didn't seem right that a man should be writing like a child.

First off when we got to Santa Fe I wanted to see Drusilla, so I went about getting my broadcloth suit brushed and pressed out. It was late afternoon when I rode to the ranch. Miguel was loafing at the gate with a rifle across his knees.

"*Señor*! It is good to see you! Every day the *señorita* has asked me if I have seen you!"

"Is she in?"

"*Señor*, it is good that you are back. Good for them, and good for us too." He indicated the door.

The house surrounded a patio, and stood itself within an adobe wall fifteen feet high. There was a walk ran around the inside near the top of the wall, and there were firing positions for at least thirty men on that wall.

Don Luis sat working at a desk. He arose. "Good afternoon, *señor*. It is good to see you. Was your venture a success?"

So I sat down and told him of our trip. A few of the cattle had carried his brand and we had kept the money for him and this I now paid.

"There is much trouble here," Don Luis said. "I fear it is only the beginning."

It seemed to me he had aged a lot in the short time since I'd last seen him. Suddenly, I realized how much I liked that stern, stiff old man with his white mustache.

Sitting back in his chair, he told me how Pritts' men made their first move. Forty in the group had moved on some flat land well within the Grant and had staked claims there, then they had dug in for a fight. Knowing the manner of the men he faced, Don Luis held back his *vaqueros*.

"There are, *señor*, many ways to victory, and not all of them through violence. And if there was a pitched battle, some of my men would be hurt. This I wished to avoid."

The invaders were watched, and it was noted when Pritts and Fetterson returned to Santa Fe on business that several bottles appeared and by midnight half the camp was drunk. Don Luis was close by, but he held back his *vaqueros* who were eager for a fight.

By three in the morning when all were in a drunken sleep, Don Luis *vaqueros* moved in swiftly.

The invaders were tied to their horses and started back down the road toward Santa Fe. Their tents and equipment were burned or confiscated, their weapons unloaded and returned to them. They were well down the trail when several riders returning from Mora engaged in a running gun battle with the *vaqueros*. Four of the invaders were killed, several wounded. Don Luis had two men wounded, none seriously.

"The advantage was ours," Don Luis explained, "but Jonathan Pritts is a very shrewd man and he is making friends, nor is he a man to suffer defeat without retaliation. It is difficult," he added, "to carry out a project with the sort of men he uses. They are toughs and evil men."

"Don Luis," I said, "have I your permission to see Miss Drusilla?"

He arose. "Of course, *señor*. I fear if the privilege

were denied that I should have another war, and one which I am much less suited to handle.

"We in New Mexico," he added, "have been closer to your people than our own. It is far to Mexico City, so our trade has been with you, our customs affected by yours. My family would disapprove of our ways, but on the frontier there is small time for formality."

Standing in the living room of the lovely old Spanish home, I felt stiff in my new clothes. Abilene had given me time to get used to them, but the awkwardness returned now that I was to see Drusilla again.

I could hear the click of her heels on the stone flags, and turned to face the door, my heart pounding, my mouth suddenly so dry I could scarcely swallow.

She paused in the doorway, looking at me. She was taller than I had remembered, and her eyes were larger. She was beautiful, too beautiful for a man like me.

"I thought you had forgotten us," she said, "you didn't answer my letter."

I shifted my hat in my hands. "It looked like I'd get here as fast as the letter, and I'm not much hand at writing."

An Indian woman came in with some coffee and some little cakes and we both sat down. Drusilla sat very erect in her chair, her hands in her lap, and I decided she was almost as embarrassed as I was.

"Ma'am, I never called on a girl before. I guess I'm almighty awkward."

Suddenly, she giggled. "And I never received a young man before," she said.

After that we didn't have much trouble. We both relaxed and I told her about our trip, about rounding up wild cattle and my fight with the Indians.

"You must be very brave."

Well, now. I liked her thinking that about me but fact is, I hadn't thought of much out there but keeping my head and tail down so's not to get shot, and I recalled being in something of a sweat to get out of there.

I've nothing against a man being scared as long as he does what has to be done ... being scared can keep a man from getting killed and often makes a better fighter of him.

We sat there in that cool, spacious room with its dark, massive furniture and tiled floors and I can tell you it was a wonderful friendly feeling. I'd never known a house like that before, and it seemed very grand and very rich.

Dru was worried about her grandfather. "He's getting old, Tyrel, and I'm afraid for him. He doesn't sleep well, and sometimes he paces the floor all night long."

Torres was waiting for me when I went to get my horse almost an hour later. "Señor," he said carefully, "Don Luis likes you and so does the señorita. Our people, they like you too."

He studied me searchingly. "Señor Pritts hates us, and he is winning friends among your people. He spends much money. I believe he would take everything from us."

"Not while I'm alive."

"We need a sheriff in this country, a man who will see justice done." He looked at me. "We ask only for justice."

"What you say is true. We do need a sheriff."

"The don grows old, and he does not know what to do, but all my life I have been with him, señor, and I do not think that to fight is enough. We must do something else, as your people would. There are, señor, still more Mexicans than Anglos. Perhaps if there was an election. . . ."

"A Mexican sheriff would not be good, Juan. The Americans would not be willing to recognize him. Not those who follow Pritts."

"This I know, señor. We will talk of this again."

When I walked into the La Fonda that night Ollie Shaddock was standing at the bar having a drink. He was a broad man with a shock of blond hair and a broad, cheerful face.

"Have a drink," he said, "I resigned my sheriffing job to bring your Ma and the boys west."

"You brought Ma?"

"Sure enough. Orrin's with her now."

He filled my glass from the bottle. "Don't you be thinkin' of me as sheriff. You done right in killin' Long. I'd have had to arrest you but the law would have freed you. He had a gun pointed when you killed him."

We didn't say anything more about it. It was good to have Ollie Shaddock out here, and I owed him a debt for bringing Ma. I wanted to see her the worst way but Ollie had something on his mind.

"Folks talk you up pretty high," he said.

"It's Orrin they like."

"You know something, Tyrel? I've been giving some thought to Orrin since I got here. He's a man should run for office."

It seemed a lot of folks had running for office on their minds, but this was a new country and in need of law. "He's got it in mind," I said.

"I've been in politics all my years. I was a deputy sheriff at seventeen, sheriff at nineteen, justice of the peace at twenty-four and served a term in the state legislature before I was thirty. Then I was sheriff again."

"I know it."

"Orrin looks to me like a man who could get out the vote. Folks take to him. He talks well, and with a mite more reading he could make something of himself, if we managed it right."

"We?"

"Politics ain't much different, Tyrel, than one of these icebergs you hear tell of. Most of what goes on is beneath the surface. It doesn't make any difference how good a man is, or how good his ideas are, or even how honest he is unless he can put across a program, and that's politics.

"Statesmanship is about ten percent good ideas and motives and ninety percent getting backing for your program. Now I figure I know how to get a man elected, and Orrin's our man. Also, you can be a big advantage to him."

"Folks don't take to me."

"Now that's as may be. I find most of the Mexicans like you. They all know you and Orrin turned Pritts down when he invited you to join him, and the *vaqueros* from the Alvarado ranch have been talking real friendly about you."

He chuckled. "Seems the women like you too. They tell me you provided more entertainment in one afternoon than they had in years."

"Now, look—!" I could feel myself getting red around the ears.

"Don't let it bother you. Folks enjoyed it, and they like you. Don't ask me why."

"You seem to have learned a lot since you've been here."

"Every man to his job, mine's politics. First thing is to listen. Learn the issues, the personalities, where the votes are, where the hard feelings are."

Ollie Shaddock tasted his whiskey and put the glass back on the bar. "Tyrel, there's trouble brewing and it will come from that Pritts outfit. That's a rough bunch of boys and they'll get to drinking and there'll be a killing. Chances are, it will be a riot or something like that."

"So?"

"So we got to go up there. You and me and Orrin. When that trouble comes Orrin has to handle it."

"He's no officer."

"Leave that to me. When it happens, folks will want somebody to take over the responsibility. So Orrin steps in."

He tossed off his whiskey. "Look ... Pritts wants Torres killed, some of the other key men. When the shooting starts some of those fur thieves and rustlers he's got will go too far.

"Orrin steps in. He's Anglo, so all the better Americans will be for him. You convince the Mexicans Orrin is their man. Then we get Orrin appointed

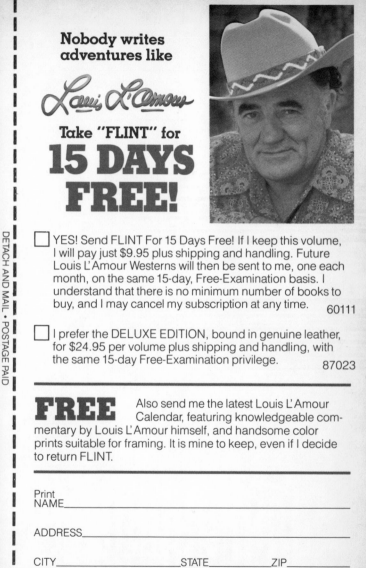

marshal, run him for sheriff, start planning for the legislature."

Ollie made a lot of sense, and it beat all how quickly he had got hold of the situation, and him here only a few weeks. Orrin was the man for it all right. Or Tom Sunday.

"What about Tom Sunday?"

"He figures he's the man for the job. But Tom Sunday can't talk to folks like Orrin can. He can't get down and be friends with everybody the way Orrin can. Orrin just plain likes people and they feel it ... like you like Mexicans and they know it. Anyway," he added, "Orrin is one of ours and one thing about Orrin. We don't have to lie."

"Would you lie?"

Ollie was embarrassed. "Tyrel, politics is politics, and in politics a man wants to win. So he hedges a little."

"Whatever we do has to be honest," I said. "Look, I'm no pilgrim. But there's nothing in this world I can't get without lying or cheating. Ma raised us boys that way, and I'm glad of it."

"All right, honesty is a good policy and if a man's honest it gets around. What do you think about Orrin?"

"I think he's the right man."

Only as I left there and started to see Ma, I was thinking about Tom Sunday. Tom was our friend, and Tom wasn't going to like this. He was a mite jealous of Orrin. Tom had the best education but folks just paid more mind to Orrin.

Ma had aged ... she was setting in her old rocker which Ollie had brought west in his wagon, and she had that old shawl over her knees. When I walked in she was puffing on that old pipe and she looked me up and down mighty sharp.

"You've filled out. Your Pa would be proud of you."

So we sat there and talked about the mountains back home and of folks we knew and I told her some of our plans. Thinking how hard her years had been, I wanted to do something for her and the boys. Bob was seventeen, Joe fifteen.

Ma wasn't used to much, but she liked flowers around her and trees. She liked meadow grass blowing in the wind and the soft fall of rain on her own roof. A good fire, her rocker, a home of her own, and her boys not too far away.

Ollie Shaddock wasted no time but rode off toward Mora. He was planning on buying a place, a saloon, or some such place where folks could get together. In those days a saloon was a meeting place, and usually the only one.

Of the books I'd bought I'd read Marcy's guide books first, and then that story, *The Deerslayer*. That was a sure enough good story too. Then I read Washington Irving's book about traveling on the prairies, and now was reading Gregg on *Commerce of the Prairies*.

Reading those books was making me talk better and look around more and see what Irving had seen, or Gregg. It was mighty interesting.

Orrin and me headed for the hills to scout a place for a home. Sate was feeling his oats and gave me a lively go-around but I figured the trip would take some of the salt out of him. That Satan horse really did like to hump his back and duck his head between his legs.

We rode along, talking land, cattle, and politics, and enjoying the day. This was a far cry from those blue-green Tennessee mountains, but the air was so clear you could hardly believe it, and I'd never seen a more beautiful land. The mountains were close above us, sharp and clear against the sky, and mostly covered with pines.

Sate wasn't cutting up any more. He was stepping right out like he wanted to go somewhere, but pretty soon I began to get a feeling I didn't like very much.

Sometimes a man's senses will pick up sounds or glimpses not strong enough to make an impression on him but they affect his thinking anyway. Maybe that's all there is to instinct or the awareness a man develops when he's in dangerous country. One thing I do know, his senses become tuned to sounds above and below the usual ranges of hearing.

We caught, of a sudden, a faint smell of dust on the air. There was no wind, but there was dust.

We walked our horses forward and I watched Sate's ears. Those ears pricked up, like the mustang he was, and I knew he was aware of something himself.

My eyes caught an impression and I walked my horse over for a look where part of the bark was peeled back from a branch. There were horses' tracks on the ground around the bush.

"Three or four, wouldn't you say, Tyrel?"

"Five. This one is different. The horses must have stood here around two hours, and then the fifth one came up but he didn't stop or get down."

Several cigarette butts were under a tree near where the horses had been tethered, and the stub of a black cigar.

We were already further north than we had planned to go and suddenly it came to me. "Orrin, we're on the Alvarado grant."

He looked around, studied our back trail and said, "I think it's Torres. Somebody is laying for him."

He walked his horse along, studying tracks. One of the horses had small feet, a light, almost prancing step. We both knew that track. A man who can read sign can read a track the way a banker would a signature. That small hoof and light step, and that sidling way of moving was Reed Carney's show horse.

Whoever the others had been, and the chances were Reed Carney had joined up with Fetterson and Pritts, they had waited there until the fifth man came along to get them. And that meant he could have been a lookout, watching for the man they were to kill.

Now we were assuming a good deal. Maybe. But there was just nothing to bring a party up here ... not in those days.

Orrin shucked his Winchester.

It was pine timber now and the trail angled up the slope through the trees. When we stopped again we were high up and the air was so clear you could see for miles. The rim was not far ahead.

We saw them.

Four riders, and below on the slope a fifth one, scouting. And off across the valley floor, a plume of dust that looked like it must be the one who was to be the target.

The men were below us, taking up position to cover a place not sixty yards from their rifles. They were a hundred feet or so higher than the rider, and he would be in the open.

Orrin and me left our horses in the trees. We stood on the edge of the mesa with a straight drop of about seventy feet right ahead of us, then the talus sloped away steeply to where the five men had gathered after leaving their horses tied to the brush a good hundred yards off.

They were well concealed from below. There was no escape for them, however, except to right or left. They could not come up the hill, and they could not go over the rim.

Orrin found himself a nice spot behind a wedged-up slab of rock. Me, I was sizing up a big boulder and getting an idea. That boulder sat right on the edge of the mesa, in fact it was a part of the edge that was ready to fall . . . with a little help.

Now I like to roll rocks. Sure, it's crazy, but I like to see them roll and bounce and take a lot of debris with them. So I walked to the rim, braced myself against the trunk of a gnarled old cedar and put my feet against the edge of that rock.

The rider they were waiting for was almost in sight. When I put my boots against that rock my knees had to be doubled up, so I began to push. I began to straighten them out. The rock crunched heavily, teetered slightly, and then with a slow, majestic movement it turned over and fell.

The huge boulder hit with a heavy thud and turned over, gained speed, and rolled down the hill.

The riders glanced around and seemed unable to move, and then as that boulder turned over and started to fall, they scattered like sheep.

At the same instant, Orrin lifted his rifle and put a bullet into the brush ahead of their horses. One of the broncs reared up and as Orrin fired again, he jerked his head and ripping off a branch of the brush, broke free and started to run, holding his head to one side to keep from tripping on the branch.

The lone horseman had come into sight, and when he stared up the mountain, I lifted my hat and waved, knowing from his fawn-colored sombrero that it was Torres. Doubtfully, he lifted a hand, unable to make us out at that distance.

One of the men started for their horses and Orrin put a bullet into the ground ahead of him and the man dove for shelter. Orrin levered another shot into the rocks where he disappeared then sat back and lighted up one of those Spanish cigars.

It was downright hot. Settling in behind some rocks I took a pull at my canteen and figured down where they were it had to be hotter than up here where we had some shade.

"I figure if those men have to walk home," Orrin said, "It might cool their tempers some."

A slow half hour passed before one of the men down below got ambitious. My rifle put a bullet so close it must have singed his whiskers and he hunkered down in the rocks. Funny part of it was, we could see them plain as day. Had we wanted to kill them we could have. And then we heard a horse coming through the trees and I walked back to meet Torres.

"What happens, *señor?*" He looked sharply from Orrin to me.

"Looks like you were expected. Orrin and me were hunting a place for ourselves and we found some tracks, and when we followed them up there were five men down there." I showed him where. Then I explained our idea about the horses and he agreed.

"It will be for me to do, *señor.*"

He went off down the slope and after awhile I saw him come out of the trees, untie the horses and run them off.

When Torres rode back Orrin came up to join us. "It is much you have done for me," Torres said. "I shall not forget."

"It is nothing," I said, "one of them is Reed Carney."

"*Gracias, Señor* Sackett," Torres said. "I believed I was safe so far from the hacienda, but a man is safe nowhere."

Riding back toward Mora I kept still and let Orrin and Torres get acquainted. Torres was a solid man and I knew Orrin would like him, and Torres liked people, so the contrary was true.

Torres turned off toward the ranch and we rode on into Mora. We got down in front of the saloon and strolled inside. It took one glance to see we weren't among friends. For one thing there wasn't a Mex in the place and this was mostly a Mexican town, and there were faces I remembered from Pawnee Rock. We found a place at the bar and ordered drinks.

There must have been forty men in that saloon, a dusty, dirty lot, most of them with uncut hair over their collars, and loaded down with six-shooters and bowie knives. Fetterson was at the other end of the bar but hadn't seen us.

We finished our drinks and edged toward the door and then we came face to face with Red . . . the one my horse had knocked down at Pawnee Rock.

He started to open his mouth, but before he could say a word, Orrin clapped him on the shoulder. "Red! You old sidewinder! Come on outside and let's talk!"

Now Red was a slow-thinking man and he blinked a couple of times, trying to decide what Orrin was talking about, and we had him outside before he could yell. He started to yell but Orrin whooped with laughter and slapped Red on the back so hard it knocked all the breath out of him.

Outside the door I put my knife against his ribs

and he lost all impulse to yell. I mean he steadied down some.

"Now wait a minute," he protested, "I never done you boys any harm. I was just—"

"You just walk steady," I told him, "I'm not in the mood for trouble myself. I got a backache and I don't feel up to a shooting, so don't push me."

"Who's pushing?"

"Red," Orrin said seriously, "you're the kind of a man we like to see. Handsome, upstanding ... and alive."

"Alive!" I added, "But you'd make a handsome corpse, Red."

By now we had him out in the dark and away from his friends, and he was scared, his eyes big as pesos. He looked like a treed coon in the lanternlight.

"What you goin' to do to me?" he protested. "Look, I—"

"Red," Orrin said, "There's a fair land up north, a wide and beautiful land. It's a land with running water, clear streams, and grass hip-high to a tall elk. I tell you Red, that's a country."

"And you know something, Red?" I put in my two-bits' worth. "We think you should see it."

"We surely do." Orrin was dead serious. "We're going to miss you if you go, Red. But Red, you stay and we won't miss you."

"You got a horse, Red?"

"Yeah, sure." He was looking from one to the other of us. "Sure, I got a horse."

"You'll like that country up north. Now it can get too hot here for a man, Red, and the atmosphere is heavy ... there's lead in it, you know, or liable to be. We think you should get a-straddle of that cayuse of yours, Red, and keep riding until you get to Pike's Peak, or maybe Montana."

"To—to*night*?" he protested.

"Of course. All your life you've wanted to see that country up north, Red, and you just can't wait."

"I—I got to get my outfit. I—"

"Don't do it, Red." Orrin shook his head, big-eyed.

"Don't you do it." He leaned closer. "*Vigilantes*, Red. *Vigilantes*."

Red jerked under my hand, and he wet his lips with his tongue. "Now, look here!" he protested.

"The climate's bad here, Red. A man's been known to die from it. Why, I know men that'd bet you wouldn't live to see daybreak."

We came to a nice little gray. "This your horse?"

He nodded.

"You get right up into the saddle, Red. No—keep your gun. If somebody should decide to shoot you, they'd want you to have your gun on to make it look right. Looks bad to shoot an unarmed man. Now don't you feel like traveling, Red?"

By this time Red may have been figuring things out, or maybe he never even got started. Anyway, he turned his horse into the street and went out of town at a fast canter.

Orrin looked at me and grinned. "Now there's a traveling man!" He looked more serious. "I never thought we'd get out of there without a shooting. That bunch was drinking and they would have loved to lynch a couple of us, or shoot us."

We rode back to join Cap and Tom Sunday. "About time. Tom has been afraid he'd have to go down and pull you out from under some Settlement man," Cap said.

"What do you mean . . . Settlement man?"

Jonathan Pritts has organized a company which he calls the Settlement Company. You can buy shares. If you don't have money you can buy them with your gun."

Orrin had nothing to say, he never did when Pritts' name was mentioned. He just sat down on his bed and pulled off a boot.

"You know," he said reflectively, "all that talk about the country up north convinced me. I think we should all go."

CHAPTER X

Mora lay quiet in the warm sun, and along the single street, nothing stirred. From the porch of the empty house in which we had been camping, I looked up the street, feeling the tautness that lay beneath the calm.

Orrin was asleep inside the house, and I was cleaning my .44 Henry. There was trouble building and we all knew it.

Fifty or sixty of the Settlement crowd were in town, and they were getting restless for something to do, but I had my own plans and didn't intend they should be ruined by a bunch of imported trouble makers.

Tom Sunday came out on the porch and stopped under the overhang where I was working on my rifle. He took out one of those thin black cigars and lighted up.

"Are you riding out today?"

"Out to the place," I said, "we've found us a place about eight or nine miles from here."

He paused and took the cigar from his mouth. "I want a place too, but first I want to see what happens here. A man with an education could get into politics and do all right out here." He walked on down the street.

Tom was no fool; he knew there was going to be a demand for some law in Mora, and he intended to be it. I knew he wouldn't take a back seat because of Orrin.

It worried me to think of what would happen when Orrin and Tom found out each wanted the same office, although I doubted if Orrin would mind too much.

When I finished cleaning my rifle I saddled up, put my blanket roll behind the saddle and got ready to ride out. Orrin crawled out of bed and came to the door.

"I'll be out later, or Cap will," he said. "I want to keep an eye on things here." He walked to the horse with me. "Tom say anything?"

"He wants to be marshal."

Orrin scowled. "Damn it, Tyrel, I was afraid of that. He'd probably make a better marshal than me."

"There's no telling about that, but I'd say it was a tossup, Orrin, but you can win in the election. I just hate to see you two set off against each other. Tom's a good man."

Neither one of us said anything for a while, standing there in the sun, thinking about it. It was a mighty fine morning and hard to believe so much trouble was building around us.

"I've got to talk to him," Orrin said at last, "this ain't right. We've got to level with him."

All I could think of was the fact that the four of us had been together two years now, and it had been a good period for all of us. I wanted nothing to happen to that. Friendships are not so many in this life, and we had put rough country behind us and kicked up some dust in our passing, and we had smelled a little powder smoke together and there's nothing binds men together like sweat and gunsmoke.

"You go ahead, Orrin. We'll talk to Tom tomorrow."

I wanted to be there when it was talked out, because Tom liked me and he trusted me. He and Orrin were too near alike in some ways, and too different in others. There was room enough for both of them, but I was quite sure that Tom would want to go first.

It took me a shade more than an hour to ride down to where we figured to start ranching. There were trees along the river there, and some good grass, and I bedded down at the mouth of the gap, in a corner among the rocks. Picketing Montana horse, I switched from boots to moccasins and scouted around, choosing the site for the house and the corrals.

The bench where the house was to be was only twenty feet above the river, but above the highest watermark. The cliff raised up behind the bench, and the location was a good one.

Peeling off my shirt, I worked through the afternoon clearing rocks and brush off the building site and pacing it off. Then I cut poles and began building a corral for our horses, for we would need that first of all.

Later, when dark began to come, I bathed in the creek and putting on my clothes, built a small fire and made coffee and chewed on some jerked beef.

After I'd eaten I dug into my saddlebags for a book and settled down to read. Time to time I'd get up and look around, or stand for a spell in the darkness away from the fire, just listening. By the time the fire was burning down I moved back from the fire and unrolled my bed. A bit of wind was blowing up and a few clouds had drifted over the stars.

Taking my rifle I went out to check on Montana horse who was close by. I shifted his picket pin a little closer and on fresh grass. There was a feel to the night that I didn't like, and I found myself wishing the boys would show up.

When I heard a sound it was faint, but Montana horse got it, too. His head came up and his ears pricked and his nostrils reached out for the smell of things. Putting a hand on his shoulder, I said, "All right, boy. You just take it easy."

Somebody was out there in the night, calling to me.

Now a man who goes rushing out into the night will sooner or later wind up with a bullet in his belly. Me, I circled around, scouting, and moving mighty easy. I had a sight more enemies in this country than friends.

It wasn't any time at all until I saw a standing horse, heard a low moan, and then I moved in. It was a man on the ground, and he was bad hurt.

"*Señor!*" the voice was faint. "Please . . . it is Miguel. I come to you . . . I bring you troubles."

So I scooped him off the ground and put him on his horse. "You hang on," I said. "Only a few yards."

"Men come to kill me, *señor*. It will be trouble for you."

"I'll talk to them," I said, "I'll read 'em from the Scriptures."

He passed out, but I got him to camp and unloaded him. He was shot all right. He'd had the hell shot out of him. There was a bullet hole in his thigh and there was another high in his right chest that had gone clean through. His clothes were soaked with blood and he was all in.

There was water by the fire so I peeled back his clothes and went to work. First off, I bathed away the blood and plugged the holes to stop the bleeding. Come daylight, if he made it, I was going to have to do more.

With the tip of my bowie I slit the hide and eased a bullet out from under the skin of his back, then bathed the wound and fixed it up as best I could. I could hear riders working their way down the country, a-hunting him. Sooner or later they'd see the reflection of my fire and then I'd have to take care of that.

Moving Miguel back out of the firelight, I got him stashed away when I heard them coming, and they came with a rush.

"Hello, the fire!"

"You're talking. Speak your piece."

"We're hunting a wounded greaser. You seen him?"

"I've seen him and he's here, but you can't have him."

They rode up to the fire then and I stepped up to the edge of the light. Trouble was, one of those riders had a rifle and it was on me, and the range wasn't fifteen feet.

That rifle worried me. They had me sweating. A fast man on the draw can beat a man who has to think before he can fire, but that first shot better be good.

"It's Sackett. The kid they say is a gunfighter."

"So it's Sackett." It was a sandy-haired man with two tied-down guns like one of these here show-off gunmen, "I ain't seen none of his graveyards."

"You just ride on," I said, "Miguel is here. He stays here."

"Talking mighty big, ain't you?" That man was Charley Smith, a big man, bearded and tough, hard to handle in a difficulty it was said. The one with the rifle was thin, angular, with a bobbing Adam's apple and a shooting look to him.

"He's wounded," I said, "I'll take care of him."

"We don't want him alive," Smith said. "We want him dead. You give him to us and you're out of it."

"Sorry."

"That's all right," Sandy said, "I like it this way. I prefer it this way."

That Sandy didn't worry me as much as the man with the rifle. Although the chances were that Sandy had practiced some with those guns. Even a show-off may be pretty fast, and I had that to think about.

Of one thing I was sure. There was no talking my way out of this. I could stand by and see them kill Miguel or I could fight them.

Now I'm not a smoking man myself, but Miguel's makings had fallen from his pocket and I'd picked them up, so I got them out and started to roll a smoke and while I talked I went right on building that smoke.

What I needed was an edge, and I needed it bad. There was the man with the rifle and Charley Smith and there was this Sandy lad who fancied himself with six-shooters. There might be more back in the dark but those three I had to think about.

"Miguel," I said, and I was talking for time, "is a good man. I like him. I wouldn't interfere in any fight of his, but on the other hand, I don't like to see a wounded man shot without a chance, either."

Smith was the cagey one. He was looking around. I

guessed Smith was worried about Orrin. He knew we
were a team, and he knew there was four of us, and
there might be, just might be, somebody out there in
the dark.

Now I was doing some serious thinking. A man
who holds a gun on somebody is all keyed up and
ready to shoot when he first gets the drop on you, but
after awhile his muscles get a little heavy, and his
reactions will be a little slower. Moreover, these fel-
lows outnumbered me three to one. They had the
advantage, so they just didn't think anybody would
be fool enough to tackle them. That there was against
them too. It sort of made them relax mentally, if you
get what I mean.

Only any move I made must be timed just right
and I had to slicker them into thinking of something
else.

If they killed Miguel when he was wounded in my
camp, I'd never feel right again . . . even if I lived.

"Miguel," Smith said, "is one of Alvarado's men.
We're running them out."

"Where's your brother?" The man with the rifle was
asking. He'd had some of his attention on the shadows
out there. In his place I'd have been giving them
plenty of thought.

"He's around. Those boys are never far off."

"Only one bed." That was Sandy shooting off his fat
mouth. "I can see it." That was the man with the two
big pistols who wanted to kill me. He could make it
sound mighty big, later.

Charley Smith was going to kill me because he
didn't want anybody around taking a shot at him
later.

Putting that cigarette between my lips I stooped
down and picked up a burning twig to light it. I
lifted it to my cigarette, holding it in my fingers while
I had my say.

"The four of us," I said, "never spread out very far.
We work together, we fight together, and we can win
together."

"They ain't around," Sandy-boy said, "only one bed, only his horse and the greaser's."

Up on the hills there was a stirring in the pines and because I'd been hearing it all evening I knew it was a wind along the ridge, but they stopped talking to listen.

"I'm a Sackett," I said conversationally, "out of Tennessee. We finished a feud a couple of years ago ... somebody from the other outfit shot a Sackett and we killed nineteen Higginses in the next sixteen years. Never stop huntin'. I got a brother named Tell Sackett ... best gunshot ever lived."

I was just talking, and the twig was burning. Charley Smith saw it. "Hey!" he said. "You'll burn—!"

The fire touched my fingers and I yelped with pain and dropped the twig and with the same continuing movement I drew my gun and shot that rifleman out of the saddle.

Sandy was grabbing iron when I swung my gun on him and thumbed my hammer twice so it sounded like one shot and he went backwards off his horse like he'd been hit with an axe.

Swinging my gun on Smith I saw him on the ground holding his belly and Tom Sunday came riding up with a Henry rifle.

"Smartest play I ever saw," he said, watching Smith on the ground. "When I saw you lighting up I knew there had to be something . . . knowing you didn't smoke."

"Thanks, you sure picked a good time to ride up."

Sunday got down and walked over to the man who'd held the rifle. He was dead with a shot through the heart and Sandy had taken two bullets through the heart also. Sunday glanced at me. "I saw it but I still don't believe it."

Thumbing shells into my gun I walked over to Miguel. He was up on one elbow, his face whiter than I'd have believed and his eyes bigger. *"Gracias, amigos,"* he whispered.

"Orrin told me you'd come out here and I was restless so I figured I'd ride out and camp with you.

When I saw you in the middle of them I was trying to figure out what to do that wouldn't start them shooting at you. Then you did it."

"They'd have killed us."

"Pritts will take your helping Miguel as a declaration of war."

There was more sound out in the darkness and we pulled back out of the light of the fire. It was Cap Rountree and two of Alvarado's hands. One of them was Pete Romero, but the other was a man I didn't know.

He was a slim, knifelike man in a braided leather jacket, the most duded-up man I ever saw, but his pearl-handled six-shooter was hung for business and he had a look in his eyes that I didn't like.

His name was Chico Cruz.

Cruz walked over to the bodies and looked at them. He took out a silver dollar and placed it over the two bullet holes in Sandy's chest. He pocketed the dollar and looked at us.

"Who?"

Sunday jerked his head to indicate me. "His . . . and that one too." He indicated the man with the rifle. Then he explained what had happened, not mentioning the burning twig, but the fact that I'd been covered by the rifle.

Cruz looked at me carefully and I had a feeling this was a man who enjoyed killing and who was proud of his ability with a gun. He squatted by the fire and poured a cup of coffee. It was old coffee, black and strong. Cruz seemed to like it.

Out in the darkness, helping Romero get Miguel into the saddle, I asked, "Who's he?"

"From Mexico. Torres sent for heem. He is a bad man. He has kill many times."

Cruz looked to me like one of those sleek prairie rattlers who move like lightning and kill just as easily, and there was nothing about him that I liked. Yet I could understand the don sending for him. The don was up against a fight for everything he had. It worried him, and he knew he was getting old, and he was no longer sure that he could win.

When I came back to the fire, Chico Cruz looked up at me. "It was good shooting," he said, "but I can shoot better."

Now I'm not a man to brag, but how much better can you get?

"Maybe," I said.

"Someday we might shoot together," he said, looking at me through the smoke of his cigarette.

"Someday," I said quietly, "we might."

"I shall look forward to it, *señor*."

"And I," I smiled at him, "I shall look back upon it."

CHAPTER XI

We expected trouble from Pritts but it failed to show up. Orrin came out to the place and with a couple of men Don Luis loaned us and help from Cap and Tom we put a house together. It was the second day, just after work finished when we were setting around the fire that Orrin told Tom Sunday he was going after the marshal's job.

Sunday filled his cup with coffee. His mouth stiffened up a little, but he laughed. "Well, why not? You'd make a good marshal, Orrin ... if you get the job."

"I figured you wanted it ... " Orrin started to say, then his words trailed off as Tom Sunday waved a hand.

"Forget it. The town needs somebody and whoever gets it will do a job. If I don't get it and you do, I'll lend a hand ... I promise that. And if I get it, you can help me."

Orrin looked relieved, and I knew he was, because he had been worried about it. Only Cap looked over his coffee cup at Tom and made no comment, and Cap was a knowing man.

Nobody needed to be a fortuneteller to see what was happening around town. Every night there were drunken brawls in the street, and a man had been murdered near Elizabethtown, and there had been robberies near Cimarron. It was just a question of how long folks would put up with it.

Meanwhile we went on working on the house, got two rooms of it up and Orrin and me set to making furniture for them. We finished the third room on the house and then Orrin and me rode with Cap over to the Grant where we bought fifty head of young stuff

102

and drove it back and through the gap where we branded the cattle and turned them loose.

Working hard like we had, I'd not seen much of Drusilla, so I decided to ride over. When I came up Antonio Baca and Chico Cruz were standing at the gate, and I could see that Baca was on duty there. It was the first time I'd seen him since the night he tried to knife me on the trail.

When I started to ride through the gate, he stopped me. "What is it you want?"

"To see Don Luis," I replied.

"He is not here."

"To see the *señorita*, then."

"She does not wish to see you."

Suddenly I was mad. Yet I knew he would like nothing better than to kill me. Also, I detected something in his manner ... he was insolent. He was sure of himself.

Was it because of Chico Cruz? Or could it be that the don was growing old and Torres could not be everywhere?

"Tell the *señorita*," I said, "that I am here. She will see me."

"It is not necessary." His eyes taunted me. "The *señorita* is not interested in such as you."

Chico Cruz moved his shoulders from the wall and walked slowly over. "I think," he said, "you had better do like he say."

There was no burned-match trick to work on them, and anyway, I wasn't looking for a fight with any of Don Luis' people. The don had troubles of his own without me adding to them. So I was about to ride off when I heard her voice.

"Tye!" She sounded so glad I felt a funny little jump inside me. "Tye, why are you waiting out there? Come in!"

Only I didn't come in, I just sat my horse and said, "Señorita, is it all right if I call here? At any time?"

"But of course, Tye!" She came to the gate and saw Baca standing there with his rifle. Her eyes flashed. "Antonio! Put that rifle down! *Señor* Sackett is our friend! He is to come and go as he wishes, do you understand?"

He turned slowly, insolently away. *"Si,"* he said, "I understand."

But when he looked at me his eyes were filled with hatred and I glanced at Cruz, who lifted a hand in a careless gesture.

When we were inside, she turned on me. "Tye, why have you stayed away? Why haven't you been to see us? Grandfather misses you. And he wanted to thank you for what you did for Juan Torres, and for Miguel."

"They were my friends."

"And you are our friend."

She looked up at me, then took my hand and led me into another room and rang a little bell.

She had grown older, it seemed, in the short time since I had last seen her. She looked taller, more composed, yet she was worried too, I could see that.

"How is Don Luis?"

"Not well, Tye. My grandfather grows old. He is more than seventy, you know. I do not even know how old, but surely more than that, and he finds it difficult to ride now.

"He fears trouble with your people. He has many friends among them, but most of them resent the size of the ranch. He wants only to keep it intact for me."

"It is yours."

"Do you remember Abreu?"

"Of course."

"He is dead. Pete Romero found him dead last week, ten miles from here. He had been shot in the back by someone with a Sharps buffalo gun."

"That's too bad. He was a good man."

We drank tea together, and she told me all that had been happening. Some days now it was difficult for the don to get out of bed, and Juan Torres was often off across the ranch. Some of the men had become hard to handle and lazy. Apparently, what had happened today was not the only such thing.

Don Luis was losing his grip when he needed

desperately to be strong, and his son, Drusilla's father, had long been dead.

"If there is any way that I can help, you just call on me."

She looked down at her hands and said nothing at all, and I sort of felt guilty, although there was no reason why. There was nobody I loved so much as Drusilla, but I'd never talked of love to anybody, and didn't know how to go about it.

"There's going to be trouble at Mora," I said, "it would be well to keep your men away from there."

"I know." She paused. "Does your brother see *Señorita* Pritts?"

"Not lately." I paused, uncertain of what to say. She seemed older.

So I told her about the place we had found, and thanked her for the help of the men the don had sent to help us with the adobe bricks. Then I told her about Tom Sunday and Orrin, and she listened thoughtfully. All the Mexicans were interested in the selection of the marshal, for it was of great importance to them. His authority would be local, but there was a chance he could move into the sheriff's job and in any case, the selection of a man would mean a lot to the Mexicans who traded in Mora and who lived there, as many did.

What I was saying wasn't at all what I wanted to say, and I searched for the words I wanted and they would not come. "Dru," I said suddenly, "I wish—"

She waited but all I could do was get red in the face and look at my hands. Finally, I got up, angry with myself. "I've got to be going," I said, "only—"

"Yes?"

"Can I come back? I mean, can I come to see you often?"

She looked straight into my eyes. "Yes, you can, Tye. I wish you would."

When I rode away I was mad with myself for saying nothing more. This was the girl I wanted. I was no hand with women but most likely Drusilla considered me a man who knew a lot about women, and figured if I had anything to say, that I'd say it.

She had a right to think that, for a man who won't speak his mind at a time like that is no man at all. More than likely she would think I just didn't want to say anything. If she thought of me that way at all.

That was a gloomy ride home, and had anybody been laying for me that night I'd have been shot dead I was that preoccupied. When I rode up to the house I saw Ollie's horse tied outside.

Ollie was there, along with a man who operated a supply store in Mora. His name was Wilson. "The time is now, Orrin. You've got to come in and stay in town a few days. Charley Smith and that sandy-haired man who was with him have done a lot to rile folks around town, and they were mighty impressed the way Tyrel handled them."

"That was Tyrel, not me."

"They know that, but they say you're two of a kind. Only," ... Ollie looked apologetically at me, "they don't figure you're as mean as your brother. I mean they like what happened out here, only they don't hold with killing."

Orrin glanced at him. "There wasn't another thing Tyrel could have done, and mighty few who could have done what he did."

"I know that, and you know it. The fact remains that these folks want law enforced against killers but without killing. The Mexicans ... they understand the situation better than the Americans. They know that when a man takes a weapon in hand he isn't going to put it down if you hand him a bunch of roses. Men of violence only understand violence, most times."

Orrin rode into town and for two days I stayed by the place, working around. I cleared rocks using a couple of mules and a stone boat. I dragged the rocks off and piled them where they could be used later in building a stable.

Next day I rode into town, and it looked like I'd timed things dead right. There was quite a bunch gathered outside the store Ollie was running and Ollie was on the porch, and for the first time since he came out here he had a gun where you could see it.

"It's getting so a decent person can't live in this country," he was saying. "What we need is a town marshal that will send these folks packing. Somebody we can trust to do the right thing."

He paused, and there were murmurs of agreement. "Seems to me this could be a fine, decent place to live. Most of the riffraff that cause the trouble came from Las Vegas."

Across the way on the benches I could see some of the Settlement crowd loafing and watching. They weren't worried none, it seemed like it was a laughing matter with them for they'd played top dog so long, here and elsewhere.

I went on into the saloon, and Tom Sunday was there. He glanced at me, looking sour.

"I'll buy a drink," I suggested.

"And I'll take it."

He downed the one he had and the bartender filled our glasses for us.

"You Sacketts gang up on a man," Tom declared. "Orrin's got half the town working for him. Take that Ollie Shaddock. I thought he was a friend of mine."

"He is, Tom. He likes you. Only Ollie's sort of a cousin of ours and came from the same country back in the mountains. Ollie's been in politics all his life, Tom, and he's been wanting Orrin to have a try at it."

Tom said nothing for a little while, and then he said, "If a man is going to get any place in politics he has to have education. This won't help Orrin a bit."

"He's been studying, Tom."

"Like that fool Pritts girl. All she could see was Orrin. She never even looked at you or me."

"Womenfolks pay me no mind, Tom."

"They sure gave you all their attention in Santa Fe."

"That was different." He needed cheering up, so for

the first time I told him—or anybody—of what happened that day. He grinned in spite of himself.

"No wonder. Why, that story would have been all over town within an hour." He chuckled. "Orrin was quite put out."

He tossed off his drink. "Well, if he can make it, more power to him."

"No matter what, Tom," I said, "the four of us should stick together."

He shot me a hard glance and said, "I always liked you, Tye, from the first day you rode up to the outfit. And from that day I knew you were poison mean in a difficulty."

He filled his glass. I wanted to tell him to quit but he was not a man to take advice and particularly from a younger man.

"Why don't you ride back with me?" I suggested. "Cap should be out there, and we could talk it up a little."

"What are you trying to do? Get me out of town so Orrin will have a clear field?"

Maybe I got a little red around the ears. I hadn't thought anything of the kind. "Tom, you know better than that. Only if you want that job, you'd better lay off the whiskey."

"When I want your advice," he said coolly, "I'll ask for it."

"If you feel like it," I said, "ride out. I'm taking Ma out today."

He glanced at me and then he said, "Give her my best regards, Tye. Tell her I hope she will be happy there." And he meant it, too.

Tom was a proud man, but a gentleman, and a hard one to figure. I watched him standing there by the bar and remembered the nights around the campfire when he used to recite poetry and tell us stories from the works of Homer. It gave me a lost and lonely feeling to see trouble building between us, but pride and whiskey are a bad combination, and I figured it was the realization that he might not get the marshal's job that was bothering him.

"Come out, Tom, Ma will want to see you. We've talked of you so much."

He turned abruptly and walked out the door, leaving me standing there. On the porch he paused.

Some of the settlement gang were gathered around, maybe six or eight of them, the Durango Kid and Billy Mullin right out in front. And the Durango Kid sort of figured himself as a gunman.

More than anything I wanted Tom Sunday to go home and sleep it off or to ride out to our place. I knew he was on edge, in a surly mood, and Tom could be hard to get along with.

Funny thing. Ollie had worked hard to prepare the ground work all right, and Orrin had a taking way with people, and the gift of blarney if a man ever had it.

It was a funny thing that with all of that, it was Tom Sunday who elected Orrin to the marshal's job.

He did it that day there in the street. He did it right then, walking out of that door onto the porch. He was a proud and angry man, and he had a few drinks under him, and he walked right out of the door and faced the Durango Kid.

It might have been anybody. Most folks would have avoided him when he was like that, but the Kid was hunting notches for his gun. He was a lean, narrow-shouldered man of twenty-one who had a reputation for having killed three or four men up Colorado way. It was talked around that he had rustled some cows and stolen a few horses and in the Settlement outfit he was second only to Fetterson.

Anything might have happened and Tom Sunday might have gone by, but the Durango Kid saw he had been drinking and figured he had an edge. He didn't know Tom Sunday like I did.

"He wants to be marshal, Billy," the Durango Kid said it just loud enough, "I'd like to see that."

Tom Sunday faced him. Like I said, Tom was tall, and he was a handsome man, and drinking or not, he walked straight and stood straight. Tom had been an officer in the Army at one time, and that was how he looked now.

"If I become marshal," he spoke coolly, distinctly, "I shall begin by arresting you. I know you are a thief and a murderer. I shall arrest you for the murder of Martin Abreu."

How Tom knew that, I don't know, but a man needed no more than to look at the Kid's face to know Tom had called it right.

"You're a liar!" the Kid yelled. He grabbed for his gun.

It cleared leather, but the Durango Kid was dead when it cleared. The range was not over a dozen feet and Tom Sunday—I'd never really seen him draw before—had three bullets into the Kid with one rolling sound.

The Kid was smashed back. He staggered against the water trough and fell, hitting the edge and falling into the street.

Billy Mullin turned sharply. He didn't reach for a gun, but Tom Sunday was a deadly man when drinking. That sharp movement of Billy's cost him, because Tom saw it out of the tail of his eye and he turned and shot Billy in the belly.

I'm not saying I mightn't have done the same. I don't think I would have, but a move like that at a time like that from a man known to be an enemy of Tom's and a friend to the Kid ... well, Tom shot him.

That crowd across the street saw it. Ollie saw it. Tom Sunday killed the Durango Kid, and Billy Mullin was in bed for a couple of months and was never the same man again after that gunshot ... but Tom Sunday shot himself right out of consideration as a possible marshal.

The killing of the Kid ... well, they all knew the Kid had it coming, but the shooting of Billy Mullin, thief and everything else that he was, was so offhand that it turned even Tom's friends against him.

It shouldn't have. There probably wasn't a man across the street who mightn't have done the same thing.

It was a friend of Tom's who turned his back on him that day and said, "Let's talk to Orrin Sackett about that job."

Tom Sunday heard it, and he thumbed shells into his gun and walked down the middle of the street toward the house where he'd been sharing with Orrin, Cap, and me when we were in Mora.

And that night, Tom Sunday rode away.

CHAPTER XII

Come Sunday we drove around to the house where Ma was living with the two boys and we helped her out to the buckboard. Ma was all slicked out in her Sunday-go-to-meeting clothes—which meant she was dressed in black—and all set to see her new home for the first time.

Orrin, he sat in the seat alongside her to drive, and Bob and Joe, both mounted up on Indian ponies, they brought up the rear. Cap and me, we led off.

Cap didn't say much, but I think he had a deep feeling about what we were doing. He knew how much Orrin and me had planned for this day, and how hard we had worked. Behind that rasping voice and cold way of his I think there was a lot of sentiment in Cap, although a body would never know it.

It was a mighty exciting thing at that, and we were glad the time of year was right, for the trees were green, and the meadows green, and the cattle feeding there ... well, it looked mighty fine. And it was a good deal better house than Ma had ever lived in before.

We started down the valley, and we were all dressed for the occasion, each of us in black broadcloth, even Cap. Ollie was going to be there, and a couple of other friends, for we'd sort of figured to make it a housewarming.

The only shadow on the day was the fact that Tom Sunday wasn't there, and we wished he was ... all of us wished it.

Tom had been one of us so long, and if Orrin and me were going to amount to something, part of the credit had to be Tom's, because he took time to teach us things, and especially me.

When we drove up through the trees, after dipping through the river, we came into our own yard and right away we saw there were folks all around, there must have been fifty people.

The first person I saw was Don Luis, and beside him, Drusilla, looking more Irish today, than Spanish. My eyes met hers across the heads of the crowd and for an instant there we were together like we had never been, and I longed to ride to her and claim her for my own.

Juan Torres was there, and Pete Romero, and Miguel. Miguel was looking a little pale around the gills yet, but he was on his own feet and looked great.

There was a meal all spread out, and music started up, and folks started dancing a fandango or whatever they call it, and Ma just sat there and cried. Orrin, he put his arm around her and we drove all the rest of the way into the yard that way, and Don Luis stepped up and offered Ma his hand, and mister, it did us proud to see her take his hand and step down, and you'd have thought she was the grandest lady ever, and not just a mountain woman from the hills back of nowhere.

Don Luis escorted her to a chair like she was a queen, and the chair was her own old rocker, and then Don Luis spread a serape across her knees, and Ma was home.

It was quite a shindig. There was a grand meal, with a whole steer barbecued, and three or four *javelinas*, plenty of roasting ears, and all a man could want. There was a little wine but no drinking liquor. That was because of Ma, and because we wanted it to be nice for her.

Vicente Romero himself, he was there, and a couple of times I saw Chico Cruz in the crowd.

Everybody was having themselves a time when a horse splashed through the creek and Tom Sunday rode into the yard. He sat his horse looking around, and then Orrin saw him and Orrin walked over.

"Glad you could make it, Tom. It wouldn't have been right without you. Get down and step up to the table, but first come and speak to Ma. She's been asking for you."

That was all. No words, no explanations. Orrin was that way, though. He was a big man in more ways than one, and he liked Tom, and had wanted him there.

We had a fiddle going for the dancing, and Orrin took his old gee-tar and sang up some songs, and Juan Torres sang, and we had us a time. And I danced with Dru.

When I went up to her and asked her to dance, she looked right into my eyes and accepted, and then for a minute or two we danced together and we didn't say much until pausing for a bit when I looked at her and said, "I could dance like this forever ... with you."

She looked at me and said, her eyes sparkling a little, "I think you'd get very hungry!"

Ollie was there and he talked to Don Luis, and he talked to Torres, and he got Torres and Jim Carpenter together, and got them both with Al Brooks. They talked it over, and Torres said the Mexicans would support Orrin, and right then and there, Orrin got the appointment.

Orrin, he walked over to me and we shook hands. "We did it, Tyrel," Orrin said, "we did it. Ma's got herself a home and the boys will have a better chance out here."

"Without guns, I hope."

Orrin looked at me. "I hope so, too. Times are changing, Tyrel."

The evening passed and folks packed into their rigs or got back into the saddle and everybody went home, and Ma went inside and saw her house.

We'd bought things, the sort of things Ma would like, and some we'd heard her speak of. An old grandfather's clock, a real dresser, some fine tables and chairs, and a big old four-poster bed. The house only had three rooms, but there would be more—and we boys had slept out so much we weren't fit for a house, anyway.

I walked to her carriage with Dru, and we stood there by the wheel. "I've been happy today," I told her.

"You have brought your mother home," she said. "It is a good thing. My grandfather admires you very much, Tye. He says you are a thoughtful son and a good man."

Watching Dry drive away in that carriage it made me think of money again. It's a high card in a man's hand when he goes courting if he has money, and I had none of that. True, the place we had, belonged to Orrin and me but there was more to it than that. Land wasn't of much value those days nor even cattle. And cash money was almighty scarce.

Orrin was going to be busy, so the money question was my chore.

Orrin, he worked hard studying Blackstone. From somewhere he got a book by Montaigne and he read Plutarch's *Lives*, and subscribed to a couple of eastern papers, and he read all the political news he could find, and he rode around and talked to folks or listened to them tell about their troubles. Orrin was a good listener who was always ready to give a man a hand at whatever he was doing.

That was after. That was after the first big night when Orrin showed folks who was marshal of Mora. That was the night he took over, the night he laid down the law. And believe you me, when Orrin takes a-hold, he takes a-hold.

At sundown, Orrin came up the street wearing the badge, and the Settlement men were around, taking their time to look him over. Having a marshal was a new thing in town and to the Settlement outfit it was a good joke. They just wanted to see him move around so they could decide where to lay hold of him.

The first thing Orrin done was walk through the saloon to the back door and on the inside of the back door he tacked up a notice. Now that notice was in plain sight and what was printed there was in both Spanish and English.

No gun shall be drawn or fired within the town limits.

No brawling, fighting or boisterous conduct will be tolerated.

Drunks will be thrown in jail.

Repeat offenders will be asked to leave town.

No citizen will be molested in any way.

Racing horses or riding steers in the street is prohibited.

Every resident or visitor will be expected to show visible means of support on demand.

That last rule was pointed right at the riffraff which hung around the streets, molesting citizens, picking fights, and making a nuisance of themselves. They were a bad lot.

Bully Ben Baker had been a keel-boat man on the Missouri and the Platte and was a noted brawler. He was several inches taller than Orrin, weighed two hundred and forty pounds, and Bully Ben decided to find what the new marshal was made of.

Bully Ben wasted no time. He walked over to the notice, read it aloud, then ripped it from the door.

Orrin got to his feet.

Ben reached around, grinning cheerfully, and took a bottle from the bar, gripping it by the neck.

Orrin ignored him, picked up the notice and replaced it on the door, and then he turned around and hit Ben Baker in the belly.

When Orrin had gone by him and replaced the notice, Bully Ben had waited to see what would happen. He had lowered his bottle, for he was a man accustomed to lots of rough talk before fighting, and Orrin's punch caught him off guard right in the pit of the stomach and he gasped for breath, his knees buckling.

Coolly, Orrin hit him a chopping blow to the chin that dropped Ben to his knees. The unexpected attack was the sort of thing Ben himself had often done but he was not expecting it from Orrin.

Ben came up with a lunge, swinging his bottle and I could have told him he was a fool. Blocking the

descending blow with his left forearm, Orrin chopped
that left fist down to Ben's jaw. Deliberately then, he
grabbed the bigger man and threw him with a rolling
hip-lock. Ben landed heavily and Orrin stood back
waiting for him to get up.

All this time Orrin had acted mighty casual, like he
wasn't much interested. He was just giving Bully Ben
a whipping without half trying.

Ben was mighty shook up and he was astonished
too. The blood was dripping from a cut on his jaw-
bone and he was stunned, but he started to get up.

Orrin let him get up and when Ben threw a punch,
Orrin grabbed his wrist and threw him over his shoulder with a flying mare. This time Baker got up more
slowly, for he was a heavy man and he had hit hard.
Orrin waited until he was halfway to his feet and
promptly knocked him down.

Ben sat on the floor staring up at Orrin. "You're a
fighter," he said, "you pack a wallop in those fists."

The average man in those years knew little of
fist-fighting. Men in those days, except such types as
Bully Ben, never thought of fighting with anything
other than a gun. Ben had won his fights because he
was a big man, powerful, and had acquired a rough
skill on the river boats.

Pa had taught us and taught us well. He was skilled
at Cornish-style wrestling and he'd learned fist-
fighting from a bare-knuckle boxer he'd met in his
travels.

Ben was a mighty confused man. His strength was
turned against him, and everything he did, Orrin had
an answer for. On a cooler night Orrin would never
have worked up a sweat.

"You had enough?" Orrin asked.

"Not yet," Ben said, and got up.

Now that was a mighty foolish thing, a sadly foolish
thing, because until now, Orrin had been teaching
him. Now Orrin quit fooling. As Ben Baker straight-
ened up, Orrin hit him in the face with both fists
before Ben could get set. Baker made an effort to
rush and holding him with his left, Orrin smashed

three wicked blows to his belly, then pushed Ben off and broke his nose with an overhand right. Ben backed up and sat down and Orrin grabbed him by the hair and picking him off the floor proceeded to smash three or four blows into his face, then Orrin picked Ben up, shoved him against the bar and said, "Give him a drink." He tossed a coin on the bar and walked out.

Looked to me like Orrin was in charge.

After that there was less trouble than a man would expect. Drunks Orrin threw in jail and in the morning he turned them out.

Orrin was quick, quiet, and he wasted no time talking. By the end of the week he had jailed two men for firing guns in the town limits and each had been fined twenty-five dollars and costs. Both had been among the crowd at Pawnee Rock and Orrin told them to get out of town or go to work.

Bob and me rode down to Ruidoso with Cap Rountree and picked up a herd of cattle I'd bought for the ranch, nigh onto a hundred head.

Ollie Shaddock hired a girl to work in his store and he devoted much of his time to talking about Orrin. He went down to Santa Fe, over to Cimarron and Elizabethtown, always on business, but each time he managed to say a few words here and there about Orrin, each time mentioning him for the legislature.

After a month of being marshal in Mora there had been no killings, only one knifing, and the Settlement crowd had mostly moved over to Elizabethtown or to Las Vegas. Folks were talking about Orrin all the way down to Socorro and Silver City.

On the Grant there had been another killing. A cousin of Abreu's had been shot ... from the back. Two of the Mexican hands had quit to go back to Mexico.

Chico Cruz had killed a man in Las Vegas. One of the Settlement crowd.

Jonathan Pritts came up to Mora with his daughter and he bought a house there.

It was two weeks after our housewarming before I

got a chance to go see Dru. She was at the door to meet me and took me in to see her grandfather. He looked mighty frail, lying there in bed.

"It is good to see you, *señor*," he said, almost whispering. "How is your ranch?"

He listened while I told him about it and nodded his head thoughtfully. We had three thousand acres of graze, and it was well-watered. A small ranch by most accounts.

"It is not enough," he said, at last, "to own property in these days. One must be strong enough to keep it. If one is not strong, then there is no hope."

"You'll be on your feet again in no time," I said.

He smiled at me, and from the way he smiled, he knew I was trying to make him feel good. Fact was, right at that time I wouldn't have bet that he'd live out the month.

Jonathan Pritts, he told me, was demanding a new survey of the Grant, claiming that the boundaries of the Grant were much smaller than the land the don claimed. It was a new way of getting at him and a troublesome one, for those old Grants were bounded by this peak or that ridge or some other peak, and the way they were written up a man could just about pick his own ridges and his own peak. If Pritts could get his own surveyor appointed they would survey Don Luis right out of his ranch, his home, and everything.

"There is going to be serious trouble," he said at last. "I shall send Drusilla to Mexico to visit until it is over."

Something seemed to go out of me right then. If she went to Mexico she would never come back because the don was not going to win his fight. Jonathan Pritts had no qualms, and would stop at nothing.

I sat there with my hat in my hand wishing I could say something, but what did I have to offer a girl like Drusilla? I was nigh to broke. Right then I was wondering what we could do for operating expenses, and it was no time to talk marriage to a girl, even if she would listen to me, when that girl was used to more than I could ever give her.

At last the don reached for my hand, but his grip was feeble. "*Señor*, you are like a son to me. We have seen too little of you, Drusilla and I, but I have found much in you to respect, and to love. I am afraid, *señor*, that I have not long, and I am the last of my family. Only Drusilla is left. If there is anything you can do, *señor*, to help her ... take care of her, *señor*."

"Don Luis, I'd like ... I mean ... I don't have any money, Don Luis. Right now I'm broke. I must get money to keep my ranch working."

"There are other things, my son. You have strength, and you have youth, and those are needed now. If I had the strength. ..."

Drusilla and I sat at the table together in the large room, and the Indian woman served us. Looking down the table at her my heart went out to her, I wanted her so. Yet what could I do? Always there was something that stood between us.

"Don Luis tells me you are going to Mexico?"

"He wishes it. There is trouble here, Tye."

"What about Juan Torres?"

"He is not the same ... something has happened to him, and I believe he is afraid now."

Chico Cruz ...

"I will miss you."

"I do not want to go, but what my grandfather tells me to do, I must do. I am worried for him, but if I go perhaps he will do what must be done."

"Any way I can help?"

"No!" She said it so quickly and sharply that I knew what she meant. What had to be done we both knew: Chico Cruz must be discharged, fired, sent away. But Dru was not thinking of the necessity, she was thinking of me, and she was afraid for me.

Chico Cruz ...

We knew each other, that one and I, and we each had a feeling about the other.

If this had to be done, then I would do it myself.

There was no hope that the Don would recover in time, for we both knew that when we parted tonight we might not meet again. Don Luis did not have the strength, and his recovery would take weeks, or even months.

What was happening here I understood. Torres was afraid of Cruz and the others knew it, so their obedience was half-hearted. There was no leader here, and it was nothing Cruz had done or needed to do. I doubted if he had thought of it . . . it was simply the evil in him and his willingness to kill.

Whatever was to be done must be done now, at once, so as we ate and talked I was thinking it out. This was nothing for Orrin, Cap, or anyone but me, and I must do it tonight. I must do it before this went any further.

Perhaps then she would stay, for I knew that if she ever left I would never see her again.

At the door I took her hand . . . it was the first time I had found courage to do it. "Dru . . . do not worry. I will come to see you again." Suddenly, I said what I had been thinking. "Dru . . . I love you."

And then I walked swiftly away, my heels clicking on the pavement as I crossed the court. But I did not go to my horse, but to the room of Juan Torres.

It seemed strange that a man could change so in three years since we had met. Three years? He had changed in months. And I knew that Cruz had done this, not by threats, not by warnings, just by the constant pressure of his being here.

"Juan . . . ?"

"Señor?"

"Come with me. We are going to fire Chico Cruz."

He sat very still behind the table and looked at me, and then he got up slowly.

"You think he will go?"

He looked at me, his eyes searching mine. And I told him what I felt. "I do not care whether he goes or stays."

We walked together to the room of Antonio Baca.

He was playing cards with Pete Romero and some others.

We paused outside and I said, "We will start here. You tell him."

Juan hesitated only a minute, and then he stepped into the room and I followed. "Baca, you will saddle your horse and you will leave ... do not come back."

Baca looked at him, and then he looked at me, and I said, "You heard what Torres said. You tried it once in the dark when my back was turned. If you try it now you will not be so lucky."

He put his cards into a neat, compact pile, and for the first time he seemed at a loss. Then he said, "I will talk to Chico."

"We will talk to Chico. You will go." Taking out my watch, I said, "Torres has told you. You have five minutes."

We turned and went down the row of rooms and stopped before one that was in the dark. Torres struck a light and lit a lantern. He held the light up to the window and I stepped into the door.

Chico Cruz had been sitting there in the darkness. Torres said, "We don't need you any longer, Chico, you can go ... now."

He looked at Torres from his dark, steady eyes and then at me.

"There is trouble here," I said, "and you do not make it easier."

"You are to make me go?" His eyes studied me carefully.

"It will not be necessary. You will go."

His left hand and arm were on the table, toying with a .44 cartridge. His right hand was in his lap.

"I said one day that we would meet."

"That's fool talk. Juan has said you are through. There is no job for you here, and the quarters are needed."

"I like it here."

"You will like it elsewhere." Torres spoke sharply. His courage was returning. "You will go now ... tonight."

Cruz ignored him. His dark, steady eyes were on me. "I think I shall kill you, *señor*."

"That's fool talk," I said casually and swung my boot up in a swift, hard kick at the near edge of the table. It flipped up and he sprang back to avoid it and tripped, falling back to the floor. Before he could grasp a gun I kicked his hand away, then grabbed him quickly by the shirt and jerked him up from the floor, taking his gun and dropping him in one swift movement.

He knew I was a man who used a gun and he expected that, but I did not want to shoot him. He clung to his wrist and stared at me, his eyes unblinking like those of a rattler.

"I told you, Cruz."

Torres walked to the bunk and began stuffing Chico's clothes into his saddlebags, and rolling his bedroll. Chico still clung to his wrist.

"If I go they will attack the hacienda," Cruz said, "is that what you want?"

"It is not. But we will risk it. We cannot risk you being here, Chico. There is an evil that comes with you."

"And not with you?" He stared at me.

"Perhaps . . . anyway, I shall not be here."

We heard the sound of a horse outside, and glanced out to see Pete Romero leading Chico's horse.

Chico walked to the door and he looked at me. "What of my gun?" he said, and swung into the saddle.

"You may need it," I said, "and I would not want you without it."

So I handed him the gun, nor did I take the shells from it. He opened the loading gate and flipped the cylinder curiously, and then he looked at me and held the gun in his palm, his face expressionless.

For several seconds we remained like that, and I don't know what he was thinking. He had reason to hate me, reason to kill me, but he held the gun in his hand and looked down at me, and my own gun remained in its holster.

He turned his horse. "I think we will never meet," he said, "I like you, *señor*."

Juan Torres and I stood there until we could hear the gallop of his horse no longer.

CHAPTER XIII

Jonathan Pritts had brought with him an instrument more dangerous than any gun. He brought a printing press.

In a country hungry for news and with a scarcity of reading material, the newspaper was going to be read, and people believe whatever they read must be true—or it would not be in print.

Most folks don't stop to think that the writer of a book or the publisher of a newspaper may have his own axe to grind, or he may be influenced by others, or may not be in possession of all the information on the subject of which he writes.

Don Luis had known about Pritts' printing press before anybody else, and that was one reason he wanted his granddaughter out of the country, for a paper can be used to stir people up. And things were not like they had been.

Don Luis sent for me again, and made a deal to sell me four thousand acres of his range that joined to mine. The idea was his, and he sold it to me on my note.

"It is enough, *señor*. You are a man of your word, and you can use the range." He was sitting up that day. He smiled at me. "Moreover, *señor*, it will be a piece of land they cannot take from me, and they will not try to take it from you."

At the same time, I bought, also on my note, three hundred head of young stuff. In both cases the notes were made payable to Drusilla.

The don was worried, and he was also smart. It was plain that he could expect nothing but trouble. Defeat had angered Jonathan Pritts, and he would never quit until he had destroyed the don or been destroyed himself.

His Settlement crowd had shifted their base to Las Vegas although some of them were around Elizabethtown and Cimarron, and causing trouble in both places. But the don was playing it smart . . . land and cattle sold to me they would not try to take, and he felt sure I'd make good, and so Drusilla would have that much at least coming to her.

These days I saw mighty little of Orrin. Altogether we had a thousand or so head on the place now, mostly young stuff that would grow into money. The way I figured, I wasn't going to sell anything for another three years, and by that time I would be in a position to make some money.

Orrin, the boys, and me, we talked it over. We had no idea of running the big herds some men were handling, or trying to hold big pieces of land. All the land I used I wanted title to, and I figured it would be best to run only a few cattle, keep from overgrazing the grass, and sell fat cattle. We had already found out we could get premium prices for cattle that were in good shape.

Drusilla was gone.

The don was a little better, but there was more trouble. Squatters had moved into a valley on the east side of his property and there was trouble. Pritts jumped in with his newspaper and made a lot more of the trouble than there had been.

Then Orrin was made sheriff of the county, and he asked Tom to become a deputy.

Now we had a going ranch and everything was in hand. We needed money, and if I ever expected to make anything of myself it was time I had at it. There was nothing to do about the ranch that the boys could not do, but I had notes to Don Luis to pay and it was time I started raising some money.

Cap Rountree rode out to the ranch. He got down from his horse and sat down on the step beside me.

"Cap," I said, "you ever been to Montana?"

"Uh-huh. Good country, lots of grass, lots of mountains, lots of Indians, mighty few folks. Except around Virginia City. They've got a gold strike up there."

"That happened some years back."

"Still working." He gave me a shrewd look out of those old eyes. "You gettin' the itch, too?"

"Need money. We're in debt, Cap, and I never liked being beholden to anybody. Seems to me we might strike out north and see what we can find. You want to come along?"

"Might's well. I'm gettin' the fidgets here."

So we rode over to see Tom Sunday. Tom was drinking more than a man should. He had bought a ranch for himself about ten miles from us. He had him some good grass, a fair house, but it was a rawhide outfit, generally speaking, and not at all like Tom was who was a first-rate cattleman.

"I'll stay here," he told me finally. "Orrin offered me a job as deputy sheriff, but I'm not taking it. I think I'll run for sheriff myself, next election."

"Orrin would like to have you," I said. "It's hard to get good men."

"Hell," Tom said harshly, "he should be working for me. By rights that should be my job."

"Maybe. You had a chance at it."

He sat down at the table and stared moodily out the window.

Cap got to his feet. "Might's well come along," he said, "if you don't find any gold you'll still see some fine country."

"Thanks," he said, "I'll stay here."

We mounted up and Tom put a hand on my saddle. "Tye," he said, "I've got nothing against you. You're a good man."

"So's Orrin, Tom, and he likes you."

He ignored it. "Have a good time. If you get in trouble, write me and I'll come up and pull you out of it."

"Thanks. And if you get in trouble, you send for us."

He was still standing there on the steps when we

rode away, and I looked back when I could barely make him out, but he was still standing there.

"Long as I've known him, Cap," I said, "that was the first time I ever saw Tom Sunday without a shave."

Cap glanced at me out of those cold, still eyes. "He'd cleaned his gun," he said. "He didn't forget that."

The aspen were like clusters of golden candles on the green hills, and we rode north into a changing world. "Within two weeks we'll be freezin' our ears off," Cap commented.

Nonetheless, his eyes were keen and sharp and Cap sniffed the breeze each morning like a buffalo-hunting wolf. He was a new man, and so was I. Maybe this was what I was bred for, roaming the wild country, living off it, and moving on.

In Durango we hired out and worked two weeks on a roundup crew, gathering cattle, roping and branding calves. Then we drifted west into the Abajo Mountains, sometimes called the Blues. It was a mighty big country, two-thirds of it standing on edge, seemed like. We rode through country that looked like hell with the fires out, and we camped at night among the cool pines.

Our tiny fire was the only light in a vast world of darkness, for any way we looked there was nothing but night and the stars. The smell of coffee was good, and the smell of fresh wood burning. We hadn't seen a rider for three days when we camped among the pines up there in the Blues, and we hadn't seen a track in almost as long. Excepting deer tracks, cat or bear tracks.

Out of Pioche I got a job riding shotgun for a stage line with Cap Rountree handling the ribbons. We stayed with it two months.

Only one holdup was attempted while I rode shotgun because it seemed I was a talked-about man. That one holdup didn't pan out for them because I dropped off the stage and shot the gun out of one of the outlaw's hands—it was an accident, as my foot slipped on a rock and spoiled my aim—and put two holes in the other one.

We took them back into town, and the shot one lived. He lived but he didn't learn ... six months later they caught him stealing a horse and hung him to the frame over the nearest ranch gate.

At South Pass City we holed up to wait out a storm and I read in a newspaper how Orrin was running for the state legislature, and well spoken of. Orrin was young but it was a time for young men, and he was as old as Alexander Hamilton in 1776, and older than William Pitt when he was chancellor in England. As old as Napoleon when he completed his Italian campaign.

I'd come across a book by Jomini on Napoleon, and another by Vegetius on the tactics of the Roman legions. Most of the time I read penny dreadfuls as they were all a body could find, except once in a while those paper-bound classics given away by the Bull Durham company for coupons they enclosed. A man could find those all over the west, and many a cowhand had read all three hundred and sixty of them.

We camped along the mountain streams, we fished, we hunted, we survived. Here and yonder we had a brush with Indians. One time we outran a bunch of Blackfeet, another time had a set-to with some Sioux. I got a nicked ear out of that one and Cap lost a horse, so we came into Laramie astride Montana horse, the both of us riding him.

Spring was coming and we rode north with the changing weather and staked a claim on a creek in Idaho, but nothing contented me any more. We had made our living, but little more than that. We'd taken a bunch of furs and sold out well, and I'd made a payment to Don Luis and sent some money home.

There was a two-by-four town near where we staked our claim. I mean, there was no town but a cluster of shacks and a saloon called the Rose-Marie. A big man with a square red face, sandy-red hair and small blue eyes ran the place. He laid his thick hands on the bar and you saw the scars of old fist fights there, and those little eyes studied you cruel ... like he was figuring how much you'd be worth to him.

"What'll you have, gents? Something to cut the dust?"

"Out of that bottle in the cabinet," I said, as I'd seen him take a drink out of it himself. "We'll have a shot of that bourbon."

"I can recommend the barrel whiskey."

"I bet you can. Give it to us from the bottle."

"My own whiskey. I don't usually sell it."

There were two men sitting at a back table and they were sizing us up. One thing I'd noticed about those men. They got their service without paying. I had a hunch they worked for the firm, and if they did, what did they do?

"My name is Brady," the red-haired man said, "Martin Brady."

"Good," I said, "a man should have a name." We put our money on the bar and turned to go. "You keep that bottle handy. We tried that river whiskey before."

After three days we had only a spot or two of color. Straightening up from my pick I said, "Cap, the way I hear it we should have a burro, and when the burro strays, we follow him, and when we find that burro he's pawing pay dirt right out of the ground, or you pick up a chunk to chuck at the burro and it turns out to be pure-dee gold."

"Don't you believe all you hear." He pushed his hat back. "I been lookin' the ground over. Over there," he indicated what looked like an old stream bed, "that crick flowed for centuries. If there's gold in the crick there's more of it under that bench there."

Up on the bench we cut timber and built a flume to carry water and a sluice box. Placer mining isn't just a matter of scooping up sand and washing it out in a pan. The amount of gold a man can get that way is mighty little, and most places he can do as well punching cows or riding shotgun on a stage.

The thing to do is locate some color and then choose a likely spot like this bench and sink a shaft down to bedrock, panning out that gravel that comes off the bedrock, working down to get all the cracks and to peel off any loose slabs and work the gravel gathered beneath them. Gold is heavy, and over the years it works deeper and deeper through loose earth or gravel until it reaches bedrock and can go no further.

When we started to get down beyond six feet we commenced getting some good color, and we worked all the ground we removed from there on down. Of a night I'd often sit up late reading whatever came to hand, and gradually I was learning a good bit about a lot of things.

On the next claim there was a man named Clark who loaned me several books. Most of the reading a man could get was pretty good stuff ... nobody wanted to carry anything else that far.

Clark came to our fire one night. "Cap, you make the best sourdough bread I ever ate. I'm going to miss it."

"You taking out?"

"She's deep enough, Cap, I'm leaving tomorrow. I'm going back to the States, to my wife and family. I worked in a store for six, seven years and always wanted one of my own."

"You be careful," Cap said.

Clark glanced around, then lowered his voice. "Have you heard those yarns, too? About the killings?"

"They found Wilton's body last week," I said, "he'd been buried in a shallow grave but the coyotes dug him out."

"I knew him." Clark accepted another plate of beans and beef and then he said, "I believe those stories. Wilton was carrying a heavy poke, and he wasn't a man to talk it around."

He forked up some more beans, then paused. "Sackett, you've been talked up as a man who's good with a gun."

"It's exaggerated."

"If you'll ride with me I'll pay you a hundred dollars each."

"That's good money, but what about our claim?"

"This means everything to me, boys. I talked to Dickey and Wells, and they're reliable men who will watch your claim."

Cap lit up his pipe and I poured coffee for all of us. Clark just wasn't a-woofin'. Most of the miners who gambled their money away at the Rose-Marie in town had no trouble leaving. It was only those who tried to leave with their money. At least three were sitting a-top some fat pokes of gold wondering how to get out alive and still keep what they'd worked for.

"Clark," I said, "Cap and me, we need the money. We'd help even if you couldn't afford to pay."

"Believe me, it's worth it."

So I got up off the ground. "Cap, I'll just go in and have a little talk with Martin Brady."

Clark got up. "You're crazy!"

"Why, I wouldn't want him to think us deceitful, Clark, so I'll just go tell him we're riding out tomorrow. I'll also tell him what will happen if anybody bothers us."

There were thirty or forty men in the Rose-Marie when I came in. Brady came to me, drying his big hands on his apron. "We're fresh out of bourbon," he said, "you'll have to take bar whiskey."

"I just came to tell you Jim Clark is riding out of the country tomorrow and he's taking all that gold he didn't spend in here."

You could have heard a pin drop. When I spoke those words I said them out loud so everybody could hear. Brady's cigar rolled between his teeth and he got white around the eyes, but I had an eye on the two loafers at the end of the bar.

"Why tell me?" He didn't know what was coming but he knew he wouldn't like it.

"Somebody might think Clark was going alone," I said "and they might try to kill him the way Wilton and Jacks and Thompson were killed, but I figured it would be deceitful of me to ride along with

Clark and let somebody get killed trying to get his gold. You see, Clark is going to make it."

"I hope he does," Brady rolled that cigar again, those cold little eyes telling me they hated me. "He's a good man."

He started to walk away but I wasn't through with him.

"Brady?"

He turned slowly.

"Clark is going through because I'm going to see that he gets through, and when he's gone, I'm coming back."

"So?" He put his big hands on the edge of the bar. "What does that mean?"

"It means that if we have any trouble at all, I'm going to come back here and either run you out of town or bury you."

Somebody gasped and Martin Brady's face turned a kind of sick white, he was that mad.

"It sounds like you're calling me a thief." He kept both hands in plain sight. "You'd have to prove that."

"Prove it? Who to? Everybody knows what killing and robbery there has been was engineered by you. There's no court here but a six-shooter court and I'm presiding."

So nothing happened. It was like I figured and it was out in the open now, and Martin Brady had to have me killed, but he didn't dare do it right then. We put Clark on the stage and started back to our own claims.

We were almost to bedrock now and we wanted to clean up and get out. We were getting the itch to go back to Santa Fe and back to Mora. Besides, I kept thinking of Drusilla.

Bob Wells was sitting on our claim with a rifle across his knees when we came in. "I was gettin' spooked," he said, "it don't seem like Brady to take this layin' down."

Dickey came over from his claim and several others, two of whom I remembered from the Rose-Marie Saloon the night I told off Martin Brady.

"We been talking it around," Dickey said, "and we figure you should be marshal."

"No."

"Can you name anybody else?" Wells asked reasonably. "This gold strike is going to play out, but a few of the mines will continue to work, and I plan to stay on here. I want to open a business, and I want this to be a clean town."

The others all pitched in, and finally Dickey said, "Sackett, with all respect, I believe it's your public duty."

Now I was beginning to see where reading can make a man trouble. Reading Locke, Hume, Jefferson, and Madison, had made me begin to think mighty high of a man's public duty.

Violence is an evil thing, but when the guns are all in the hands of the men without respect for human rights, then men are really in trouble.

It was all right for folks back east to give reasons why trouble should be handled without violence. Folks who talk about no violence are always the ones who are first to call a policeman, and usually they are sure there's one handy.

"All right," I said, "on two conditions: first, that somebody else takes over when the town is cleaned up. Second, that you raise money enough to buy out Martin Brady."

"*Buy* him out? I say, run him out!"

Who it was yelled, I don't know, but I spoke right up in meeting. "All right, whoever you are. You run him out."

There was a silence then, and when they had gathered the fact that the speaker wasn't goir to offer I said, "We run him out and we're no better than he is."

"All right," Wells agreed, "buy him out."

"Well, now," I said, "we can be too hasty. I didn't say we should buy him out, what I say is we should *offer*. We make him a cash offer and whatever he does then is up to him."

Next day in town I got down from my horse in

front of the store. Wind blew dust along the street and skittered dry leaves along the boardwalk. It gave me a lonesome feeling. Looking down the street I had a feeling the town would die.

No matter what happened here, what I was going to do was important. Maybe not for this town, but for men everywhere, for there must be right. Strength never made right, and it is an indecency when it is allowed to breed corruption. The west was changing. One time they would have organized vigilantes and had some necktie parties, but now they were hiring a marshal, and the next step would be a town meeting and a judge or a mayor.

Martin Brady saw me come in. His two men standing at the bar saw me too, and one of them moved a mite so his gun could be right under his hand and not under the edge of the bar.

There was nothing jumpy inside me, just a slow, measured, waiting feeling.

Around me everything seemed clearer, sharper in detail, the shadows and lights, the grain of wood on the bar, the stains left by the glasses, a slight tic on the cheek of one of Brady's men, and he was forty feet away.

"Brady, this country is growing up. Folks are moving in and they want schools, churches, and quiet towns where they can walk in the streets of an evening."

He never took his eyes from me, and I had a feeling he knew what was coming. Right then I felt sorry for Martin Brady, although his kind would outlast my kind because people have a greater tolerance for evil than for violence. If crooked gambling, thieving, and robbing are covered over, folks will tolerate it longer than outright violence, even when the violence may be cleansing.

Folks had much to say about the evil of those years, yet it took hard men to live the life, and their pleasures were apt to be rough and violent. They came from the world around, the younger sons of fine families, the ne'er-do-wells, the soldiers of fortune, the drifters,

the always-broke, the promoters, the con men, the
thieves. The frontier asked no questions and gave its
rewards to the strong.

Maybe it needed men like Martin Brady, even the
kind who lived on murder and robbery, to plant a
town here at such a jumping-off place to nowhere. An
odd thought occurred to me. Why had he called the
saloon and the town Rose-Marie?

"Like I said, the country is growing up, Martin.
You've been selling people rot-gut liquor, you've been
cheating them out of hide an' hair, you've been robbing and murdering them. Murdering them was going
too far, Martin, because when you start killing men,
they fight back."

"What are you gettin' at, Sackett?"

"They elected me marshal."

"So?"

"You sell out, Martin Brady, they'll pay you a fair
price. You sell out, and you get out."

He took the cigar from his teeth with his left hand
and rested that hand on the bar. "And if I don't want
to sell?"

"You have no choice."

He smiled and leaned toward me as if to say something in a low tone and when he did he touched that
burning cigar to my hand.

My hand jerked and I realized the trick too late
and those gunmen down the bar, who had evidently
seen it done before, shot me full of holes.

My hand jerked and then guns were hammering. A
slug hit me and turned me away from the bar, and
two more bullets grooved the edge of the bar where
I'd been standing.

Another slug hit me and I started to fall but my
gun was out and I rolled over on the floor with bullets
kicking splinters at my eyes and shot the big one with
the dark eyes.

He was coming up to me for a finishing shot, and I
put a bullet into his brisket and saw him stop dead
still, turn half around and fall.

Then I was rolling over and on my feet and out of

the corner of my eye I saw Martin Brady standing
with both hands on the bar and his cigar in his teeth,
watching me. My shirt was smoldering where it had
caught fire from that black powder, but I shot the
other man, taking my time, and my second bullet
drove teeth back into his mouth and I saw the blood
dribble from the corner of his mouth.

They were both down and they weren't getting up
and I looked at Martin Brady and I said, "You haven't
a choice, Martin."

His face turned strange and shapeless and I felt
myself falling and remembered Ma asking me about
Long Higgins.

There were cracks in the ceiling. It seemed I lay
there staring at them for a dozen years, and remembered that it had been a long time since I'd been in a
house and wondered if I was delirious.

Cap Rountree came into the room and I turned my
head and looked at him. "If this here is hell, they sure
picked the right people for it."

"Never knew a man to find so many excuses to get
out of his work," Cap grumbled. "How much longer do
I do the work in this shebang?"

"You're an old pirate," I said, "who never did an
honest day's work in his life."

Cap came back in with a bowl of soup which he
started spooning into me. "Last time I recollect they
were shooting holes in me. Did you plug them up?"

"You'll hold soup. Only maybe all your sand run
out."

On my hand I could see the scar of that cigar burn,
almost healed now. That was one time I was sure
enough outsmarted. It was one trick Pa never told me
about, and I'd had to learn it the hard way.

"You took four bullets," Cap said, "an' lost a sight
more blood than a man can afford."

"What about Brady?"

"He lit a shuck whilst they were huntin' a rope to

hang him." Cap sat down. "Funny thing. He showed up here the next night."

"Here?"

"Stopped by to see how you was. Said you were too good a man to die like that—both of you were damned fools but a man got into a way of livin' and there was no way but to go on."

"The others?"

"Those boys of his were shot to doll rags."

Outside the door I could see the sunshine on the creek and I could hear the water chuckling over the rocks, and I got to thinking of Ma and Drusilla, and one day when I could sit up I looked over at Cap.

"Anything left out there?"

"Ain't been a day's wages in weeks. If you figure to do any more minin' you better find yourself another crick."

"We'll go home. Come morning you saddle up."

He looked at me skeptically. "Can you set a saddle?"

"If I'm going home. I can sit a saddle if I'm headed for Santa Fe."

Next morning, Cap and me headed as due south as the country would allow, but it is a long way in the saddle from Idaho to New Mexico.

From time to time we heard news about Sacketts. Men on the trail carried news along with them and everybody was on the prod to know all that was going on. The Sackett news was all Orrin ... it would take awhile for the story of what happened at Rose-Marie to get around and I'd as soon it never did. But Orrin was making a name for himself. Only there was a rumor that he was to be married.

Cap told me that because he heard it before I did and neither of us made comments. Cap felt as I did about Laura Pritts and we were afraid it was her.

We rode right to the ranch.

Bob came out to meet us, and Joe was right behind him. Ma had seen us coming up the road.

She came to the steps to meet me. Ma was better than she had been in years, a credit to few worries and a better climate, I suppose. There was a Navajo woman helping with the housework now, and for the first time Ma had it easier.

There were bookshelves in the parlor and both the boys had taken to reading.

There was other news. Don Luis was dead ... had been buried only two days ago, but already the Settlement crowd had moved in. Torres was in bad shape ... he had been ambushed months ago and from what I was told there was small chance he'd be himself again.

Drusilla was in town.

And Orrin was married to Laura Pritts.

CHAPTER XIV

Orrin came out to the ranch in the morning, driving a buckboard. He got down and came to me with his hand out, a handsome man by any standards, wearing black broadcloth now like he was born to it.

He was older, more sure of himself, and there was a tone of authority in his voice. Orrin had done all right, no doubt of that, and beneath it all he was the same man he had always been, only a better man because of the education he had given himself and the experience behind him.

"It's good to see you, boy." He was sizing me up as he talked, and I had to grin, for I knew his way.

"You've had trouble," he said suddenly, "you've been hurt."

So I told him about Martin Brady and the Rose-Marie, my brief term as marshal, and the showdown.

When he realized how close I'd come to cashing in my chips he grew a little pale. "Tyrel," he said slowly, "I know what you've been through, but they need a man right here. They need a deputy sheriff who is honest and I sure know you'd never draw on anybody without cause."

"Has somebody been saying the contrary?" I asked him quietly.

"No . . . no, of course not." He spoke hastily, and I knew he didn't want to say who, which was all the answer I needed. "Of course, there's always talk about a man who has to use a gun. Folks don't understand."

He paused. "I suppose you know I'm married?"

"Heard about it. Has Laura been out to see Ma?"

Orrin flushed. "Laura doesn't take to Ma. Says a woman smoking is indecent, and smoking a pipe is worse."

"That may be true," I replied carefully. "Out here you don't see it much, but that's Ma."

He kicked at the earth, his face gloomy. "You may think I did wrong, Tyrel, but I love that girl. She's ... she's different, Tyrel, she's so pretty, so delicate, so refined and everything. A man in politics, he needs a wife like that. And whatever else you can say about Jonathan, he's done everything he could to help me."

I'll bet, I said to myself. I'll just bet he has. And he'll want a return on it too. So far I hadn't noticed Jonathan Pritts being freehanded with anything but other folks' land.

"Orrin, if Laura suits you, and if she makes you happy, then it doesn't matter who likes her. A man has to live his own life."

Orrin walked out of the corral with me and leaned on the rail and we stood there and talked the sun out of the sky and the first stars up before we went in to dinner. He had learned a lot, and he had been elected to the legislature, and a good part of it had been the Mexican vote, but at the last minute the Pritts crowd had gotten behind him, too. He had won by a big majority and in politics a man who can command votes can be mighty important.

Already they were talking about Orrin for the United States Senate, or even for governor. Looking at him across the table as he talked to Ma and the boys, I could see him as a senator ... and he'd make a good one.

Orrin was a smart man who had grown smarter. He had no illusions about how a man got office or kept it, yet he was an honest man, seeking nothing for himself beyond what he could make in the natural way of things.

"I wanted Tom Sunday for the deputy job," Orrin said, "he turned it down, saying he didn't need any handouts." Orrin looked at me. "Tye, I didn't mean it that way. I liked Tom, and I needed a strong man here."

"Tom could have handled it," Cap said. "That's bad, Tom feelin' thataway."

Orrin nodded. "It doesn't seem right without Tom. He's changed, Cap. He drinks too much, but that's only part of it. He's like an old bear with a sore tooth, and I'm afraid there'll be a killing if it keeps up."

Orrin looked at me. "Tom always liked you. If there is anybody can keep him in line it will be you. If anybody else even tried, and that includes me, he would go for his gun."

"All right."

Miguel rode over on the second day and we talked. Drusilla did not want to see me—he'd been sent to tell me that.

"Why, Miguel?"

"Because of the woman your brother has married. The *señorita* believes the hatred of Jonathan Pritts killed her father."

"I am not my brother's keeper," I replied slowly, "nor did I choose his wife." I looked up at him. "Miguel, I love the *señorita*."

"I know, *señor*. I know."

The ranch was moving nicely. The stock we had bought had fattened out nicely, and some had been sold that year.

Bill Sexton was sheriff, and I took to him right off, but I could also see that he was an office man, built for a swivel chair and a roll-top desk.

Around Mora I was a known man, and there was mighty little trouble. Once I had to run down a couple of horse thieves, but I brought them in, without shooting, after trailing them to where they had holed up, then—after they'd turned in—I Injuned down there and got their guns before I woke them up.

Only once did I see Tom Sunday. He came into town, unshaven and looking mighty unpleasant, but when he saw me he grinned and held out his hand. We talked a few minutes and had coffee together, and it seemed like old times.

"One thing," he said, "you don't have to worry about. Reed Carney is dead."

"What happened?"

"Chico Cruz killed him over to Socorro."

It gave me a cold feeling, all of a sudden, knowing that gun-slinging Mexican was still around, and I found myself hoping that he did not come up this way.

When I'd been on the job about a week I was out to the ranch one day when I saw that shining black buckboard coming, only it wasn't Orrin driving. It was Laura.

I walked down from the steps to meet her. "How are you, Laura? It's good to see you."

"It isn't good to see you." She spoke sharply, and her lips thinned down. Right at that moment she was a downright ugly woman. "If you have any feeling for your brother, you will leave here and never come back!"

"This is my home."

"You'd better leave," she insisted, "everybody knows you're a vicious killer, and now you've wheedled the deputy's job out of Sexton, and you'll stay around here until you've ruined Orrin and me and everybody."

She made me mad so I said, "What's the difference between being a killer and hiring your killing done."

She struck at me, but I just stepped back and she almost fell out of the buckboard. Catching her arm, I steadied her, and she jerked away from me. "If you don't leave, I'll find a way to make you. You hate me and my father and if it hadn't been for you there wouldn't have been any of this trouble."

"I'm sorry. I'm staying."

She turned so sharply that she almost upset the buggy and drove away, and I couldn't help wondering if Orrin had ever seen her look like that. She wasn't like that hammer-headed roan I'd said she was like. That roan was a whole damned sight better.

Ma said nothing to me but I could see that she missed Orrin's visits, which became fewer and fewer. Laura usually contrived to have something important to do or somewhere important for him to be whenever he thought about coming out.

There was talk of rustling by Ed Fry who ranched near Tom's place, and we had several complaints about Tom Sunday. Whatever else Tom might be, he was an honest man. I got up on Kelly and rode the big red horse out to Sunday's place.

It was a rawhide outfit. I mean it the western way where a term like that is used to mean an outfit that's held together with rawhide, otherwise it would fall apart.

Tom Sunday came to the door when I rode up and he stood leaning against the doorjamb watching me tie my horse.

"That's a good horse, Tye," he said, "you always had a feeling for a good horse."

He squatted on his heels and began to build a smoke. Hunkering down beside him I made talk about the range and finally asked him about his trouble with Fry.

He stared at me from hard eyes. "Look, Tye, that's my business. You leave it alone."

"I'm the law, Tom," I said mildly. "I want to keep the peace if I can do it."

"I don't need any help and I don't want any interference."

"Look, Tom, look at it this way. I like this job. The boys do all there is to do on the ranch, so I took this job. If you make trouble for me, I may lose out."

His eyes glinted a little with sardonic humor. "Don't try to get around me, Tye. You came down here because you've been hearing stories about me and you're worried. Well, the stories are a damned lie and you know it."

"I do know it, Tom, but there's others."

"The hell with them."

"That may be all right for you, but it isn't for me. One reason I came down was to check on what's been happening, another was to see you. We four were mighty close for a long time, Tom, and we should stay that way."

He stared out gloomily. "I never did get along with

that high-and-mighty brother of yours, Tye. He always thought he was better than anybody else."

"You forget, Tom. You helped him along. You helped him with his reading, almost as much as you did me. If he is getting somewhere it is partly because of you."

I figured that would please him but it didn't seem to reach him at all. He threw his cigarette down. "I got some coffee," he said, and straightening up he went inside.

We didn't talk much over coffee, but just sat there together, and I think we both enjoyed it. Often on the drives we would ride for miles like that, never saying a word, but with a kind of companionship better than any words.

There was a book lying on the table called *Bleak House* by Charles Dickens. I'd read parts of some of Dickens' books that were run as serials in papers. "How is it?" I asked.

"Good . . . damned good."

He sat down opposite me and tasted the coffee. "Seems a long time ago," he said gloomily, "when you rode up to our camp outside of Baxter Springs."

"Five years," I agreed. "We've been friends a long time, Tom. We missed you, Cap and me, on this last trip."

"Cap and you are all right. It's that brother of yours I don't like. But he'll make it all right," he added grudgingly, "he'll get ahead and make the rest of us look like bums."

"He offered you a job. That was the deal: if you won you were to give him a job, if he won he would give you a job."

Tom turned sharply around. "I don't need his damned job! Hell, if it hadn't been for me he'd never have had the idea of running for office!"

Now that wasn't true but I didn't want to argue, so after awhile I got up and rinsed out my cup. "I'll be riding. Come out to the house and see us, Tom. Cap would like to see you and so would Ma." Then I added, "Orrin isn't there very much."

Tom's eyes glinted. "That wife of his. You sure had her figured right. Why, if I ever saw a double-crossing no-account female, she's the one. And her old man . . . I hate his guts."

When I stepped into the saddle I turned for one last word. "Tom, stay clear of Ed Fry, will you? I don't want trouble."

"You're one to talk." He grinned at me. "All right, I'll lay off, but he sticks in my craw."

Then as I rode away, he said, "My respects to your mother, Tye."

Riding away I felt mighty miserable, like I'd lost something good out of my life. Tom Sunday's eyes had been bloodshot, he was unshaven and he was careless about everything but his range. Riding over it, I could see that whatever else Tom might be, he was still a first-rate cattleman. Ed Fry and some of the others had talked of Tom's herds increasing, but by the look of things it was no wonder, for there was good grass, and he was keeping it from overgrazing, which Fry nor the others gave no thought to . . . and his water holes were cleaned out, and at one place he'd built a dam in the river to stop the water so there would be plenty to last.

There was no rain. As the months went by, the rains held off, and the ranchers were worried, yet Tom Sunday's stock, in the few times I rode that way, always looked good. He had done a lot of work for a man whose home place was in such rawhide shape, and there was a good bit of water damned up in several washes, and spreader dams he had put in had used the water he had gotten to better effect, so he had better grass than almost anybody around.

Ed Fry was a sorehead. A dozen times I'd met such men, the kind who get something in their craw and can't let it alone. Fry was an ex-soldier who had never seen combat, and was a man with little fighting experience anywhere else, and in this country, a man who wasn't prepared to back his mouth with action was better off if he kept still. But Ed Fry was a big man who talked big, and was too egotistical to believe anything could happen to him.

One morning when I came into the office I sat down and said, "Bill, you could do us both a favor if you'd have a talk with Ed Fry."

Sexton put down some papers and rolled his cigar in his jaws. "Has he been shooting off his mouth again?"

"He sure has. It came to me secondhand, but he called Tom Sunday a thief last night. If Tom hears about that we'll have a shooting. In fact, if Cap Rountree heard it there would be a shooting."

Sexton glanced at me. "And I wouldn't want you to hear it," he said bluntly, "or Orrin, either."

"If I figured to do anything about it, I'd take off this badge. There's no place in this office for personal feelings."

Sexton studied the matter. "I'll talk to Ed. Although I don't believe he'll listen. He only gets more bullheaded. He said the investigation you made was a cover-up for Sunday, and both you and Orrin are protecting him."

"He's a liar and nobody knows it better than you, Bill. When he wants to bear down, Tom Sunday is the best cattleman around. Drunk or sober he's a better cattleman than Ed Fry will ever be."

Sexton ran his fingers through his hair. "Tye, let's make Ed put up or shut up. Let's demand to know what cattle he thinks he has missing, and what, exactly, makes him suspect Sunday. Let's make him put his cards on the table."

"You do it," I said, "he would be apt to say the wrong thing to me. The man's a fool, talking around the way he is."

Since taking over my job as deputy sheriff and holding down that of town marshal as well, I'd not had to use my gun nor had there been a shooting in town in that time. I wanted that record to stand, but what concerned me most was keeping Tom Sunday out of trouble.

Only sometimes there isn't anything a man can do,

and Ed Fry was a man bound and determined to have his say. When he said it once too often it was in the St. James Hotel up at Cimarron, and there was quite a crowd in the saloon.

Clay Allison was there, having a drink with a man from whom he was buying a team of mules. That man was Tom Sunday.

Cap was there, and Cap saw it all. Cap Rountree had a suspicion that trouble was heading for Sunday when he found out that Fry was going to Cimarron. Cap already knew that Sunday had gone there, so he took off himself, and he swapped horses a couple of times but didn't beat Fry to town.

Ed Fry was talking when Cap Rountree came into the St. James. "He's nothing but a damned cow thief!" Fry said loudly. "That Tom Sunday is a thief and those Sacketts protect him."

Tom Sunday had a couple of drinks under his belt and he turned slowly and looked at Ed Fry.

Probably Fry hadn't known until then that Sunday was in the saloon, because according to the way Cap told it, Fry went kind of gray in the face and Cap said you could see the sweat break out on his face. Folks had warned him what loose talk would do, but now he was face to face with it.

Tom was very quiet. When he spoke you could hear him in every corner of the room, it was that still.

"Mr. Fry, it comes to my attention that you have on repeated occasions stated that I was a cow thief. You have done this on the wildest supposition and without one particle of evidence. You have done it partly because you are yourself a poor cowman as well as a very inept and stupid man."

When Tom was drinking he was apt to fall into a very precise way of speaking as well as using all that highfalutin language he knew so well.

"You can't talk to me like—"

"You have said I was a cow thief, and you have said the Sacketts protect me. I have never been a cow thief, Mr. Fry, and I have never stolen anything in my life, nor do I need protection from the Sacketts or anyone else. Anyone that says I have stolen cattle or that I have been protected is a liar, Mr. Fry, a very fat-headed and stupid liar."

He had not raised his voice but there was something in his tone that lashed a man like a whip and in even the simplest words, the way Tom said them, there was an insult.

Ed Fry lunged to his feet and Tom merely watched him. "By the Lord—"

Ed Fry grabbed for his gun. He was a big man but a clumsy one, and when he got the gun out he almost dropped it. Sunday did not make a move until Fry recovered his grip on the gun and started to bring it level, and then Tom palmed his gun and shot him dead.

Cap Rountree told Bill Sexton, Orrin, and me about it in the sheriff's office two days later. "No man ever had a better chance," Cap said, "Tom, he just stood there and I figured for a minute he was going to let Fry kill him. Tom's fast, Tye, he's real fast."

And the way he looked at me when he said it was a thing I'll never forget.

CHAPTER XV

It was only a few days later that I rode over to see Drusilla.

Not that I hadn't wanted to see her before, but there had been no chance. This time there was nobody to turn me away and I stopped before an open doorway.

She was standing there, tall and quiet, and at the moment I appeared in the door she turned her head and saw me.

"Dru," I said, "I love you."

She caught her breath sharply and started to turn away. "Please," she said, "go away. You mustn't say that."

When I came on into the room she turned to face me. "Tye, you shouldn't have come here, and you shouldn't say that to me."

"You know that I mean it?"

She nodded. "Yes . . . I know. But you love your brother, and his wife's family hate me, and I ... I hate them too."

"If you hate them, you're going about it as if you tried to please them. They think they've beaten your grandfather and beaten you because you live like a hermit. What you should do is come out, let people see you, go to places."

"You may be right."

"Dru, what's happening to you? What are you going to do with yourself? I came here today to pay you money, but I'm glad I came and for another reason.

"Don Luis is gone, and he was a good man, but he would want you to be happy. You are a beautiful girl, Dru, and you have friends. Your very presence

150

around Santa Fe would worry Laura and Jonathan Pritts more than anything we could think of. Besides, I want to take you dancing. I want to marry you, Dru."

Her eyes were soft. "Tye, I've always wanted to marry you. A long time ago I would have done it had you asked me, that first time you visited us in Santa Fe. . . ."

"I didn't have anything. I was nobody. Just another drifter with a horse and a gun."

"You were you, Tye."

"Sometimes there were things I wanted to say so bad I'd almost choke. Only I never could find the words."

So we sat down and we had coffee again like we used to and I told her about Laura and Ma, which made Dru angry.

"There's trouble shaping, Dru. I can't read the sign clear enough to say where it will happen, but Pritts is getting ready for a showdown.

"There's a lot could happen, but when it happens, I want you with me."

We talked the sun down, and it wasn't until I got up to go that I remembered the money.

She pushed it away. "No, Tyrel, you keep it for me. Invest it for me if you want to. Grandfather left me quite a bit, and I don't know what to do with it now."

That made sense, and I didn't argue with her. Then she told me something that should have tipped me off as to what was coming.

"I have an uncle, Tye, and he is an attorney. He is going to bring an action to clear the titles to all the land in our Grant. When they are clear," she added, "I am going to see the United States Marshal moves any squatters off the land."

Well . . . what could I say? Certainly it was what needed to be done and what had to be done sooner or later, but there was nothing I could think of that was apt to start more trouble than that.

Jonathan Pritts had settled a lot of his crowd on land belonging to the Alvarado Grant. Then he had

bought their claims from them, and he was now laying claim to more than a hundred thousand acres.
Probably Pritts figured when the don died that he
had no more worries . . . anyway, he was in it up to
his ears and if the title of the Alvarado Grant proved
itself, he had no more claim than nothing. I mean, he
was broke.

Not that I felt sorry for him. He hadn't worried
about what happened to the don or his granddaughter, all he thought of was what he wanted. Only if
there was anything that was figured to blow the lid
off this country it was such a suit.

"If I were you," I advised her, "I'd go to Mexico
and I'd stay there until this is settled."

"This is my home," Dru said quietly.

"Dru, you don't seem to realize. This is a shooting
matter. They'll kill you . . . or they'll try."

"They may try," she said quietly. "I shall not
leave."

When I left the house I was worried about Dru. If I
had not been so concerned with her situation I might
have given some thought to myself.

They would think I had put her up to it.

From the day that action was announced I would
be the Number-One target in the shooting gallery.

When I was expecting everything to happen, nothing happened. There were a few scattered killings
further north. One was a Settlement man who had
broken with Jonathan Pritts and the Settlement Company . . . it was out of my bailiwick and the killing
went unsolved, but it had an ugly look to it.

Jonathan Pritts remained in Santa Fe, Laura was
receiving important guests at her parties and fandan-
gos most every night. Pritts was generally agreed to
have a good deal of political power. Me, I was a
skeptic . . . because folks associate in a social way
doesn't mean they are political friends, and most everybody likes a get-together.

One Saturday afternoon Orrin pulled up alongside

me in a buckboard. He looked up at me and grinned as I sat Sate's saddle.

"Looks to me like you'd sell that horse, Tyrel," he said. "He was always a mean one."

"I like him," I said. "He's contrary as all get-out, and he's got a streak of meanness in him, but I like him."

"How's Ma?"

"She's doing fine." It was a hot day and the sweat trickled down my face. The long street was busy. Fetterson was down there with the one they called Paisano, because he gave a man a feeling that he was some kin to a chaparral cock or road runner. Folks down New Mexico way called them *paisanos*.

Only I had a feeling about Paisano. I didn't care for him much.

"Ma misses you, Orrin. You should drive out to see her."

"I know . . . I know. Damn it, Tyrel, why can't womenfolks get along?"

"Ma hasn't had any trouble with anybody. She's all right, Orrin, the same as always. Only she still smokes a pipe."

He mopped his face, looking mighty harried and miserable. "Laura's not used to that." He scowled. "She raises hell every time I go out to the place."

"Womenfolks," I said, "sometimes need some handling. You let them keep the bit in their teeth and they'll make you miserable and themselves too. You pet 'em a little and keep a firm hand on the bridle and you'll have no trouble."

He stared down the sun-bright street, squinting his eyes a little. "It sounds very easy, Tyrel. Only there's so many things tied in with it. When we become a state I want to run for the Senate, and it may be only a few years now."

"How do you and Pritts get along?"

Orrin gathered the reins. He didn't need to tell me. Orrin was an easygoing man, but he wasn't a man you could push around or take advantage of. Except maybe by that woman.

"We don't." He looked up at me. "That's between

us, Tyrel. I wouldn't even tell Ma. Jonathan and I
don't get along, and Laura . . . well, she can be difficult."

"You were quite a bronc rider, Orrin."

"What's that mean?"

"Why," I pushed my hat back on my head, "I'd say
it meant your feet aren't tied to the stirrups, Orrin. I'd
say there isn't a thing to keep you in the saddle but
your mind to stay there, and nobody's going to give
you a medal for staying in the saddle when you can't
make a decent ride of it.

"Take Sate here," I rubbed Sate's neck and that
bronc laid back his ears, "you take Sate. He's a mean
horse. He's tough and he's game and he'll go until the
sun comes up, but Orrin, if I could only have one
horse, I'd never have this one. I'd have Dapple or
that Montana horse.

"It's fun to ride a mean one when you don't have to
do it every day, but if I stay with Sate long enough
he'll turn on me. And there's some women like that."

Orrin gathered the reins. "Too hot . . . I'll see you
later, Tyrel."

He drove off and I watched him go. He was a fine,
upstanding man but when he married that Laura girl
he bought himself a packet of grief.

Glancing down the street I saw Fetterson hand
something to Paisano. It caught the sunlight an instant, then disappeared in Paisano's pocket. But the
glimpse was enough. Paisano had gotten himself a
fistful of gold coins from Fetterson, which was an
interesting thought.

Sometimes a man knows something is about to
happen. He can't put a finger on a reason, but he gets
an itch inside him, and I had it now.

Something was building up. I could smell trouble in
the making, and oddly enough it might have been
avoided by a casual comment. The trouble was that I
did not know that Torres was coming up from Socorro, and that he was returning to work for Dru.

Had I known that, I would have known what Jonathan Pritts' reaction was to be.

If Dru had happened to mention the fact that Torres was finally well and able to be around and was coming back, I would have gone down to meet him and come back with him.

Juan Torres was riding with two other Mexicans, men he had recruited in Socorro to work for Dru, and they were riding together. They had just ridden through the gap about four miles from Mora when they were shot to doll rags.

Mountain air is clear, and sound carries, particularly when it has the hills behind it. The valley was narrow all the way to town, and it was early morning with no other sound to interfere.

Orrin had come up from Santa Fe by stage to Las Vegas and had driven up to town from there. We had walked out on the street together for I'd spent the night in the back room at the sheriff's office.

We all heard the shots, there was a broken volley that sounded like four or five guns at least, and then, almost a full half minute later, a single, final shot.

Now nobody shoots like that if they are hunting game. For that much shooting it has to be a battle, and I headed for Orrin's buckboard on the run with him right behind me. His Winchester was there and each of us wore a belt gun.

Dust lingered in the air at the gap, only a faint suggestion of it. The killers were gone and nobody was going to catch up with them right away, especially in a buckboard, so I wasted no time thinking about that.

Juan Torres lay on his back with three bullet holes in his chest and a fourth between his eyes, and there was a nasty powder burn around that.

"You know what that means?" I asked Orrin.

"Somebody wanted him dead. Remember that final shot?"

There was a rattle of hoofs on the road and I looked around to see my brother Joe and Cap Rountree riding bareback. The ranch was closer than the town and they must have come as fast as they could get to their horses.

They knew better than to mess things up.

Juan Torres had been dead when that final shot was fired, I figured, because at least two of the bullets in the chest would have killed him. The two others were also dead.

I began casting for sign. Not thirty feet off the trail I found where several men had waited for quite some time. There were cigarette stubs there and the grass was matted down.

Orrin had taken one look at the bodies and had walked back to the buckboard and he stood there, saying no word to anybody, just staring first at the ground and then at his hands, looking like he'd never seen them before.

A Mexican I knew had come down the road from town, and he was sitting there on his horse looking at those bodies.

"*Bandidos?*" he looked at me with eyes that held no question.

"No," I said, "assassins."

He nodded his head slowly. "There will be much trouble," he said, "this one," he indicated Torres, "was a good man."

"He was my friend."

"*Si.*"

Leaving the Mexican to guard the road approaching the spot—just beyond the gap—I put Joe between the spot and the town. Only I did this after we loaded the bodies in the buckboard. Then I sent Orrin and Cap off to town with the bodies.

Joe looked at me, his eyes large. "Keep anybody from messing up the road," I said, "until I've looked it over."

First I went back to the spot in the grass where the drygulchers had waited. I took time to look all around very carefully before approaching the spot itself.

Yet even as I looked, a part of my mind was thinking this would mean the lid was going to blow off. Juan Torres had been a popular man and he had been killed, the others, God rest their souls, were incidental. But it was not that alone, it was what was going to happen to my own family, and what Orrin already knew. Only one man had real reason to want Juan Torres dead. . . .

One of the men had smoked his cigarettes right down to the nub. There was a place where he had knelt to take aim, the spot where his knee had been and where his boot toe dug in was mighty close. He was a man, I calculated, not over five feet-four or-five. A short man who smoked his cigarettes to the nub wasn't much to go on, but it was a beganning.

One thing I knew. This had been a cold-blooded murder of men who had had no chance to defend themselves, and it had happened in my bailiwick and I did not plan to rest until I had every man who took part in it . . . no matter where the trail led.

It was a crime on my threshold, and it was a friend of mine who had been killed. And once before Orrin and I had prevented his murder . . . and another time Torres had been shot up and left for dead.

I was going to get every man Jack of them.

There had been five of them here and they had gathered up all the shells before leaving . . . or had they?

Working through the tall grass that had been crushed down by them, I found a shell and I struck gold. It was a .44 shell and it was brand, spanking new. I put that shell in my pocket with a mental note to give some time to it later.

Five men . . . and Torres himself had been hit by four bullets. Even allowing that some of them might have gotten off more than one shot, judging by the bodies there had been at least nine shots fired before that final shot.

Now some men can lever and fire a rifle mighty fast, but it was unlikely you'd find more than one man, at most two, who could work a lever and aim a shot as fast as those bullets had been, in one group of five men.

Torres must have been moving, maybe falling after that first volley, yet somebody had gotten more bullets into him. The answer to that one was simple. There were more than five.

Thoughtfully, I looked up at the hill crested with cedar which arose behind the place where they'd been waiting. They would have had a lookout up there, someone to tell them when Torres was coming.

For a couple of hours I scouted around. I found where they had their horses and they had seven of them, and atop the ridge I found where two men had waited, smoking. One of them had slid right down to the horses, and a man could see where he had dug his heels into the bank to keep from sliding too fast.

Cap came and lent me a hand and after a bit, Orrin came out and joined us.

One more thing I knew by that time. The man who had walked up to Torres' body and fired that last shot into his head had been a tall man with fairly new boots and he had stepped in the blood.

Although Orrin held off and let me do it—knowing too many feet would tramp everything up—he saw enough to know here was a plain, outright murder, and a carefully planned murder at that.

First off, I had to decide whether they expected to be chased or not and about how far they would run. How well did they know the country? Were they likely to go to some ranch owned by friends, or hide out in the hills?

Cap had brought back Kelly all saddled and ready, so when I'd seen about all I could see there, I got into the saddle and sent Joe back to our ranch. He was mighty upset, wanting to go along with a posse, but if it was possible I wanted to keep Joe and Bob out of any shooting and away from the trouble.

"What do you think, Tyrel?" Orrin watched me carefully as he spoke.

"It was out-and-out murder," I said, "by seven men who knew Torres would be coming to Mora. It was planned murder, with the men getting there six to seven hours beforehand. Two of them came along later and I'd guess they watched Torres from the hills to make sure he didn't turn off or stop."

Orrin stared at the backs of his hands and I didn't say anything about what I suspected nor did Cap.

"All right," Orrin said, "you go after them and bring them in, no matter how long it takes or what money you need."

I hesitated. Only Cap, Orrin, and me were there together. "Orrin," I said, "you had me hired, and you can fire me. You can leave it to Bill Sexton or you can put in someone else."

Orrin seldom got mad but he was angry when he stared back at me. "Tyrel, that's damn-fool talk. You do what you were hired to do."

Not one of the three of us could have doubted where that trail would lead, but maybe even then Orrin figured it would lead to Fetterson, maybe, but not Pritts.

Bill Sexton came up just then. "You'll be wanting a posse," he said, "I can get a few good men."

"No posse . . . I want Cap, that's all."

"Are you crazy? There's seven of them . . . at least."

"Look, if I take a posse there's apt to be one in the crowd who's trigger happy. If I can avoid it I don't want any shooting. If I can take these men alive, I'm going to do it."

"You're looking to lose your scalp," Sexton said doubtfully, "but it's your hair. You do what you've a mind to."

"Want me to come along?" Orrin asked.

"No." I wanted him the worst way but the less involved he was, the better. "Cap will do."

The way I looked at it, the chances were almighty slim that the seven would stay together very long. Some of them would split off and that would shorten the odds.

The Alvarado Ranch lay quiet under low gray clouds when Cap and I rode up to the door. Briefly, I told Miguel about Torres. "I will come with you," he said instantly.

"You stay here." I gave it to him straight. "They thought by killing Torres they would ruin any chance the *señorita* would have. Torres is killed but you are not. You're going to take his place, Miguel. You are going to be foreman."

He was startled. "But I—"

"You will have to protect the *señorita*," I said, "and you will have to hire at least a dozen good men. You'll have to bunch what cattle she has left and guard them. It looks to me like the killing of Juan Torres was the beginning of an attempt to put her out of business."

I went on inside, walking fast, and Dru was there to meet me. Quietly as possible, I told her about Juan Torres' death and what I had told Miguel.

"He's a good man," I said, "a better man than he knows, and this will prove it to him and to you. Give him authority and give him responsibility. You can trust him to use good judgment."

"What are you going to do?"

"Why, what a deputy sheriff has to do. I am going to run down the killers."

"And what does your brother say?"

"He says to find them, no matter what, no matter how long, and no matter who."

"Tyrel—be careful!"

That made me grin. "Why, ma'am," I said, grinning at her, "I'm the most careful man you know. Getting myself killed is the last idea in my mind . . . I want to come back to you."

She just looked at me. "You know, Dru, we've waited long enough. When I've caught these men I am going to resign and we are going to be married . . . and I'm not taking no for an answer."

Her eyes laughed at me. "Who said no?"

At the gap Cap and I picked up the trail and for several miles it gave us no trouble at all. Along here they had been riding fast, trying to put distance between themselves and pursuit.

It was a green, lovely country, with mountain meadows, the ridges crested with cedar that gave way to pine as we climbed into the foothills. We camped that night by a little stream where we could have a fire without giving our presence away.

Chances were they would be expecting a large party and if they saw us, would not recognize us. That was one reason I was riding Kelly. Usually I was up on Dapple or Montana horse, and Kelly was not likely to be known.

Cap made the coffee and sat back into the shadows. He poked sticks into the fire for a few minutes the way he did when he was getting ready to talk.

"Figured you'd want to know. Pritts has been down to see Tom Sunday."

I burned my mouth on a spoonful of stew and when I swallowed it I looked at him and said, "*Pritts* to see *Tom?*"

"Uh-huh. Dropped by sort of casual-like, but stayed some time."

"Tom tell you that?"

"No . . . I've got a friend down thataway."

"What happened?"

"Well, seems they talked quite some time and when Pritts left, Tom came out to the horse with him and they parted friendly."

Jonathan Pritts and Tom . . . it made no kind of sense. Or did it?

The more thought I gave to it the more worried I became, for Tom Sunday was a mighty changeable man, and drinking as he was, with his temper, anything might happen.

Orrin had had trouble with Pritts—of this I was certain sure—and Pritts had made a friendly visit to Tom Sunday. I didn't like the feel of it. I didn't like it at all.

CHAPTER XVI

There was a pale lemon glow over the eastern mountains when we killed the last coals of our fire and saddled up. Kelly was feeling sharp and twisty, for Kelly was a trail-loving horse who could look over big country longer than any horse I ever knew, except maybe Montana horse.

Inside me there was a patience growing and I knew I was going to need it. We were riding a trail that could only bring us to trouble because the men we were seeking had friends who would not take lightly to our taking them. But the job was ours to do and those times a man didn't think too much of consequences but crossed each bridge as he came to it.

It was utterly still. In this, the last hour before dawn, all was quiet. Even with my coat on, the sharp chill struck through and I shivered. There was a bad taste in my mouth and I hated the stubble on my jaws ... I'd gotten used to shaving living in town and being an officer. It spoiled a man.

Even in the vague light we could see the lighter trail of pushed-down grass where the riders had ridden ahead of us. Suddenly, the trail dipped into a hollow in the trees and we found their camp of the night before.

They were confident, we could see that, for they had taken only the usual, normal precaution in hiding their camp, and they hadn't made any effort to conceal that they'd been there.

We took our time there for much can be learned of men at such a time, and to seek out a trail it is well to know the manner of men you seek after. If Cap Rountree and me were to fetch these men we would have to follow them a far piece.

They ate well. They had brought grub with them and there was plenty of it. At least a couple of them were drinking, for we found a bottle near the edge of camp ... it looked like whoever was drinking didn't want the others to know, for the bottle had been covered over with leaves.

"Fresh bottle," I said to Cap and handed it to him. He sniffed it thoughtfully. "Smells like good whiskey, not none of this here Indian whiskey."

"They don't want for anything. This outfit is traveling mighty plush."

Cap studied me carefully. "You ain't in no hurry."

"They finished their job, they'll want their pay. I want the man who pays them."

"You figured out who it'll be?"

"No ... all I want is for these men to take me there. Twice before they tried to kill Juan and now they got him. I'm thinking they won't stop there and the only way to stop it is to get the man who pays out the money."

As I was talking a picture suddenly came to mind. It was Fetterson passing out gold to that renegade Paisano. It was a thing to be remembered.

"Bearing west," Cap said suddenly, "I think they've taken a notion."

"Tres Ritos?"

"My guess." Cap considered it. "That drinkin' man now. Supposin' he's run out of whiskey? The way I figure, he's a man who likes his bottle and whoever is bossin' the bunch has kept him off it as much as possible.

"Drinkin' man now, he gets mighty canny about hidin' his stuff. He figures he got folks fooled ... trouble is, it becomes mighty obvious to everybody but the one drinkin'. They may believe that because the job's finished they can have a drink, and Tres Ritos is the closest place."

"I'd guess it's about an easy two-hour ride from here," I looked ahead, searching out the way the riders had gone. "They've taken themselves a notion, all right. Tres Ritos, it is."

Nevertheless, we kept a close watch on the trail. Neither of us had a good feeling about it. A man living in wild country develops a sense of the rightness of things ... and he becomes like an animal in sensing when all is not well.

So far it had been easy, but I was riding rifle in hand now and ready for trouble. Believe me, I wanted that Henry where I could use it. We had seven tough men ahead of us, men who had killed and who did not wish to be caught. I believe we had them fooled, for they would expect to be followed by a posse, but only a fool depends on a feeling like that.

Against such men you never ride easy in the saddle, you make your plans, you figure things out, and then you are careful. I never knew a really brave man yet who was reckless, nor did I ever know a red fighting man who was reckless ... maybe because the reckless ones were all dead.

Cap drew up. "I think I'll have a smoke," he said. Cap got down from his saddle, keeping his rifle in his hand.

He drew his horse back under the trees out of sight and I did likewise. Only one fault with Kelly. That big red horse stood out like a forest fire in this green country.

We sat there studying the country around but doing no talking until Cap smoked his pipe out. Meanwhile both of us had seen a long bench far above the trail that led in the direction of Tres Ritos.

"We might ride along there," I suggested, "I'm spooky about that trail ahead."

"If they turn off we'll lose 'em."

"We can come back and pick up the trail."

We started off at an easy lope, going up through the trees, cutting back around some rocks. We'd gone about a mile when Cap pointed with his rifle.

Down the hill, not far off the trail, we could see some horses tied in the trees. One of them was a dark roan that had a familiar look. Reminded me of a horse I'd seen Paisano riding. And Paisano had taken money from Fetterson. This trail might take us some-where at that.

We dusted the trial into Tres Ritos shy of sundown. We had taken our own time scouting around and getting the country in our minds.

We headed for the livery stable. The sleepy hostler was sitting on the ground with his back to the wall. He had a red headband and looked like a Navajo. He took our horses and we watched him stall them and put corn in the box. Cap walked down between the rows of stalls and said, "Nobody ... we beat 'em to town."

The barkeep in the saloon was an unwashed half-breed with a scar over his left eye like somebody had clouted him with an axe.

We asked for coffee and he turned and yelled something at a back door. The girl his yell brought out was Tina Fernandez. She knew me all right. All those Santa Fe women knew me.

Only she didn't make out like she knew me. She was neat as a new pin, and she brought a pot of coffee and two cups and she poured the coffee and whispered something that sounded like *cuidado*—a word meaning we should be careful.

We drank our coffee and ate some chili and beans with tortillas and I watched the kitchen door and Cap watched the street.

The grub was good, the coffee better, so we had another cup. "Behind the corral," she whispered, "after dark."

Cap chewed his gray mustache and looked at me out of those old, wise-hard eyes. "You mixin' pleasure with business?"

"This is business."

We finished our coffee and we got up and I paid the bartender while Cap studied the street outside. The bartender looked at my face very carefully and then he said, "Do I know you?"

"If you do," I said, "you're going to develop a mighty bad memory."

The street was empty. Not even a stray dog ap-

peared. Had we guessed wrong? Had they gone
around Tres Ritos? Or were they here now, waiting
for us?

Standing there in the quiet of early evening I had a
dry mouth and could feel my heart beating big inside
of me. Time to time I'd seen a few men shot and had
no idea to go out that way if I could avoid it.

We heard them come into town about an hour
later. Chances are they grew tired of waiting for us, if
that was what they had been doing. They came down
the street strung out like Indians on the trail, and
from where we lay in the loft over the livery stable
we could not see them but we could hear their
horses.

They rode directly to the saloon and got down
there, talking very little. As we had ridden into Tres
Ritos by a back trail they would have seen no tracks,
so unless they were told by the bartender they were
not likely to realize we were around.

Lying there on the hay, listening out of the back of
my mind for any noise that would warn us they were
coming our way, I was not thinking of them, but of
Orrin, Laura, Tom Sunday, Dru, and myself. And
there was a lot to think about.

Jonathan Pritts would not be talking to Tom Sunday unless there was a shady side to his talk, for
Jonathan was a man who did nothing by accident. I
knew Tom had no use for the man, but as far back as
the night Jonathan had sent for us in Santa Fe there
had been a streak of compromise in Tom. He had
hesitated that night, recognizing, I think, that Jonathan was a man who was going to be a power.

What was Jonathan Pritts up to? The thought
stayed with me and I worried it like a dog at a bone,
trying to figure it out. Of one thing I was sure: it
promised no good for us.

Cap sat up finally and took out his pipe. "You're
restless, boy."

"I don't like this."

"You got it to do. A man wants peace in a country
he has to go straight to the heart of things." He

smoked in silence for a few minutes. "Time to time I've come across a few men like Pritts ... once set on a trail they can't see anything but that and the more they're balked the stiffer they get." He paused a moment. "As he gets older he gets meaner ... he wants what he's after and he knows time is short."

The loft smelled of the fresh hay and of the horses below in their stalls. The sound of their eating was a comfortable sound, a good sleeping sound, but I could not sleep, tired as I was.

If I was to do anything with my life it had to be now and when this trail had been followed to the end I was going to quit my job, marry Dru, and settle down to build something.

We'd never rightly had a real home and for my youngsters I wanted one. I wanted a place they could grow up with, where they could put down roots. I wanted a place they'd be proud to come back to and which they could always call home ... no matter how far they went or what happened.

Getting up I brushed off the hay, hitched my gun belt into position, and started for the ladder.

"You be careful."

"I'm a careful man by nature."

At the back of the corral I squatted on my heels against a corral post and waited.

Time dragged and then I heard a soft rustle of feet in the grass and saw a shadow near me and smelled a faint touch of woman-smell.

"You all right?"

It was scarcely a whisper but she came to me and I stood up keeping myself in line with that corral post at the corner.

"They are gone," Tina said.

"*What?*"

"They are gone," she repeated. "I was 'fraid for you."

She explained there had been horses for them hidden in the woods back of the saloon, and while they were inside drinking, their saddles had been switched and they had come out one by one and gone off into the woods.

"Fooled us . . . hornswoggled us."

"The other one is there. He is upstairs but I think he will go in the morning."

"Who?"

"The man who gave them money. The blond man."

Fetterson? It could be.

"You saw the money paid?"

"Yes, *señor*. With my two eyes I saw it. They were paid much in gold . . . the balance, he said."

"Tina, they killed Juan Torres . . . did you know him?"

"*Si* . . . he was a good man."

"In court, Tina. Would you testify against them? Would you tell you saw money paid? It would be dangerous for you."

"I will testify. I am not afraid." She stood very still in the darkness. "I know, *señor*, you are in love with the *Señorita* Alvarado, but could you help me, *señor*? Could you help me to go away from here? This man, the one you talked to, he is my . . . how do you call it? He married my mother."

"Stepfather."

"*Si* . . . and my mother is dead and he keeps me here and I work, *señor*. Some day I will be old. I wish now to go to Santa Fe again but he will not let me."

"You shall go. I promise it."

The men had gone and we had not seen them but she told me one had been Paisano. Only one other she knew. A stocky, very tough man named Jim Dwyer . . . he had been among those at Pawnee Rock. But Fetterson was here and he was the one I wanted most.

We slept a little, and shy of daybreak we rolled out and brushed off the hay. I felt sticky and dirty and wanted a bath and a shave the worst way but I checked my gun and we walked down to the hotel. There was a light in the kitchen and we shoved open the back door.

The bartender was there in his undershirt and pants and sock feet. There was the tumbled, dirty bedding where he had slept, some scattered boots, dirty socks, and some coats hung on the wall, on one nail a gun belt hung. I turned the cylinder and shucked out the shells while the bartender watched grimly.

"What's all this about?"

Turning him around we walked through the dark hall with a lantern in Cap's hand to throw a vague light ahead.

"Which room is he in?"

The bartender just looked at me, and Cap, winking at me, said, "Shall I do it here? Or should we take him out back where they won't find the body so soon?"

The bartender's feet shifted. "No, look!" he protested. "I ain't done nothing."

"He'd be in the way," I said thoughtfully, "and he's no account to us. We might as well take him out back."

Cap looked mean enough to do it, and folks always figured after a look at me that killing would be easier for me than smiling.

"Wait a minute ... he ain't nothin' to me. He's in Room Six, up the stairs."

Looking at him, I said "Cap, you keep him here." And then looking at the bartender I said, "You know something? That had better be the right room."

Up the stairs I went, tiptoeing each step and at the top, shielding the lantern with my coat, I walked down the hall and opened the door to Room Six.

His eyes opened when I came through the door but the light was in his eyes when I suddenly unveiled the lantern and his gun was on the table alongside the bed. He started to reach for it and I said, "Go ahead, Fetterson, you pick it up and I can kill you."

His hand hung suspended above the gun and slowly he withdrew it. He sat up in bed then, a big, raw-boned man with a shock of rumpled blond hair and his hard-boned, wedgelike face. There was nothing soft about his eyes.

"Sackett? I might have expected it would be you." Careful to make no mistakes he reached for the makings and began to build a smoke. "What do you want?"

"It's a murder charge, Fett. If you have a good lawyer you might beat it, but you make a wrong move and nothing will beat what I give you."

He struck a match and lit up. "All right . . . I'm no Reed Carney and if I had a chance I'd try shooting it out, but if that gun stuck in the holster I'd be a dead man."

"You'd never get a hand on it, Fett."

"You takin' me in?"

"Uh-huh. Get into your clothes."

He took his time dressing and I didn't hurry him. I figured if I gave him time he would decide it was best to ride along and go to jail, for with Pritts to back him there was small chance he would ever come to trial. My case was mighty light on evidence, largely on what Tina could tell us and what I had seen myself, which was little enough.

When he was dressed he walked ahead of me down the hall to where Cap was waiting with a gun on the bartender. We gathered up Fetterson's horse and started back to town. I wasn't through with that crowd I'd trailed, but they would have to wait.

Our return trip took us mighty little time because I was edgy about being on the trail, knowing that the bartender might get word to Fetterson's crowd. By noon the next day we had him behind bars in Mora and the town was boiling.

Fetterson stood with his hands on the bars. "I won't be here long," he said, "I'd nothing to do with this."

"You paid them off. You paid Paisano an advance earlier."

There was a tic in his eyelid, that little jump of the lid that I'd noticed long ago in Abilene when he had realized they were boxed and could do nothing without being killed.

"You take it easy," I said, "because by the time this case comes to court I'll have enough to hang you."

He laughed, and it was a hard, contemptuous laugh, too. "You'll never see the day!" he said. "This is a put-up job."

When I walked outside in the sunlight, Jonathan Pritts was getting down from his buckboard.

One thing I could say for Jonathan ... he moved fast.

CHAPTER XVII

It had been a long time since I'd stood face to face with Jonathan Pritts. He walked through the open door and confronted me in the small office, his pale blue eyes hard with anger. "You have Mr. Fetterson in prison. I want him released."

"Sorry."

"On what charge are you holding him?"

"He is involved in the murder of Juan Torres."

He glared at me. "You have arrested this man because of your hatred for me. He is completely innocent and you can have no evidence to warrant holding him. If you do not release him I will have you removed from office."

He had no idea how empty that threat was. He was a man who liked power and could not have understood how little I wanted the job I had, or how eager I was to be rid of it.

"He will be held for trial."

Jonathan Pritts measured me carefully. "I see you are not disposed to be reasonable." His tone was quieter.

"There has been a crime committed, Mr. Pritts. You cannot expect me to release a prisoner because the first citizen who walks into my office asks me to. The time has come to end crimes of violence, and especially," I added this carefully, "murder that has been paid for."

This would hit him where he lived, I thought, and maybe it did, only there was no trace of feeling on his face. "Now what do you mean by that?"

"We have evidence that Fetterson paid money to the murderers of Juan Torres."

Sure, I was bluffing. We had nothing that would stand up in court, not much, actually, on which to hold him. Only that I had seen him paying money to Paisano, and he had been at Tres Ritos when the killers arrived, and that Tina would testify to the fact that he had paid money there.

"That is impossible."

Picking up a sheaf of papers, I began sorting them. He was a man who demanded attention and my action made him furious.

"Mr. Pritts," I said, "I believe you are involved in this crime. If the evidence will substantiate my belief you will hang also, right along with Fetterson and the others."

Why, he fooled me. I expected him to burst out with some kind of attack on me, but he did nothing of the kind.

"Have you talked to your brother about this?"

"He knows I have my duty to do, and he would not interfere. Nor would I interfere in his business."

"How much is the bail for Mr. Fetterson?"

"You know I couldn't make any ruling. The judge does that. But there's no bail for murder."

He did not threaten me or make any reply at all, he just turned and went outside. If he had guessed how little I had in the way of evidence he would have just sat still and waited. But I have a feeling about this sort of thing ... if you push such men they are apt to move too fast, move without planning, and so they'll make mistakes.

Bill Sexton came in, and Ollie was with him. They looked worried.

"How much of a case have you got against Fetterson?" Sexton asked me.

"Time comes, I'll have a case."

Sexton rubbed his jaw and then took out a cigar. He studied it while I watched him, knowing what was coming and amused by all the preliminaries, but kind of irritated by them, too.

"This Fetterson," Sexton said, "is mighty close to Jonathan Pritts. It would be a bad idea to try to stick him with these killings. He's got proof he wasn't anywhere around when they took place."

"There's something to that, Tye," Ollie said. "It was Jonathan who helped put Orrin in office."

"You know something?" I had my feet on the desk and I took them down and sat up in that swivel chair. "He did nothing of the kind. He jumped on the band wagon when he saw Orrin was a cinch to win. Fetterson stays in jail or I resign."

"That's final?" Ollie asked.

"You know it is."

He looked relieved, I thought. Ollie Shaddock was a good man, mostly, and once an issue was faced he would stand pat and I was doing what we both believed to be right.

"All right," Sexton said, "if you think you've got a case, we'll go along."

It was nigh to dark when Cap came back to the office. There was no light in the office and sitting back in my chair I'd been doing some thinking.

Cap squatted against the wall and lit his pipe. "There's a man in town," he said, "name of Wilson. He's a man who likes his bottle. He's showing quite a bit of money, and a few days ago he was broke."

"Pretty sky," I said, "the man who named the Sangre de Cristos must have seen them like this. That red in the sky and on the peaks ... it looks like blood."

"He's getting drunk," Cap said.

Letting my chair down to an even keel I got up and opened the door that shut off the cells from the office. Walking over to the bars and stopping there, I watched Fetterson lying on his cot. I could not see his face, only the dark bulk of him and his boots. Yes, and the glow of his cigarette.

"When do you want to eat?"

He swung his boots to the floor. "Any time. Suit yourself."

"All right." I turned to go and then let him have it easy. "You know a man named Wilson?"

He took the cigarette from his mouth. "Can't place him. Should I?"

"You should ... he drinks too much. Really likes

that bottle. Some folks should never be trusted with money."

When I'd closed the door behind me Cap lit the lamp. "A man who's got something to hide," Cap said, "has something to worry about."

Fetterson would not, could not know what Wilson might say, and a man's imagination can work overtime. What was it the Good Book said? "The guilty flee when no man pursueth."

The hardest thing was to wait. In that cell Fetterson was thinking things over and he was going to get mighty restless. And Jonathan Pritts had made no request to see him. Was Jonathan shaping up to cut the strings on Fetterson and leave him to shift for himself? If I could think of that, it was likely Fetterson could too.

Cap stayed at the jail and I walked down to the eating house for a meal. Tom Sunday came in. He was a big man and he filled the door with his shoulders and height. He was unshaved and he looked like he'd been on the bottle. Once inside he blinked at the brightness of the room a moment or two before he saw me and then he crossed to my table. Maybe he weaved a mite in walking ... I wouldn't have sworn to it.

"So you got Fetterson?" He grinned at me, his eyes faintly taunting. "Now that you've got him, what will you do with him?"

"Convict him of complicity," I replied. "We know he paid the money."

"That's hitting close to home," Sunday's voice held a suggestion of a sneer. "What'll your brother say to that?"

"It doesn't matter what he says," I told him, "but it happens it has been said. I cut wood and let the chips fall where they may."

"That would be like him," he said, "the sanctimonious son-of-a-bitch."

"Tom," I said quietly, "that term could apply to both of us. We're brothers, you know."

He looked at me, and for a moment there I thought

he was going to let it stand, and inside me I was praying he would not. I wanted no fight with Tom Sunday.

"Sorry," he said, "I forgot myself. Hell," he said then, "we don't want trouble. We've been through too much together."

"That's the way I feel," I said, "and Tom, you can take my say-so or not, but Orrin likes you, too."

"Likes me?" he sneered openly now. "He likes me, all right, likes me out of the way. Why, when I met him he could scarcely read or write ... I taught him. He knew I figured to run for office and he moved right in ahead of me, and you helping him."

"There was room for both of you. There still is."

"The hell there is. Anything I tried to do he would block me. Next time he runs for office he won't have the backing of Jonathan Pritts. I can tell you that."

"It doesn't really matter."

Tom laughed sardonically. "Look, kid, I'll tip you to something right now. Without Pritts backing him Orrin wouldn't have been elected ... and Pritts is fed up."

"You seem to know a lot about Pritts' plans."

He chuckled. "I know he's fed up, and so is Laura. They're both through with Orrin, you wait and see."

"Tom, the four of us were mighty close back there a while. Take it from me, Tom, Orrin has never disliked you. Sure, the two of you wanted some of the same things but he would have helped you as you did him."

He ate in silence for a moment or two, and then he said, "I have nothing against you, Tye, nothing at all."

After that we didn't say anything for a while. I think both of us were sort of reaching out to the other, for there had been much between us, we had shared violence and struggle and it is a deep tie. Yet when he got up to leave I think we both felt a sadness, for there was something missing.

He went outside and stood in the street a minute and I felt mighty bad. He was a good man, but nobody can buck liquor and a grudge and hope to come out of it all right. And Jonathan Pritts was talking to him.

I arrested Wilson that night. I didn't take him to jail where Fetterson could talk to him. I took him to that house at the edge of town where Cap, Orrin, and me had camped when we first came up to Mora.

I stashed him there with Cap to mount guard and keep the bottle away. Joe came in to guard Fetterson and I mounted up and took to the woods, and I wasn't riding on any wild-goose chase ... Miguel had told me that a couple of men were camped on the edge of town, and one of them was Paisano.

From the ridge back of their camp I studied the layout through a field glass. It was a mighty cozy little place among boulders and pines that a man might have passed by fifty times without seeing had it not been for Miguel being told of it by one of the Mexicans.

The other man must be Jim Dwyer—a short, thickset man who squatted on his heels most of the time and never was without his rifle.

There was no hurry. There was an idea in my skull to the effect these men were camping here for the purpose of breaking Fetterson out of jail. I wanted those men the worst way but I wanted them alive, and that would be hard to handle as both men were tough, game men who wouldn't back up from a shooting fight.

There was a spring about fifty yards away, out of sight of the camp. From the layout I'd an idea this place had been used by them before. There was a crude brush shelter built to use a couple of big boulders that formed its walls. All the rest of the day I lay there watching them. From time to time one of them would get up and stroll out to the thin trail that led down toward Mora.

They had plenty of grub and a couple of bottles but neither of them did much drinking.

By the time dark settled down I knew every rock, every tree, and every bit of cover in that area. Also I had spotted the easiest places to move quietly in the dark, studying the ground for sticks, finding openings in the brush.

Those men down there were mighty touchy folks with whom a man only made one mistake.

Come nightfall I moved my horse to fresh grass after watering him at the creek. Then I took a mite of grub and a canteen and worked my way down to within about a hundred feet of their camp.

They had a small fire going, and coffee on. They were broiling some beef, too, and it smelled almighty good. There I was, lying on my belly smelling that good grub and chewing on a dry sandwich that had been packed early in the day. From where I lay I could hear them but couldn't make out the words.

My idea was that with Fetterson in jail it was just a chance Jonathan Pritts might come out himself.

He was a cagey man and smart enough to keep at least one man between himself and any gun trouble. But Pritts wanted Fetterson out of jail.

It seemed to me that in the time I'd known Jonathan Pritts he had put faith in nobody. Such a man was unlikely to have confidence in Fetterson's willingness to remain silent when by talking he might save his own skin. Right now I thought Pritts would be a worried man, and with reason enough.

Fetterson had plenty to think about too. He knew that we had Wilson, and Wilson was a drinker who would do almost anything for his bottle. If Wilson talked, Fetterson was in trouble. His one chance to get out of it easier was to talk himself. Personally, I did not believe Fetterson would talk—there was a loyalty in the man, and a kind of iron in him, that would not allow him to break or be broken.

I was counting on the fact that Pritts believed in nobody, was eternally suspicious and would expect betrayal.

What I did not expect was the alternative on which Jonathan Pritts had decided. I should have guessed, but did not. Jonathan was a hard man, a cold man, a resolute man.

Now it can be mighty miserable lying up in the

brush, never really sleeping, and keeping an eye on a camp like that. Down there, they'd sleep awhile and then rouse up and throw some sticks on the fire, and go back to sleep again. And that's how the night run away.

It got to be the hour of dawn with the sun some time away but crimson streaking the sky, and those New Mexico sunrises ... well, there's nothing like the way they build a glory in the sky.

Paisano stood up suddenly. He was listening. He was lower in the canyon and might hear more than I.

Would it be Jonathan Pritts himself? It it was, I would move in, taking the three of them in a bundle. Now that might offer a man a problem, and I wanted them all alive, which would not be a simple thing. Yet I had it to do.

What made me turn my head, I don't know.

There was a man standing in the brush about fifty feet away, standing death-still, his outline vague in the shadowy brush. How long that man had been there I had no idea, but there he was, standing silent and watching.

It gave me a spooky feeling to realize that man had been so close all the while and I'd known nothing about it. Not one time in a thousand could that happen to me. Trouble was, I'd had my eyes on that camp, waiting, watching to miss nothing.

Suddenly, that dark figure in the brush moved ever so slightly, edging forward. He was higher than I, and could see down the canyon, although he was not concealed nearly so well as I was. My rifle was ready, but what I wanted was the bunch of them, and all alive so they could testify. And I'd had my fill of killing and had never wished to use my gun against anyone.

It was growing lighter, and the man in the brush was out further in the open, looking down as if about to move down there into the camp. And then he turned his head and some of the light fell across his face and I saw who it was.

It was Orrin.

CHAPTER XVIII

Orrin. . . .

It was so unexpected that I just lay there staring and then I began to bring my thoughts together and when I considered it I couldn't believe it. Sure, Orrin was married to Pritts' daughter, but Orrin had always seemed the sort of man who couldn't be influenced against his principles. We'd been closer even than most brothers.

So where did that leave me? Our lives had been built tightly around our blood ties for Lord knows how many years. Only I knew that even if it was Orrin, I was going to arrest him. Brother or not, blood tie or not, it was my job and I would do it.

And then I had another thought. Sure, I could see then I was a fool. There had to be another reason. My faith in Orrin went far beyond any suspicion his presence here seemed to mean.

So I got up.

His attention was on that camp as mine had been, and I had taken three steps before he saw me.

He turned his head and we looked into each other's eyes, and then I walked on toward him.

Before I could speak he lifted a hand. "Wait!" he whispered, and in the stillness that followed I heard what those men down below must have heard some time before . . . the sound of a buckboard coming.

We stood there with the sky blushing rose and red and the gold cresting the far-off ridges and the shadows still lying black in the hollows.

We stood together there, as we had stood together before, against the Higginses, against the dark demons of drought and stones that plagued our hillside farm in Tennessee, against the Utes, and against Reed

Carney. We stood together, and in that moment I suddenly knew why he was here, and knew before the buckboard came into sight just who I would see.

The buckboard came into the trail below and drew up. And the driver was Laura.

Paisano and Dwyer went out to meet her and we watched money pass between them and watched them unload supplies from the back of the buckboard.

Somehow I'd never figured on a woman, least of all, Laura. In the west in those years we respected our women, and it was not in me to arrest one although I surely had no doubts that a woman could be mighty evil and wrong.

Least of all could I arrest Laura. It was a duty I had, but it was her father I wanted and the truth was plain to see. A man who would send his daughter on such a job . . . he was lower than I figured.

Of course, there were mighty few would believe it or even suspect such a frail, blond, and ladylike girl of meeting and delivering money to murderers.

Orrin shifted his feet slightly and sighed. I never saw him look the way he did, his face looking sick and empty like somebody had hit him in the midsection with a stiff punch.

"I had to see it," he said to me, "I had to see it myself to believe it. Last night I suspected something like this, but I had to be here to see."

"You knew where the camp was?"

"Jonathan gave her most careful directions last night."

"I should arrest her," I said.

"As you think best."

"It isn't her I want," I said, "and she would be no good to me. She'd never talk."

Orrin was quiet and then he said, "I think I'll move out to the ranch, Tyrel. I'll move out today."

"Ma will like that. She's getting feeble, Orrin."

We went back into the brush a mite and Orrin rolled a smoke and lit up. "Tyrel," he said after a minute, "what's he paying them for? Was it for Tor-res?"

"Not for Torres," I said, "Fetterson already paid them."

"For you?"

"Maybe ... I doubt it."

Suddenly I wanted to get away from there. Those two I could find them when I wanted them for they were known men, and the man I had wanted had been cagey enough not to appear.

"Orrin," I said, "I've got to head Laura off. I'm not going to arrest her, I just want her to know she has been seen and I know what's going on. I want them to know and to worry about it."

"Is that why you're holding Wilson apart?"

"Yes."

We went back to our horses and then we cut along the hill through the bright beauty of the morning to join the trail a mile or so beyond where Laura would be.

When she came up, for a minute I thought she would try to drive right over us, but she drew up.

She was pale, but the planes of her face had drawn down in hard lines and I never saw such hatred in a woman's eyes.

"Now you're spying on me!" There was nothing soft and delicate about her voice then, it was strident, angry.

"Not on you," I said, "on Paisano and Dwyer."

She flinched as if I'd struck her, started to speak, then pressed her lips together.

"They were in the group that killed Juan Torres," I said, "along with Wilson."

"If you believe that, why don't you arrest them? Are you afraid?"

"Just waiting ... sometimes if a man let's a small fish be his bait he can catch a bigger fish. Like you, bringing supplies and money to them. That makes you an accessory. You can be tried for aiding and abetting."

For the first time she was really scared. She was a

girl who made much of position, a mighty snooty sort, if you ask me, and being arrested would just about kill her.

"You wouldn't dare!"

She said it, but she didn't believe it. She believed I would, and it scared the devil out of her.

"Your father has been buying murder too long, and there is no place for such men. Now you know."

Her face was pinched and white and there was nothing pretty about her then. "Let me pass!" she demanded bitterly.

We drew aside, and she looked at Orrin. "You were nothing when we met, and you'll be nothing again."

Orrin removed his hat, "Under the circumstances," he said gently, "you will pardon me if I remove my belongings?"

She slashed the horses with the whip and went off. Orrin's face was white as we cut over across the hills. "I'd like to be out of the house," he said, "before she gets back."

The town was quiet when I rode in. Fetterson came to the bars of his cell and stared at me when I entered. He knew I'd been away and it worried him he didn't know what I was doing.

"Paisano and Dwyer are just outside the town," I said, "and no two men are going to manage a jail delivery, but Pritts was paying them . . . what for?"

His eyes searched my face and suddenly he turned and looked at the barred window. Beyond the window, three hundred yards away, was the wooded hillside . . . and to the right, not over sixty yards off, the roof of the store.

He turned back swiftly. "Tye," he said, "you've got to get me out of here."

Fetterson was no fool and he knew that there was no trust in Jonathan Pritts. Fetterson would die before he would talk, but Pritts did not for a minute believe that. Consequently he intended that Fetterson should die before he could talk.

"Fett," I said, "it's up to you not to get in front of

that window. Or," I paused and let the word hang for a minute, "you can talk and tell me the whole story."

He turned sharply away and walked back to his cot and lay down. I knew that window would worry him, Wilson would worry him, and he would worry about how much I knew.

"You might as well tell me and save your bacon," I said, "Wilson hasn't had a drink in three days and he'll tell all he knows any day now. After that we won't care about you."

Right then I went to Ceran St. Vrain. He was the most influencial man in Mora, and I had Vicente Romero come in, and we had a talk. Ollie Shaddock was there, Bill Sexton, and Orrin.

"I want ten deputies," I said, "I want Ceran to pick five of them and Romero to pick the other five. I want solid, reliable men. I don't care whether they are good men with guns or not, I want substantial citizens."

They picked them and we talked the whole thing over. I laid all my cards on the table. Told them just what the situation was and I didn't beat around the bush.

Wilson was talking, all right. He had a hand in the killing of Torres and the others and he named the other men involved, and I told them that Paisano and Dwyer were out in the hills and that I was going after them myself. I made good on my word to Tina Fernandez and got a promise from Ceran himself to go after her with a couple of his riders to back him up. He was a man respected and liked and feared.

On Jonathan Pritts I didn't pull my punches. Telling them of our meeting with him in Abilene, of our talk with him in Santa Fe, of the men waiting at Pawnee Rock, and of what he had done since. St. Vrain was an old friend to the Alvarado family . . . he knew much of what I said.

"What is it, señor? What do you wish to do?"

"I believe Fetterson is ready to talk." I said, "We will have Wilson, we will have Tina, and Cap's evidence as well as my own, for we trailed the killers to Tres Ritos."

"What about Mrs. Sackett?" St. Vrain asked.

Right there I hesitated. "She's a woman and I'd like to keep her out of it."

They all agreed to this and when the meeting broke up, I was to have a final talk with Fetterson.

So this was to be an end to it. There was no anger in me any more. Juan Torres was gone and another death could not bring him back. Jonathan Pritts would suffer enough to see all his schemes come to nothing, and they would, now. I knew that Vicente Romero was the most respected man in the Spanish-speaking group, and St. Vrain among the Anglos. Once they had said what they had to say, Jonathan Pritts would no longer have influence locally nor in Santa Fe.

Orrin and me, we walked back to the jail together and it was good to walk beside him, brothers in feeling as well as in blood.

"It's tough," I said to him, "I know how you felt about Laura, but Orrin, you were in love with what you thought she was. A man often creates an image of a girl in his mind but when it comes right down to it that's the only place the girl exists."

"Maybe," Orrin was gloomy, "I was never meant to be married."

We stopped in front of the sheriff's office and Cap came out to join us.

"Tom's in town," he said, "and he's drunk and spoilin' for a fight."

"We'll go talk to him," Orrin said.

Cap caught Orrin's arm. "Not you, Orrin. You'd set him off. If you see him now there'll be a shootin' sure."

"A shooting?" Orrin smiled disbelievingly. "Cap, you're clean off the trail. Why, Tom's one of my best friends!"

"Look," Cap replied shortly, "you're no tenderfoot. How much common sense or reason is there behind two-thirds of the killings out here? You bump into a man and spill his drink, you say the wrong thing ... it doesn't have to make sense."

"There's no danger from Tom," Orrin insisted quietly. "I'd stake my life on it."

"That's just what you're doing," Cap replied. "The man's not the Tom Sunday that drove cows with us. He's turned into a mighty mean man, and he's riding herd on a grudge against you. He's been living alone down there and he's been hitting the bottle."

"Cap's right." I told him, "Tom's carrying a chip on his shoulder."

"All right. I want no trouble with him or anyone."

"You got an election comin' up," Cap added. "You get in a gun battle an' a lot of folks will turn their backs on you."

Reluctantly, Orrin mounted up and rode out to the ranch, and for the first time in my life, I was glad to see him go. Things had been building toward trouble for months now, and Tom Sunday was only one small part of it, but the last thing I wanted was a gun battle between Tom and Orrin.

At all costs that fight must be prevented both for their sakes and for Orrin's future.

Ollie came by the office after Orrin had left. "Pritts is down to Santa Fe," he said, "and he's getting himself nowhere. Vicente Romero has been down there, and so has St. Vrain and it looks like they put the kibosh on him."

Tina was in town and staying with Dru and we had our deposition from Wilson. I expect he was ready to get shut of the whole shebang, for at heart Wilson was not a bad man, only he was where bad company and bad liquor had taken him.

He talked about things clear back to Pawnee Rock, and we took that deposition in front of seven witnesses, three of them Mexican, and four Anglos. When the trial came up I didn't want it said that we'd beaten it out of him, but once he started talking he left nothing untold.

On Wednesday night I went to see Fetterson for I'd been staying away and giving him time to think.

He looked gaunt and scared. He was a man with plenty of sand but nobody likes to be set up as Number-One target in a shooting gallery.

"Fett," I said, "I can't promise you anything but a chance in court, but the more you co-operate the better. If you want out of this cell you'd better talk."

"You're a hard man, Tyrel," he said gloomily. "You stay with a thing."

"Fett," I said, "men like you and me have had our day. Folks want to settle affairs in court now, and not with guns. Women and children coming west want to walk a street without stray bullets flying around. A man has to make peace with the times."

"If I talk I'll hang myself."

"Maybe not . . . folks are more anxious to have an end to all this trouble than to punish anybody."

He still hesitated so I left him there and went out into the cool night. Orrin was out at the ranch and better off there, and Cap Rountree was some place up the street.

Bill Shea came out of the jail house. "Take a walk if you're of a mind to, Tyrel," he suggested, "there's three of us here."

Saddling the Montana horse I rode over to see Dru. It was a desert mountain night with the sky so clear and the stars so close it looked like you could knock them down with a stick. Dru had sold the big house that lay closer to Santa Fe, and was spending most of her time in this smaller but comfortable house near Mora.

She came to the door to meet me and we walked back inside and I told her about the meeting with Romero and St. Vrain, and the situation with Fetterson.

"Move him, Tye, you must move him out of there before he is killed. It is not right to keep him there."

"I want him to talk."

"Move him," Dru insisted, "you must. Think of how you would feel if he was killed."

She was right, of course, and I'd been thinking of it. "All right," I said, "first thing in the morning."

Sometimes the most important things in a man's life are the ones he talks about least. It was that way with Dru and me. No day passed that I did not think of her much of the time, she was always with me, and even when we were together we didn't talk a lot because so much of the time there was no need for words, it was something that existed between us that we both understood.

The happiest hours of my life were those when I was riding with Dru or sitting across a table from her. And I'll always remember her face by candlelight ... it seemed I was always seeing it that way, and soft sounds of the rustle of gowns, the tinkle of silver and glass, and Dru's voice, never raised and always exciting.

Within the thick adobe walls of the old Spanish house there was quiet, a shadowed peace that I have associated with such houses all my years. One stepped through the door into another world, and left outside the trouble, confusion, and storm of the day.

"When this is over, Dru," I said, "we'll wait no longer. And it will soon be over."

"We do not need to wait." She turned from the window where we stood and looked up at me. "I am ready now."

"This must be over first, Dru. It is a thing I have to do and when it is finished I shall take off my badge and leave the public offices to Orrin."

Suddenly there was an uneasiness upon me and I said to her, "I must go."

She walked to the door with me. "*Vaya con Dios,*" she said, and she waited there until I was gone.

And that night there was trouble in town but it was not the trouble I expected.

CHAPTER XIX

It happened as I left my horse in front of the saloon and stepped in for a last look around. It was after ten o'clock and getting late for the town of Mora, and I went into the saloon and stepped into trouble.

Two men faced each other across the room and the rest were flattened against the walls.

Chico Cruz, deadly as a sidewinder, stood posed and negligent, a slight smile on his lips, his black eyes flat and without expression.

And facing him was Tom Sunday.

Big, blond, and powerful, unshaven as always these days, heavier than he used to be, but looking as solid and formidable as a blockhouse.

Neither of them saw me. Their attention was concentrated on each other and death hung in the air like the smell of lightning on a rocky hillside. As I stepped in, they drew.

With my own eyes I saw it. Saw Chico's hand flash. I had never believed a man could draw so fast, his gun came up and then he jerked queerly and his body snapped sidewise and his gun went off into the floor and Tom Sunday was walking.

Tom Sunday was walking in, gun poised. Chico was trying to get his gun up and Tom stopped and spread his legs and grimly, brutally, he fired a shot into Chico's body, and then coolly, another shot.

Chico's gun dropped, hit the floor with a thud. Chico turned and in turning his eyes met mine across the room, and he said very distinctly into the silence that followed the thundering of the guns, "It was not you."

He fell, then, fell all in a piece and his hat rolled free and he lay on the floor and he was dead.

Tom Sunday turned and stared at me and his eyes

were blazing with a hot, hard flame. "You want me?" he said, and the words were almost a challenge.

"It was a fair shooting, Tom," I said quietly. "I do not want you."

He pushed by me and went out of the door, and the room broke into wild talk. "Never would have believed it. . . . Fastest thing I ever saw. . . . But *Chico!*" The voice was filled with astonishment. "He killed *Chico Cruz!*"

Until that moment I had always believed that if it came to a difficulty that Orrin could take care of Tom Sunday, but I no longer believed it.

More than any of them I knew the stuff of which Orrin was made. He had a kind of nerve rarely seen, but he was no match for Tom when it came to speed. And there was a fatal weakness against him, for Orrin truly liked Tom Sunday.

And Tom?

Somehow I didn't think there was any feeling left in Tom, not for anyone, unless it was me.

The easy comradeship was gone. Tom was ingrown, bitter, hard as nails.

When Chico's body was moved out I tried to find out what started the trouble, but it was like so many bar-room fights, just sort of happened. Two, tough, edgy men and neither about to take any pushing around. Maybe it was a word, maybe a spilled drink, a push, or a brush against each other, and then guns were out and they were shooting.

Tom had ridden out of town.

Cap was sitting in the jail house with Babcock and Shea when I walked in. I could see Fetterson through the open door, so walked back to the cells.

"That right? What they're saying?"

"Tom Sunday killed Chico Cruz . . . beat him to the draw."

Fetterson shook his head unbelievingly. "I never would have believed it. I thought Chico was the fastest thing around . . . unless it was you."

Fetterson grinned suddenly. "How about you and Tom? You two still friends?"

It made me mad and I turned sharply around and he stepped back from the bars, but he was grinning when he moved back. "Well, I just asked," he said, "some folks never bought that story about you backin' Cruz down."

"Tom is my friend," I told him, "we'll always be friends."

"Maybe," he said, "maybe." He walked back to the bars. "Looks like I ain't the only one has troubles."

Outside in the dark I told Cap about it, every detail. He listened, nodding thoughtfully.

"Tyrel," Cap said, "we've been friends, and trail dust is thicker'n blood, but you watch Tom Sunday. You watch him. That man's gone loco like an old buffalo bull who's left the herd."

Cap took his pipe out of his mouth and knocked out the ashes against the awning post. "Tyrel, mark my words! He's started now an' nuthin's goin' to stop him. Orrin will be next an' then you."

That night I got into the saddle and rode all the way out to the ranch to sleep, pausing only a moment at the gap where the river flowed through, remembering Juan Torres who died there. It was bloody country and time it was quieted down. Inside me I didn't want to admit that Cap was right, but I was afraid, I was very much afraid.

As if the shooting, which had nothing to do with Pritts, Alvarado, or myself, had triggered the whole situation from Santa Fe to Cimarron, the lid suddenly blew off. Maybe it was that Pritts was shrewd enough to see his own position weakening and if anything was to be done it had to be done now.

Jonathan and Laura, they moved back up to Mora and it looked like they had come to stay.

Things were shaping up for a trial of Wilson and Fetterson for the murder of Juan Torres.

We moved Fetterson to a room in an old adobe up the street that had been built for a fort. We moved him by night and the next morning we stuck a dummy up in the window of the jail. We put that dummy up just before daylight and then Cap, Orrin, and me, we took to the hills right where we knew we ought to be.

We heard the shots down the slope from us and we went down riding fast. They were wearing Sharps buffalo guns. They both fired and when we heard those two rifles talk we came down out of the higher trees and had them boxed. The Sharps buffalo was a good rifle, but it was a single shot, and we had both those men covered with Winchesters before they could get to their horses or had time to load.

Paisano and Dwyer. Caught flat-footed and red-handed, and nothing to show for it but a couple of bullets through a dummy.

That was what broke Jonathan Pritts' back. We had four of the seven men now and within a matter of hours after, we tied up two more. That seventh man wasn't going to cause anybody any harm. Seems he got drunk one night and on the way home something scared his horse and he got bucked off and with a foot caught in the stirrup there wasn't much he could do. Somewhere along the line he'd lost his pistol and couldn't kill the horse. He was found tangled in some brush, his foot still in the stirrup, and the only way they knew him was by his boots, which were new, and his saddle and horse. A man dragged like that is no pretty sight, and he had been dead for ten to twelve hours.

Ollie came down to the sheriff's office with Bill Sexton and Vicente Romero. They were getting up a political rally and Orrin was going to speak. Several of the high mucky-mucks from Santa Fe were coming up, but this was to be Orrin's big day.

It was a good time for him to put himself forward and the stage was being set for it. There was to be a real ol' time fandango with the folks coming in from back at the forks of the creeks. Everybody was to be there and all dressed in their Sunday-go-to-meeting clothes.

In preparation for it I made the rounds and gave several of the trouble makers their walking papers. What I mean is, I told them they would enjoy Las Vegas or Socorro or Cimarron a whole sight better and why didn't they start now.

They started.

"Have you heard the talk that's going around?" Shea asked me.

"What talk?"

"It's being said that Tom Sunday is coming into town after Orrin."

"Tom Sunday and Orrin are friends," I said, "I know Tom's changed, but I don't believe he'll go that far."

"Put no faith in that line of thought, Tyrel. Believe me, the man hasn't a friend left. He's surely as a grizzly with a sore tooth, and nobody goes near him any more. The man's changed, and he works with a gun nearly every day. Folks coming by there say they can hear it almost any hour."

"Tom never thought much of Orrin as a fighter. Tom never knew him like I have."

"That isn't all." Shea put his cigar down on the edge of the desk. "There's talk about what would happen if you and Tom should meet."

Well, I was mad. I got up and walked across the office and swore. Yes, and I wasn't a swearing man.

Oddly enough, thinking back, I can't remember many gunfighters who were. Most of them I knew were sparing in the use of words as well as whiskey.

But one thing I knew: Orrin must not meet Tom Sunday. Even if Orrin beat him, Orrin would lose. A few years ago it would not have mattered that he had been in a gun battle, now it could wreck his career.

If Orrin would get out of town ... but he couldn't. He had been selected as the speaker for the big political rally and that would be just the time when Tom Sunday would be in town.

"Thanks," I said to Shea, "thanks for telling me."

Leaving Cap in charge of the office I mounted up and rode out to the ranch. Orrin was there, and we sat down and had dinner with Ma. It was good to have our feet under the same table again, and Ma brightened up and talked like her old self.

Next day was Sunday and Orrin and me decided to take Ma to church. It was a lazy morning with bright sunshine and Orin took Ma in the buckboard and we boys rode along behind.

We wore our broadcloth suits and the four of us dressed in black made a sight walking around Ma, who was a mighty little woman among her four tall sons, and Dru was with us, standing there beside Ma and me, and I was a proud man.

It was a meeting I'll not soon forget, that one was, because when Ollie heard the family was going, he came along and stood with us at the hymn singing and the preaching.

Whether or not Orrin had heard any of the stories going round about Tom I felt it necessary to warn him. If I expected him to brush it off, I was wrong. He was dead serious about it when I explained. "But I can't leave," he added, "everybody would know why I went and if they thought I was afraid, I'd lose as many votes as if I actually fought him."

He was right, of course, so we prepared for the meeting with no happy anticipation of it, although this was to be Orrin's big day, and his biggest speech, and the one that would have him fairly launched in politics. Men were coming up from Santa Fe to hear him, all the crowd around the capital who pulled the political strings.

Everybody knew Orrin was to speak and everybody knew Tom would be there. And nothing any of us could do but wait.

Jonathan Pritts knew he had been left out and he knew it was no accident. He also knew that it was to be Orrin's big day and that Laura's cutting loose had not hurt him one bit.

Also Jonathan knew the trial was due to come off soon, and before the attorney got through cross-examining Wilson and some of the others the whole story of his move into the Territory would be revealed. There was small chance it could be stopped, but if something were to happen to Orrin and me, if there was to be a jail delivery. . . .

He wouldn't dare.

Or would he?

CHAPTER XX

The sun was warm in the street that morning, warm even at the early hour when I rode in from the ranch. The town lay quiet and a lazy dog sprawled in the dust opened one eye and flapped his tail in a I-won't-bother-you-if-you-don't-bother-me sort of way, as I approached.

Cap Rountree looked me over carefully from those shrewd old eyes as I rode up. "You wearing war paint, boy? If you ain't, you better. I got a bad feeling about today."

Getting down from the saddle I stood beside him and watched the hills against the skyline. People were getting up all over town now, or lying there awake and thinking about the events of the day. There was to be the speaking, a band concert, and most folks would bring picnic lunches.

"I hope he stays away."

Cap stuffed his pipe with tobacco. "He'll be here."

"What happened, Cap? Where did it start?"

He leaned a thin shoulder against the awning post. "You could say it was at the burned wagons when Orrin and him had words about that money. No man likes to be put in the wrong.

"Or you could say it was back there at the camp near Baxter Springs, or maybe it was the day they were born. Sometimes men are born who just can't abide one another from the time they meet ... don't make no rhyme nor reason, but it's so."

"They are proud men."

"Tom's gone killer, Tyrel, don't you ever forget that. It infects some men like rabies, and they keep on killing until somebody kills them."

We stood there, not talking for awhile, each of us

busy with his own thoughts. What would Dru be doing about now? Rising at home, and planning her day, bathing, combing her long dark hair, having breakfast.

Turning away I went inside and started looking over the day's roundup of mail. This morning there was a letter from Tell, my oldest brother. Tell was in Virginia City, Montana, and was planning to come down and see us. Ma would be pleased, mighty pleased. It had been a sorry time since we had seen Tell.

There was a letter from that girl, too. The one we had sent the money we found in that burned wagon ... she was coming west and wanted to meet us. The letter had been forwarded from Santa Fe where it had been for weeks ... by this time she must be out here, or almost here.

It gave me an odd feeling to get that letter on this morning, thinking back to the trouble it had caused.

Cap came in from outside and I said, "I'm going to have coffee with Dru. You hold the fort, will you?"

"You do that, boy. You just do that."

Folks were beginning to crowd the streets now, and some were hanging out bunting and flags. Here and there a few rigs stood along the street, all with picnic baskets in the back. There were big, rawboned men in the Sunday-go-to-meeting clothes and women in fresh-washed ginghams and sunbonnets. Little boys ran and played in the streets, and their mothers scolded and called after them while little girls, starched and ribboned, looked on enviously and disdainfully.

It was good to be alive. Everything seemed to move slow today, everything seemed to take its time ... was this the way a man felt on his last day? Was it to be my last day?

When I knocked on the door Dru answered it herself. Beyond the welcome I could see the worry.

"How's about a poor drifter begging a cup of coffee, ma'am? I was just passin' through and the place had a kindly look."

"Come in, Tye. You don't have to knock."

"Big day in town. Biggest crowd I ever saw. Why, I've seen folks from Santa Fe ... as far as Raton or Durango."

The maid brought in the coffee and we sat at the breakfast table looking out the low-silled window over the town and the hillside and we sat talking for awhile and at last I got up and she came with me to the door. She put her hand on my sleeve. "Stay here, Tye ... don't go."

"Got to ... busy day today."

Folks were crowded along the street and there were wagons drawn up where the speaking was to be—with many people taking their places early so they could be close enough to hear. When I got down to the office Orrin was there in his black frock coat and string tie. He grinned at me, but beyond the grin his eyes were serious. "You get up there and talk," I said, "you're the speaker of this family."

Me, I stayed at the office. Cap was out and around, nosing after news like a smart old coon dog looking up trails in the dust or the berry patches.

There was no sign of Tom Sunday, and around the jail everything was quiet. Nor was Jonathan Pritts anywhere in sight. My guards were restless, most of them men with families who wanted to be with them on a big day like this.

Ma and the boys came in about noon, Ma riding in the buckboard with Joe driving. Ollie had held a place for them where Ma could hear the speaking, and it would be the first time she had ever heard Orrin make a speech. Folks were mighty impressed with speech-making those days, and a man who could talk right up and make his words sound like something, well, he rated mighty high up there. He was a big man.

That day I was wearing black broadcloth pants down over my boots, a style just then coming in, and I had on a gray shirt with a black string tie and a black, braided Spanish-style jacket and a black hat.

My gun was on, and I was carrying a spare tucked into my waistband out of sight under my jacket.

About noon Caribou Brown rode into town with Doubleout Sam. Shea saw them ride in and reported to me at once and I went down to the saloon where they had bellied up to the bar.

"All right, boys. Finish your drink and ride out."

They turned around on me, the both of them, but they knew me pretty well by then. "You're a hard man" Brown said. "Can't a man stay around for the fun?"

"Sorry."

They had their drinks but they didn't like it and when they finished them I was standing right there. "If you boys start right now you can make Vegas," I told them. "You'll have trouble if you think you can stay. I'll throw you both in jail and you'll be there next month at this time."

"On what charge?" Sam didn't like it.

"Loitering, obstructing justice, interfering with an officer, peddling without a license ... I'll think of something."

"Oh, damn you!" Brown said. "Come on, Sam ... let's ride."

They started for the door.

"Boys?"

They turned. "Don't circle around. I've got some deputies who are mighty concerned about the town today. You're known men and if you come back they'll be shooting on sight."

They rode out of town and I was glad to see them go. Both were known trouble makers of the old Settlement crowd and they had been in several shootings.

The streets began to grow empty as folks drifted toward the speech-making and the band concert, which was going full blast. Going slow along the walks the streets were so empty the sound of my heels was loud. When I reached the adobe where Fetterson was held, I stopped by. Shea was on guard there.

"Hello, Fett," I said.

He got up and came to the bars. "That right? That they shot into my cell? Into a dummy?"

"What did you expect? You can hang him, Fetterson, and he knows that. He's got to do something ... or run!"

Fetterson rubbed his jaw. The man looked worried. "How does a man get into these things?" he asked suddenly. "Damn it, I played square with him."

"He's wrong, Fett. He cares nothing for you except in so far as you are useful and when your usefulness is ended, so's his interest. You're too good a man to be wasted, Fett ... you're loyal to a man who does not understand loyalty."

"Maybe ... maybe."

He listened to the band, which was playing *My Darling Nelly Gray*. "Sounds like a good time," he said wistfully.

"I've got to go," I said, "the speaking starts in a few minutes."

He was still standing by the bars when I went out. Shea got up and walked outside with me. "Are you expecting trouble?"

"At any minute."

"All right," he cradled the shotgun in his arms, "I just don't want to miss all the fun."

From the gathering place beyond the buildings I could hear Ollie introducing somebody. Pausing, I listened. It was the speaker from Santa Fe—the one who preceded Orrin—and I could hear his rolling tones, although he was too far away to distinguish more than a word or two, and when it happened, it happened so suddenly that I was taken by surprise.

They came into the street below the jail and they came suddenly and they were on foot. Obviously they had been hidden during the night in the houses of some of the citizens, and there were eight of them and they had rifles. Every one of them was a familiar face, all were from the old Settlement crowd, and they had me dead to rights.

They were near the jail and there was a man

inside. There were probably two men inside. Up the street behind me Shea could do little unless I gave him room, but I had to be where I could do the most damage.

Turning at right angles I walked into the middle of the street and then I faced them. Sixty yards separated us. Looking at those rifles and shotguns I knew I was in trouble and plenty of it, but I knew this was what I had been waiting for.

There were eight of them and they would be confident, but they would also be aware that I was going to get off at least one shot and probably one man would be killed ... nobody would want to be that man.

"What are you boys getting out of this?" I asked them coolly. "Fifty dollars apiece? It's a cinch Jonathan isn't going to pay more than that ... hope you collected in advance."

"We want the keys!" The man talking was named Stott. "Toss them over here!"

"You're talking, Stott ... but are you watching? You boys are going to get it from the jail."

"The keys!"

Stott I was going to kill. He was the leader. I was going to get him and as many more as possible.

There was a rustle of movement down the street behind them. There was movement down there but I didn't dare take my eyes off them. So I started to walk. I started right down the street toward them, hoping to get so close they would endanger each other if they started shooting. Beyond them I could see movement and when I realized who it was I was so startled they might have killed me.

It was Dru.

She wasn't alone. She had six buckskin-clad riders with her and they all had Winchesters and they looked like they wanted to start shooting.

"All right," I said, "the fun's over. Drop your gun belts."

Stott was angry. "What are you trying—" Behind him seven Winchesters were cocked on signal, and he

looked sharply around. And after that it was settled
... they were not nearly so anxious for trouble and
when they were disarmed, they were jailed along
with the others.

Dru walked her horse up to the front of the jail.
"Miguel saw them coming," she said, "so we rode
down to help."

"Help? You did it all."

We talked there in the street and then I walked
beside her horse over to the speaking. When this was
over I was going to go after Jonathan Pritts. I was
going to arrest him but oddly enough, I did not want
him jailed. He was an old man, and defeat now would
ruin him enough and he was whipped. When this was
over he would be arrested, but if St. Vrain, Romero,
and the others agreed, I'd just send him out of town
with his daughter and a buckboard ... they deserved
each other.

Orrin was introduced. He got up and walked to the
front of the platform and he started to speak in that
fine Welsh voice of his. He spoke quietly, with none of
that oratory they had been hearing. He just talked to
them as he would to friends in his own home, yet as
he continued his voice grew in power and conviction,
and he was speaking as I had never heard him speak.

Standing there in the shade of a building I listened
and was proud. This was my brother up there ... this
was Orrin. This was the boy I'd grown up with, left
the mountains with, herded cattle, and fought Indians
beside.

There was a strange power in him now that was
born of thought and dream and that fine Welsh magic
in his voice and mind. He was talking to them of what
the country needed, of what had to be done, but he
was using their own language, the language of the
mountains, the desert, the cattle drives. And I was
proud of him.

Turning away from the crowd, I walked slowly
back to the street and between the buildings and
when I emerged on the sunlit street, Tom Sunday
was standing there.

I stopped where I stood and could not see his eyes but as flecks of light from the shadow beneath his hat brim.

He was big, broad, and powerful. He was unshaved and dirty, but never in my life had I seen such a figure of raw, physical power in one man.

"Hello, Tom."

"I've come for him, Tyrel. Stay out of the way."

"He's building his future," I said, "you helped him start it, Tom. He's going to be a big man and you helped him."

Maybe he didn't even hear me. He just looked at me straight on like a man staring down a narrow hallway.

"I'm going to kill him," he said, "I should have done it years ago."

We were talking now, like in a conversation, yet something warned me to be careful. What had Cap said? He was a killer and he would go on killing until something or somebody stopped him.

This was the man who had killed the Durango Kid, who had killed Ed Fry and Chico Cruz ... Chico never even got off a shot.

"Get out of the way, Tye," he said, "I've nothing against you, I—"

He was going to kill me.

I was going to die ... I was sure of it.

Only he must not come out of it alive. Orrin must have his future. Anyway, I was the mean one ... I always had been.

Once before I had stepped in to help Orrin and I would now.

There was nobody there on the street but the two of us, just Tom Sunday, the man who had been my best friend, and me. He had stood up for me before this and we had drunk from the same rivers, fought Indians together. ...

"Tom," I said, "remember that dusty afternoon on that hillside up there on the Purgatoire when we. ..."

Sweat trickled down my spine and tasted salt on my lips. His shirt was open to his belt and I could see the hair on his big chest and the wide buckle of his belt. His hat was pulled low but there was no expression on his face.

This was Tom Sunday, my friend ... only now he was a stranger.

"You can get out of the way, Tye," he said, "I'm going to kill him."

He spoke easily, quietly. I knew I had it to do, but this man had helped teach me to read, he had loaned me books, he had ridden the plains with me.

"You can't do it," I said. Right then, he went for his gun.

There was an instant before he drew when I knew he was going to draw. It was an instant only, a flickering instant that triggered my mind.

My hand dropped and I palmed my gun, but his came up and he was looking across it, his eyes like white fire, and I saw the gun blossom with a rose of flame and felt my own gun buck in my hand, and then I stepped forward and left—one quick step—and fired again.

He stood there looking across his gun at me and then he fired, but his bullet made a clean miss. Thumbing back the hammer I said, "Damn it, Tom. ..." and I shot him in the chest.

He still stood there but his gun muzzle was lowering and he was still looking at me.

A strange, puzzled expression came into his eyes and he stepped toward me, dropping his gun. "Tyrel ... Tye, what. ..." He reached out a hand toward me, but when I stepped quickly to take it, he fell.

He went full face to the dust, falling hard, and when he hit the ground he groaned, then he half-turned and dropping to my knees I grabbed his hand and gripped it hard.

"Tye ... Tye, damn it, I. ..." He breathed hoarsely, and the front of his shirt was red with blood.

"The books," he whispered, "take the ... books."

He died like that, gripping my hand, and when I looked up the street was full of people, and Orrin was there, and Dru.

And over the heads of some of the nearest, Jonathan Pritts.

Pushing through the crowd I stopped, facing Jonathan. "You get out of town," I told him, "you get out of the state. If you aren't out of town within the hour, or if you ever come back, for any reason at all, I'll kill you."

He just turned and walked away, his back stiff as a ramrod . . . but it wasn't even thirty minutes until he and Laura drove from town in a buckboard.

"That was my fight, Tye," Orrin said quietly, "it was my fight."

"No, it was mine. From the beginning it was mine. He knew it would be, I think. Maybe we both knew it . . . and Cap. I think Cap Rountree knew it first of all."

We live on the hill back of Mora, and sometimes in Santa Fe, Dru and me . . . we've sixty thousand acres of land in two states and a lot of cattle. Orrin, he's a state senator now, and pointing for greater things.

Sometimes of an evening I think of that, think when the shadows grow long of two boys who rode out of the high hill country of Tennessee to make a home in the western lands.

We found our home, and we graze and work our acres, and since that day in the street of Mora when I killed Tom Sunday I have never drawn a gun on any man.

Nor will I. . . .